# PERSONALITY AND PSYCHOLOGICAL DISORDERS

ARNOLD

# Dedication

To the 21 Oxford students on whom we tested an early version of this book.

Current Check-Outs summary for Cupp, Kri
    Tue Feb 22 10:27:39 PST 2011

BARCODE: 33371000771340
TITLE: Personality and psychological dis
DUE DATE: Mar 24 2011

BARCODE: 33371000736744
TITLE: Mental disorders in older adults
DUE DATE: Mar 24 2011

BARCODE: 33371002133783
TITLE: Clinical handbook of psychologica
DUE DATE: Mar 24 2011

BARCODE: 33371002017390
TITLE: The anxiety & phobia workbook / E
DUE DATE: Mar 24 2011

RANGO
TICKETS

# PERSONALITY AND PSYCHOLOGICAL DISORDERS

GORDON CLARIDGE and
CAROLINE DAVIS

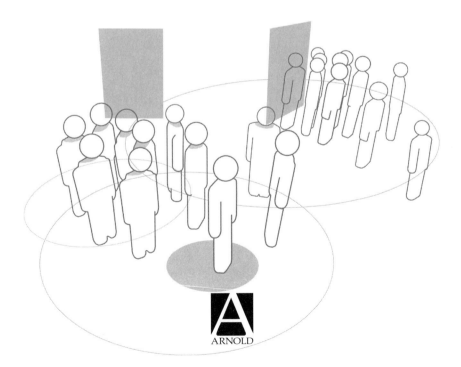

ARNOLD

First published in Great Britain in 2003 by
Arnold, a member of the Hodder Headline Group,
338 Euston Road, London NW1 3BH

http://www.arnoldpublishers.com

Distributed in the United States of America by
Oxford University Press Inc.
198 Madison Avenue, New York, NY10016

*British Library Cataloguing in Publication Data*
A catalogue record for this book is available from the British Library

*Library of Congress Cataloging-in-Publication Data*
A catalog record for this book is available from the Library of Congress


ISBN 0 340 807148 (hb)
ISBN 0 340 807156 (pb)

iv

1 2 3 4 5 6 7 8 9 10

Typeset in 11/12.5pt Garamond 3 by Dorchester Typesetting Group Ltd
Printed and bound in Great Britain by MPG Books Ltd

What do you think about this book? Or any other Arnold title?
Please send your comments to feedback.arnold@hodder.co.uk

# Contents

| | | |
|---|---|---|
| Preface | | ix |
| | | |
| **Chapter 1   Connecting personality and disorder** | | 1 |
| Some theoretical issues | | 1 |
| An historical perspective | | 6 |
| Layout of the book | | 8 |
| | | |
| **Chapter 2   Description, classification, and models of disorder** | | 11 |
| The medical classification | | 11 |
| The dimensional approach | | 16 |
|    Historical considerations: HJ Eysenck | | 16 |
|    Comments on Eysenck's theory | | 19 |
|    A dimensional model of psychological disorder | | 20 |
|    From continuity to discontinuity | | 23 |
| Summary and conclusions | | 28 |
| | | |
| **Chapter 3   Personality dimensions: description and biology** | | 31 |
| Historical antecedents and Eysenck's theory | | 31 |
|    The Eysenck dimensions | | 33 |
|    Eysenck's 'causal' theories | | 34 |
|    A note on the status of Psychoticism (P) | | 37 |
| Temperament and personality compared | | 38 |
| Contemporary theorists | | 40 |
|    Gray | | 40 |
|    Cloninger | | 44 |
|    Zuckerman | | 46 |
|    Five-factor theory (Costa & McCrae) | | 48 |
| An integrated view of the theories | | 50 |

Genetic considerations                                              53
  Behaviour genetics                                               53
  Molecular genetics                                               56
The developmental perspective                                      57
Summary and conclusions                                            59

**Chapter 4   Personality disorders**                              60
Some basic features                                                60
Personality disorders in DSM-IV                                    62
Personality disorders and models of the abnormal                   66
Approaches to the explanation of personality disorders             67
  Five-factor theory and Axis II                                   68
  Cloninger revisited                                              70
  The work of Millon                                               71
  Beck's cognitive approach                                        72
Particular personality disorders                                   74
  Antisocial personality disorder (psychopathy)                    75
  Borderline personality disorder                                  80
Summary and conclusions                                            86

**Chapter 5   Mood and anxiety disorders**                         88
Introduction                                                       88
Animal models                                                      91
Common symptoms of mood and anxiety disorders                      95
  Fearfulness                                                      96
  Anxiousness                                                      101
  Melancholy                                                       106

**Chapter 6   Obsessive–Compulsive Disorder**                      113
Introduction                                                       113
Natural history of the disorder                                    115
Causal explanations of OCD                                         117
  Biological models                                                117
  Cognitive models of OCD                                          121
Personality factors in OCD                                         124
Obsessive-Compulsive spectrum disorders                            128

## Chapter 7    Addictive behaviours      131

Introduction    131
Clinical features    133
The neurobiology of addiction    136
Chronic use of addictive behaviours    140
Vulnerability to addiction    141
     Sensitivity to reward (SRT)    143
     Impulsive behaviour    147
     Proneness to anxiety and negative mood    150

## Chapter 8    Eating disorders      155

Introduction    155
Clinical features    156
Historical perspectives    158
Research methodology    160
Temperament and personality    164
     Obsessionality and the eating disorders    165
     Perfectionism and the eating disorders    167
     Impulsivity and the eating disorders    169
     Anxiousness and the eating disorders    170
     Sensitivity to reward, addiction, and the eating disorders    175
The pathophysiology of eating disorders    177
Conclusions    180

## Chapter 9    Psychotic disorders      181

Definitions and descriptions    181
The issue of heterogeneity    185
     One psychosis or two?    185
     One schizophrenia or several?    186
Dimensional aspects of schizophrenia    187
     Quasi- versus fully dimensional models    188
     Measurement of schizotypy    190
Explaining schizophrenia    192
     Research problems and strategies    192
     Genetics and risk for schizophrenia    193
     Experimental psychopathology of schizophrenia    197

Brain systems in schizophrenia     201
Manic depression     205
    The unitary psychosis issue     205
    Dimensionality of manic depression     206
Conclusions     207

**Chapter 10   Final remarks**     211
**References**     217
**Index**     245

# Preface

As is often the case, this book had a serendipitous beginning. More precisely, it started after one of us could not resist voicing his opinion to Arnold that there was a need for a book like 'Personality and Psychological Disorders'. Before we knew it, we were writing one! And having finished it we can now see why there hasn't been one before, at least one at a factual level of complexity sufficient to be informative, but not too detailed to be inaccessible to the readers for whom it is mainly intended. We hope we have come some way towards striking that difficult balance; for each of the two areas covered is itself a huge branch of psychology, with many different viewpoints and examples that clamour to be represented. Indeed, the two topics – individual differences and psychological disorders – are generally taught separately in psychology degree courses and, in our experience, reference from one to the other, even if occurs, is sketchy and tentative. This is a pity because, as we try to show in this book, the study of personality may be usefully enriched by looking beyond the average and the healthy; whilst the deviant states of mind and behaviour that constitute the subject matter of abnormal and clinical psychology can scarcely be understood without reference to some concept of normality.

As described in the early chapters of the book, the arguments we develop and the material we present, concentrate on a certain way of thinking about the connection between normal and abnormal: one that draws particularly on its biology, yet without embracing a straightforwardly disease view of psychological disorder. This perspective has not always been uncontroversial – and that is still the case in some quarters. We chose it because it is well-grounded in the history of ideas about the topic, is supported by considerable past and present scientific evidence, and, looking to the future, is likely to assume increasing importance as we begin to understand more about the origins of personality and its occasional manifestations in mental illness.

Although, as co-authors, we naturally share a common interest in this approach, we don't necessarily agree on every implication of it – at the very least, we are sometimes led to place our emphases differently. We have not tried to conceal this by seeking to homogenize the text. On the contrary, we have allowed our respective interpretations of the book's title to flourish, on the grounds that the learning process is a matter of finding out about different viewpoints and different interpretations of evidence, and then making up one's own mind.

There are a number of people we need to thank for their help and understanding during the course of constructing this book. There are those among our respective family circles who did not see enough of us, or when they did found us distracted and preoccupied. At Arnold we wish to thank Christina Wipf Perry, formerly Publisher for psychology, for commissioning us to write the book in the first place and, currently, Emma Woolf, Commissioning Editor for Psychology, and Jasmine Brown, Senior Desk Editor, for seeing it through to production.

Lastly, we thank the goddess for our shared sense of humour and each other for mutual support and encouragement during moments of writing crisis.

Gordon Claridge
Oxford
Caroline Davis
Toronto
July 2002

# CHAPTER 1

## CONNECTING PERSONALITY AND DISORDER

### SOME THEORETICAL ISSUES

That psychological disorders are intimately connected to personality might seem self-evident. Yet the idea may be interpreted in several ways and has been studied from a number of different perspectives. In this opening chapter we will discuss some of those views and, in so doing, draw out the particular themes that form the content of the rest of the book.

One interpretation refers to the impact of having a psychological disorder upon the individual; how the onset and progression of a mental illness can temporarily or permanently alter sufferers' personal reactions to events and others around them. This can be reflected in lowered self-esteem, increased emotional sensitivity, a greater tendency to depression, the exaggeration of temperamental tendencies which in the healthy state may be hidden or scarcely visible, yet, in the presence or aftermath of mental illness help to re-define the individual's here-and-now personality. Although we shall not emphasize this aspect of the link between personality and disorder, we should at the very beginning stress its importance. Personality is a dynamic feature of individuality, constantly changing, progressing (or regressing) according to environmental demands and internal developments of the organism. Although this evolution of the person is most salient in the early years – infancy, childhood and adolescence – nevertheless it continues throughout life. Indeed, the development of a psychological disorder as an adult may be seen as a particularly dramatic example of how apparently quite stable propensities to action, motivations, and other characteristics that constitute the personality can be thrown into disarray. This is particularly true in the case of the serious mental illnesses, such as schizophrenia, but it is also noticeably so in other intractable disorders like obsessive–compulsive neurosis, a point we shall return to it in the chapter devoted to that condition.

Another interpretation of the title of this book – closer to its actual subject matter – approaches the question from the opposite direction. That is to say, it examines how personality can *predispose* to disorder, influence an individual's response to stress, shape its severity and its progression. A straightforward example would be a client who complains to the clinical psychologist or psychiatrist of excessive anxiety, to the extent of agoraphobia, usually defined as a fear of public places and often seen as a refusal to leave the safety of the home. Whatever other formative factors, such as immediate life circumstances or recent traumatic experience, have contributed to this person's condition, it is an interesting fact that not everyone faced with such exigencies will develop agoraphobia or, indeed, any form of maladaptive behaviour. Examples abound of individuals who, exposed to the most traumatic circumstances, should by rights be mental wrecks – yet they emerge as perfectly healthy, adapted persons, able to cope with whatever life throws at them. Why is this?

One explanation is that of 'toughening up'. That is to say, exposure to early adversity might, in conjunction with certain psychosocial protective factors, make some individuals better able to cope with later stress (Masten, 1994). Another explanation – and one we shall particularly emphasize here – is that those who survive trauma possess temperamental or personality characteristics that make them inherently less likely to be affected by stressors that cause others to succumb; as a generalization, that people simply differ in the extent to which personal tendencies make them more or less liable to psychological breakdown. In the course of the book we shall see that there is good reason to believe that this is true, and we will examine some of the intrinsic differences that cause some people to become seriously mentally ill, others mildly disordered only, and yet others not disturbed at all.

As a corollary to the above, there is another, more specific question we shall address. It concerns the actual *form* of disorder a person develops if he or she does break down into mental illness. It would be surprising, too, if this were unconnected to the individual's personality. Indeed, the idea is not new; it traditionally forms part of clinical approaches to personality, the abnormal manifestations of which have been of obvious interest. The classic example was Freud's theory about the developmental stages through which individuals are supposed to go in their passage to mature adulthood (Freud, 1940). Freud labelled these so-called 'psychosexual' stages – oral, anal, phallic, and genital – according to the biological sources of satisfaction attached to them. He proposed that people normally pass from one stage to the next in an orderly sequence, resolving as they go conflicts which he believed were commonly encountered at each point. But Freud also suggested that individuals may sometimes get fixated, or stuck, at an earlier developmental stage than necessary for full maturity – and, furthermore, that this lays the groundwork for specific forms of neurotic illness or other disordered behaviour. Thus,

2

fixation at the anal stage is supposed to lead to extreme obsessive–compulsiveness; oral fixation to unhealthy narcissism (abnormal preoccupation with the self) or, even worse, what can be diagnosed as narcissistic personality disorder. Yet, in a more healthy form, both of these features – self-regard and a touch of obsessionality – are perfectly adaptive traits, sitting easily alongside the many other characteristics that serve to describe the well-rounded personality.

Like many aspects of Freud's writings, his explanation of why different personality types develop different psychological disorders has found limited support from empirical study (Kline, 1972). Although still popular in literary and artistic circles, the theory therefore rarely figures among discussions of personality development in mainstream academic psychology. Nevertheless, it does state an important point of principle: that it is impossible to understand the nature of psychological disorders, including the form they take in particular individuals, without knowing something about the personality characteristics from which they spring.

Contemporary psychologists formulate the question differently. This stems from the prevailing view that, at least as the starting-point for studying it, personality is best considered as being made up of a collection of traits – relatively stable tendencies, inherent in the person, which define unique ways of behaving, thinking, and feeling. What makes people different from one another is that they differ in the profiles they show across the various traits that constitute personality. Traits themselves can be, and frequently are, described with commonsense adjectives – *honest, worrying, confident, shy, rigid,* etc. – but, in the hands of personality researchers, the use of such labels is not just an armchair exercise. On the contrary, as will be discussed in Chapter 3, quite sophisticated statistical methods are required to identify those traits which, for scientific purposes, may be judged both reliable to measure and useful as predictors of behaviours that each trait is supposed to describe.

Although adopting basically the same statistical method, some personality theorists prefer to work, not with a large number of narrow traits, but with just a few broad dimensions: the most commonly quoted example of the latter is 'introversion–extraversion'. Choosing the broad dimension, as against the narrow trait, approach (or vice versa) has influenced how psychologists have then proceeded to explore personality further. But, that aside, the approaches are very similar, and identical in two important respects.

First, it is known – and this can be demonstrated statistically – that broad dimensions *encompass* narrow traits. In fact, one is a summary of the other: each broad dimension acts as a sort of collecting-point for the traits that help to define it. This may be illustrated in the case of introversion–extraversion, cited above as a typical broad personality dimension. 'Underneath' this dimension, as it were, there are several narrower traits that elaborate on what, at the more general level, we mean by extraversion (or its opposite, introversion):

3

extraverts are more sociable, cheerful, talkative and so on. Broad dimension and narrow trait descriptions of personality are not, therefore, incompatible; they are merely alternative ways of expressing the same thing.

The second reason the two approaches are virtually identical is that both assume *continuity* in the features – whether broad or narrow – that they use to describe personality. Individuals are *more or less* honest, worrying, confident, shy or rigid, being ranged at various points along unbroken continua that describe the traits or dimensions in question. This way of describing personality is therefore tailor-made for examining associations to the psychological disorders. The clinically abnormal can easily be visualized as, in some regard, an extension of the normal, defining the extremes of the dimensions that describe personality.

In fact, the picture is not quite as simple as that. For, as we shall see, people who have already developed a mental disorder are not *merely* individuals occupying the end-point of some normal personality dimension, even if the latter does describe part of their condition. Again, consider the agoraphobic. He or she would almost certainly be found to score highly on a rating scale or personality inventory of trait anxiety. But, by the time they are formally diagnosed as agoraphobic – and probably even before – such individuals will have developed new, pathological, behaviours (symptoms); for example they refuse to leave the house and express irrational fears that they did not have before. In other words, they are now *more* than just people of very anxious personality; so new facts are needed to explain their transition from extreme *trait* anxiety to *symptomatic* anxiety. Nonetheless, this does not alter the working rule that personality and psychological disorder are connected by virtue of the fact that one reflects, in some sense, an exaggeration of the other.

The view of individual differences just outlined is very superficial, accounting only for the *structure* of personality, how the clustering of traits or the combining of dimensions helps us to describe the variations between people. But most theories of this type try to go one step further and look for explanations or underlying causes of the personality differences – and, by extrapolation, the disorders to which they connect. This has frequently been done from a biological standpoint and has two themes.

One involves trying to characterize the neural basis of traits or dimensions, discovering what facets of brain activity might account for, or at the very least correlate with, personality variations. It then becomes possible to build up a picture of how the nervous system works in people who are, say, impulsive, sensation-seeking, or of depressive temperament. Here, personality psychologists make use of techniques or draw upon existing information, where available, from all branches of neuroscience, including psychophysiology, neurophysiology and neurochemistry, as well as studies of drugs that affect brain function. At our present stage of knowledge there is still a fair amount of approximation in all of this and the exercise very much amounts to what the eminent Canadian psychologist, Donald Hebb (Hebb, 1955) once referred to as building a 'conceptual nervous system', an imaginary model which hopefully will eventually be found to correspond to how the real nervous system works. Hebb himself was referring to the general case in neuropsychology. But all systems show fluctuation and variation, and the brain is no exception. This rule – that nervous systems differ in the way they work – coupled to the principle that such variations partly explain why people have different personalities, provides the key to understanding much that we shall be writing about here (see Claridge, 1995) for a general introduction to these ideas).

A second important theme in the biological account of personality is genetics. Almost all theories that explain personality by referring to biology also propose that the differences observed are under some degree of genetic control. Here, two strands of evidence may be distinguished. One is represented in the search for genes that could contribute to nervous system variability in brain function, which could, in turn, find expression in psychological and behavioural differences. The other comes from use of the statistical procedures of *behaviour* genetics; that is, seeking evidence for hereditary influences by examining how far family members selected for their degree of kinship resemble one another on some personality trait or dimension – or indeed an appropriate physiological correlate of it. The classic method involves comparing twins, classified according to whether or not they are genetically identical. In these cases the aim is to arrive at a statistical estimate of the so-called 'heritability' of the trait being studied. Behaviour genetics is the older discipline and was the only source of evidence available to individual differences workers until the advent of the new era in genetics research. Nevertheless, it still has a crucial role to play in contemporary enquiry: in bolstering evidence from molecular genetics that genes do play a part in some chosen feature of human variation, and in leading researchers to possible sources of variation where such genes might be worth looking for.

Before leaving the theme of genetics we feel we should insert some cautionary remarks. It is currently fashionable, not just in popular writing but also in scientific publications, to claim that there are, or could be, genes for complex behavioural traits. We believe this to be very misleading. Genes code for very precise, literally microscopic, bits of biological material (proteins) that are both physically and conceptually very distant from the complex behavioural and psychological characteristics which they are supposed to – and perhaps in some sense – do influence. But it is unlikely that there are genes, or sets of genes, 'for' impulsivity, the preference for gay relationships, religiosity, anxiety, or even serious mental disorders, such as schizophrenia. The route from genes to behaviour is likely to be much more tortuous than that and, for any particular characteristic, to involve a multitude of genes and interactions among them – as well as an interplay between genes and environmental factors. The reason for taking an interest in the genetic effects on individual differences – and there is good evidence that they do exist – is therefore not in order to *reduce* everything to heredity, but to see where such influences fit into the larger picture about personality.

Pursuing the above point, we should also state that, although we will be mainly emphasizing the biological aspects, our overall view of the material to be presented is, strictly speaking, *psycho*biological. That is to say, it assumes that human variation, both normal and abnormal, is an integrated whole, of biological and psychological influences, both equally legitimate fields of enquiry and sources of information. In practice, of course, it is frequently difficult to bring them together, except in parallel as alternative descriptions or explanations of the same factual data. The language used in each domain is different, it is possible only to talk in one of them at a time, and a bias towards one or the other is bound, as here, to predominate. Nevertheless, we shall, where possible, try to remind the reader from time to time of the psychobiological nature of the phenomena we are describing and draw upon more 'psychological' ideas. This especially includes reference, where appropriate, to the *cognitive* viewpoint, which is currently the one that prevails at the clinical end of the subject. At least, that is the case among psychologists, though less so in psychiatry where biological explanations of mental illness predominate. These differences of viewpoint – their history and the tensions to which they have given and still give rise – are themselves of interest and deserve further comment here, in order to place the material presented in our book in its proper context.

## AN HISTORICAL PERSPECTIVE

Dispute about the relative importance of biological and non-biological explanations of personality and abnormal mental states has always existed and is merely a particular case of the age old philosophical preoccupation with brain/mind relationships. The issue has frequently been discussed around the value of the medical model in psychiatry, articulated as the question: How far can psychological disorders be judged similar to physical diseases? The contemporary scene contains several shades of opinion that mirror historically distinct disagreements, sometimes within psychiatry, sometimes between psychiatry and psychology, and sometimes between clinical psychology and its parent discipline of academic psychology.

Historically, the most publicized part of the debate was in psychiatry, stemming from challenges, for a period from the 1960s onwards, to the received wisdom of mental illnesses as brain diseases. The two pivotal critics of that view were the Scottish radical psychiatrist, R.D. Laing (1960), and the American anti-psychiatrist, Thomas Szasz (1974). Although arguing from (sometimes very) different standpoints, Laing and Szasz did agree on one thing: that biology was not relevant to disorders of the mind and behaviour.

These, they said, could only be fully understood from a social or sociological point of view. In the event, Establishment psychiatry won out: Laing drifted into mysticism and alcoholism, and Szasz became marginalized as a still vociferous, but largely ignored, polemicist. The triumph of biological psychiatry came about because of advances in the neurosciences, including pharmacology, so that, at the beginning of the twenty-first century it is impossible to ignore the fact that, whatever else one wants to believe, the brain has *something* to do with mental disorder.

Notably, the mid-twentieth century disputes within psychiatry were mostly fuelled by differences of opinion about schizophrenia and other forms of serious mental illness. This might be crucial to understanding the course of subsequent events: the biologists could not fail to win the argument given that, even in the absence of precise knowledge about why they are like they are, schizophrenic individuals have always 'looked' as though their brains were acting up. The evidence that did eventually accumulate to support this conclusion therefore very easily spearheaded a general shift towards biological explanations of *all* forms of psychological disorder. Indeed, some would argue that the trend has gone too far towards an expectation that everything that is deviant about the human condition may be explained by reference to biology. Whether or not that is true, the fact remains that the brain is here to stay in psychiatry.

The Laing/Szasz attack on psychiatrists for their overenthusiasm for the medical model was not the only one, however. At about the same time as psychiatry was being challenged from within its own ranks, it was also coming under fire from psychology, specifically from Hans Eysenck, one of the founding fathers of the dimensional, trait, view of personality that we have already introduced here. Eysenck, whose writings we shall often have occasion to refer to again, also disliked the prevailing psychiatric construction of psychological abnormality. But his arguments against it could not have been more different from those of Laing, Szasz, and their followers. Eysenck's criticism was more along the lines that, rather than being discrete disease entities, as the medical model demands, mental illnesses merely form the end-points of normal personality dimensions. Furthermore, contrary to the radicalists within psychiatry, Eysenck very much argued for there being essential biological roots to disorder. So, although being on the side of psychiatry over the importance of looking at the brain, he construed its involvement in mental illness differently. For Eysenck – in line with the view to be presented here – understanding the biology of mental illnesses was very much an extension of understanding the biology of the personality traits that predispose to them (Eysenck, 1960).

A third element in this history was the emergence of clinical psychology as an offshoot of academic abnormal psychology, separate from the latter but influenced by and influencing its ideas. It should be noted that the theoretical stance and attitudes found among clinical psychologists have always been

7

somewhat coloured by professional considerations; an evolving need of a group of practitioners seeking a role, independent of psychiatry, in the treatment of the mentally ill. In the early days of this new profession many clinical psychologists – mostly those of a social constructionist persuasion – were delighted by, and fiercely joined in with, the attacks launched by Laing and Szasz on their colleagues in psychiatry (Bannister and Fransella, 1971). However, this was not true of all clinical psychologists. Others, schooled – indeed sometimes through Eysenck's influence – in more behaviourist accounts (and treatments) of psychological disorder, were just as much at loggerheads with other clinical psychologists. But even they took some satisfaction at the rifts occurring within psychiatry at that time.

It would be an oversimplification to suggest that the contemporary scene in clinical psychology may be traced in a straightforwardly linear fashion to these early differences of opinion. Nevertheless, some continuity can be observed: the emergence of a predominantly cognitive view of mental disorder; the confluence, on the therapeutic front, of behavourist and mentalistic traditions, leading to the almost universal preference for so-called 'cognitive–behavioural' treatments; and a lasting indifference, in some quarters even hostility, to things biological, whether coming from psychology or from psychiatry.

The professional side of this development in clinical psychology has continued to be strongly shaped by the need, referred to above, for an independent practitioner identity, separate from that of the psychiatrist. Current practical questions are therefore often articulated in the form of, say, a comparison of the relative efficacy for panic disorder of some drug regime versus an appropriate cognitive–behavioural manipulation. Theories in clinical psychology correspondingly tend to be driven by these same treatment concerns and to be formulated in the language of cognitive psychology, with little reference to biological ideas, even of the kind found in personality psychology.

There may be two reasons why clinical psychology has been reluctant to seek a meeting-point with biological personality theory. One is that, on the face of it, the latter appears to offer little in the way of practical guidance on treatment issues. Indeed, as we will touch upon briefly in the final chapter, the reverse might be true: the idea of biological vulnerabilities (and invulnerabilities) could imply restraints on the upper limits for change in the mentally ill. Another reason is that embracing *any* kind of biological explanation might take clinical psychology too close to the psychiatric model of psychological disorder that it has tried hard, for professional reasons, to avoid.

## LAYOUT OF THE BOOK

It is clear from the above that there are some subtle (as well as not so subtle) shades of opinion in the field of study covered by this book. In the following chapters we shall try to disentangle these: to provide a view of psychological disorders that takes account of the personality factors from which they

originate, and a view of personality that helps to define the abnormal. Since we shall be attempting to span two domains – or, more accurately, explore the spectrum that joins them – there is a choice of where to start. Should we first outline the personality theories that are relevant to the topic? Or should we start by saying something about the nature of psychological disorder? We decided that the latter is the more appropriate, for the following reasons.

We have already sketched out in this chapter the kind of personality theories upon which we shall draw; the bare bones of them, admittedly, but in sufficient detail to make clear the drift of the argument about how the study of personality can inform our understanding of psychological disorder. The notion of dimensionality lies at the heart of that connection and there are some issues about this that we have not yet discussed, except in our brief reference above to different views that have been expressed about the status of mental illness as medical disease. In the next chapter, therefore, we shall examine that question in more detail, explaining how psychological disorders are classified and diagnosed, the principal theoretical model that lies behind that process, and some criticisms of and alternatives to it.

This will lay the groundwork for returning, in Chapter 3, to the personality side, when, starting from an historical perspective, we shall consider various competing dimensional theories and how these might help us to describe predispositions to disorder. The discussion there will include something on the biological underpinnings of dimensions proposed in such theories: their developmental and genetic origins; brain systems which might account for healthy variations along the dimensions; and how the idea of abnormal functioning in such systems could reveal clues to the mechanisms of disorder.

Subsequent chapters will then look at specific disorders and groups of disorder. These have been chosen as illustrative rather than comprehensive, selected so as to bring out the salient themes that we wish to develop.

The personality disorders are discussed first (Chapter 4) because they represent the clearest evidence of continuity between normal and abnormal. Anxiety disorders and depression (Chapter 5) similarly illustrate this well: in addition to being diagnosable illnesses in their own right, they are universal accompaniments of most other forms of dysfunction (physical and mental) and their underlying mechanisms have a good reference point in normal psychology and biology. Then, in Chapter 6, obsessive–compulsive disorder is introduced as a more specialized, but very informative, example of the dimensionality of psychiatric illness. Chapters 7 and 8 discuss, respectively, substance abuse and eating disorders. Taken together, these illustrate several points. In addition to being relatively common, both are good examples of the truly psychobiological nature of disorder: there are personality correlates, social factors in their aetiology, cognitive explanations of their symptoms, and strong biological statements to be made about the progression once the behaviours associated with them have been established. In Chapter 9 we extend the discussion to the psychotic disorders and demonstrate how the dimensional model can even be applied to these more serious illnesses.

Lastly, we should state that we both believe strongly in the importance of taking an historical perspective on ideas. Explanations and theories are rarely entirely novel. Instead they almost always build upon earlier formulations and, however 'modern' a fresh viewpoint might seem, it is generally a revision or a modification of something that went before. The reader will come across several examples of this historicism in the book and sometimes we will deliberately draw the connection. The main point is to bear in mind the long time factor of the ideas to be presented, and to appreciate that this, in itself, helps to give them some credence.

# C H A P T E R 2

## DESCRIPTION, CLASSIFICATION, AND MODELS OF DISORDER

### THE MEDICAL CLASSIFICATION

Whenever natural variations are seen in some phenomenon there is always a need to classify them – to arrive at what in biology is termed a *taxonomy,* an orderly descriptive system for bringing together subsets of examples that share similar features. In the case of psychological disorders, attempts to construct such a taxonomy – in this case called a *nosology* – has traditionally been in the hands of psychiatrists. Consequently, as will be evident from our introductory chapter, the form and thinking behind psychiatric nosologies have been very much dictated by a medical model, a belief in the need to identify distinct psychological diseases. This has often attracted criticism. But it should not blind us to the fact that, irrespective of how it is done, *some* way of systematically distinguishing between the various psychological disorders is required. Why is this? There are three main reasons.

First, it provides clinicians and others involved in the management of the mentally ill with a language in which to communicate with one another about individual cases with whom they are dealing. It obviously helps, when exchanging information about a patient or client, if some commonly agreed terminology is available and if a label can be assigned, which differentiates one person's disorder from another's. Second, classification helps in the choice of treatment. Indeed, if it did not do so, the nosology would be of limited use, since one of the main purposes of the labelling process is to match the client to a suitable form of therapy. Third, classification serves a scientific need, by defining the guidelines for studying different types of disorder; it allows researchers interested in a particular disorder to select for investigation only those cases that share defined features of the condition they wish to study. Of course, since such research has to be done in order to help to establish the nosology in the first place, there is an element here of what is often called 'bootstrapping', that is, gradually refining the classification on the strength of new knowledge that accumulates from its use.

It is evident from the above – and emphasized in the last point – that there is nothing that is cast in stone about current attempts to classify psychological disorders. Nosologies only represent a present state of affairs, an accumulated wisdom, as interpreted by contemporary experts in the field. This is illustrated by considering the two systems of psychiatric classification currently in use. One is the *International Classification of Mental and Behavioural Disorders (ICD)* (World Health Organization, 1992); the other is the *Diagnostic and Statistical Manual of Mental Disorders (DSM)* (American Psychiatric Association, 1994). The former, as the name implies, is a universal publication: it provides diagnostic guidelines for clinicians throughout the world and forms the basis for collating cross-national statistics on mental disorder. The *DSM*, on the other hand, is of North American origin but is also widely referred to outside the USA.

Both the *ICD* and the *DSM* are essentially handbooks, consisting of lists of disorders, each accompanied by the defining characteristics by which the clinician arrives at a diagnosis in a particular case, Both glossaries are quite similar (or can be translated across from one to the other), but the fact that they are not identical indicates that the diagnostic categories they suggest are somewhat arbitrary and often represent compromise. This is bound to be the case, since the contents of both merely result from decisions made in committee by groups of professionals, experienced in their own fields, but often of differing theoretical persuasion or clinical expertise.

Illustrating an earlier point, it should also be noted that these glossaries are not static in their definitions of disorder. At the time of writing the ICD is in its tenth edition, whereas the DSM has reached its fourth edition (DSM-IV), having gone through two previous editions since 1980 and already being in the process of revision to DSM-V. In the meantime an intermediate version has been introduced, known as DSM-IV-TR (American Psychiatric Association, 2000). There is therefore continual 'tweaking' of psychiatrists' definitions of psychological disorders, even over relatively short periods of time.

12

Here, whenever we have occasion to refer to these psychiatric classifications, we shall use the DSM-IV, for two reasons: it is more detailed than the ICD in its descriptions of psychological disorders; and it is much more commonly adopted as the nosology of choice for selecting subjects in research studies, even outside North America. Before considering the DSM from this more academic standpoint it will be helpful to get some idea of its structure, purely as a practitioner's diagnostic manual.

DSM-IV, like its two immediate predecessors, is organized around what is referred to as a 'multi-axial' approach to diagnosis. This means that a clinician making full use of it to assess a patient at first interview reaches a decision on five facets of the individual's condition. For information, these are listed in

Table 2.1. But note that here we shall be mostly concerned with just two components: Axis I (the classes of major clinical disorders) and the personality disorders listed under Axis II. Together these form the centrepiece of the DSM system of psychiatric classification.

**Table 2.1**  DSM Axes.

| Axis I | Clinical disorders |
|---|---|
| Axis II | Personality disorders<br>Mental retardation |
| Axis III | General medical conditions |
| Axis IV | Psychosocial problems |
| Axis V | Global functioning |

The thinking behind the DSM (and the ICD) approach is explicitly categorical, drawing on the medical model of defining classes of disease according to their superficial features, before (or in conjunction with) trying to identify their causes. The general assumption of this method is that the diseases in question form relatively discrete, homogeneous entities, without overlap between them and with fairly clear boundaries between illness and health. Judged in this way, how does the DSM-IV fare? In the Introduction the authors admit that the DSM system is far from ideal, falling well short of the standards for a strictly categorical model of the kind that works well in physical medicine; they defend it largely on the practical grounds we mentioned earlier – as a vehicle for communicating between professionals in the field. But, doubts remain about it on the scientific front: whether the DSM or similar categorical systems are best suited to taking forward our *understanding* of psychological disorders. There are several areas of concern.

A central problem is that of *comorbidity*, the tendency for an individual to meet the diagnostic criteria for more than one disorder. This can genuinely occur; as in the case of someone having, by coincidence, the symptoms of two quite separate conditions. After all, it is common enough in physical medicine: diabetic individuals catch the 'flu like anyone else, and patients with cystitis can suffer hair loss. But in those cases there is factual evidence that each illness has a distinct aetiology – and anyway the disorders in question simply *look* quite different. By comparison, in psychiatry comorbid disorders often seem suspiciously similar, as though they share some common cause or underlying mechanism (One notable example, relevant to our discussion in later chapters, is the conjunction of eating disorders and substance abuse disorder).

An extension of the comorbidity problem is the overlap between what in the DSM are regarded as two separate types of disorder: the major mental illnesses in Axis I and the personality disorders in Axis II. Several Axis II disorders are descriptively similar to and have an apparent counterpart in an equivalent Axis I disorder; for example, Obsessive Compulsive Disorder (Axis I) and Obsessive Compulsive *Personality* Disorder (Axis II). Although these two are by no means always comorbid, there is evidence suggesting – not surprisingly – that there is some relationship (continuity) between them (Nigg & Goldsmith, 1994). To consider them as belonging to two totally different classes, and as sitting on two different axes, of abnormality therefore looks very artificial. It also tempts us to believe that their respective aetiologies are quite unconnected, which is almost certainly not true. The same problem will be seen to arise in an even more serious form when we come to address associations between Axis II disorders and the psychotic illnesses.

Equally unconvincing is the DSM formulation of the Axis II disorders themselves as categorical. Even if the main mental illnesses could be said to be in some sense qualitatively distinct, the personality disorders definitely seem less like that. To view them as categorical appears to be taking the 'medical model' too far. To make matters worse, the personality disorders subsumed under Axis II are themselves highly comorbid. As we shall see when we discuss Axis II in more detail in Chapter 4, the DSM deals with the problem by acknowledging the existence of related 'clusters' of personality disorder. But this does not instil much confidence that we are dealing in that case with recognizably disparate classes of abnormal behaviour.

Another criticism to be made of the categorical approach is that it does not deal all that well with the fact that the distinction between illness (or dysfunction) and health is not itself clear-cut. Of course, this is by no means confined to psychological disorders: people with physical diseases can also experience these to a varying degree. There, too, decisions constantly have to be made – both by the sufferer and by doctors – about whether the symptoms are bad enough for the person to be considered unwell. Nevertheless, psychological disorders *are* uniquely different. In physical diseases the primary fault lies in just one part of the organism and the evidence for its failure or deficiency is usually fairly objective. Psychological disorders, on the other hand, are defined more in terms of the person's *whole* behaviour and mental functioning. This means that what is judged psychologically abnormal can sometimes seem quite arbitrary, and it may often depend on changing social criteria of what is healthy and unhealthy. In other words, the idea of 'disease process' as the *sole* cause of psychological disorders is less helpful than in the case of physical illness. To explain this point further let us consider one other, very important, distinction that needs to be made in our definition of psychological disorder – and therefore what it is we shall be covering in this book.

We are referring to the comparison between, on the one hand, the psychiatric disorders and, on the other, the *neurological* diseases. Well-known examples of the latter are Alzheimer's disease and Huntington's chorea. We shall not be

considering this type of disorder in this book. It might be asked how we justify that. After all, neurological diseases also affect a person's 'whole behaviour and mental functioning' – a criterion we used above to mark out the psychological disorders. Furthermore, the examples just quoted actually appear in the DSM, as do several other conditions that traditionally, and until recently, have been studied more within the medical specialty of neurology, rather than psychiatry.

The answer lies in the way the nervous system is implicated in the two types of disorder: neurological and psychiatric. In the former, illness results from some pathological process in the nervous system, either one that is already known or one that can be confidently assumed and therefore, at some point in the future, discovered. In other words, neurological diseases are exactly like any other physical disease: they just happen to affect the brain. The disease process involved, whatever it is, can produce a quite gross change in the brain and is often not static, causing a progressive deterioration in mental functioning. Put simply, neurological diseases *destroy* the healthy brain, either partly or completely; they never contain any element that is compatible with full health. This contrasts with the disorders we shall be considering here, where – as we shall explain more fully below – the biology of disorder is more continuous with the biology of health. Before elaborating that point, let us summarize the types of disorder we shall be discussing, either in passing or in detail, in the book. Table 2.2 will act as a guide to this, showing how the disorders are broadly distinguished, as well as how they relate to one another. The table is *not* intended as a summary of the DSM (or the ICD); in fact some terms, for example 'neurotic', no longer appear in the DSM, even though they are still in common use.

The table first draws the general distinction between the psychotic and the non-psychotic disorders and then, for each of these, makes further subdivisions. The exact details of the individual conditions will emerge in later chapters, but one point needs clarifying here: the difference between 'psychotic' and 'non-psychotic'.

**Table 2.2** Main types of psychological disorder.

| Non-psychotic disorders | Psychotic disorders |
|---|---|
| *Neuroses* | *Personality disorders* |
| Anxiety disorders | Schizophrenia |
| Obsessive–compulsive disorder | |
| Dissociative ('hysterical') & somatoform disorders | Manic-depressive (bipolar affective) disorder |
| Neurotic (mild) depression | Psychotic (severe) depression |

In practice – and further illustrating the limitations of categorical description – the distinction between the two expressions of disorder is not all that easy to make. Three criteria have often been adopted, as follows:

- Psychotic illnesses are mostly more severe and psychologically disabling. But that is not always the case: some people receiving a diagnosis of psychotic illness are actually quite mildly affected.

- The label 'psychotic' usually indicates symptoms that are more weird or bizarre, like believing aliens are invading one's mind. But again some 'neurotic' symptoms, for example obsessional thoughts, can also be very strange.

- Psychotic people are more likely to lose touch with reality and lack insight that there is anything worrisome about their behaviour and their ideas. But that is relative and mostly only true in the acute phases of their illnesses.

Of course, if all three of these criteria are met then we can be fairly safe in use of the term 'psychotic' to describe the disorder and so this combination will help, for the moment, to capture what we mean when we refer to psychotic as against non-psychotic.

## THE DIMENSIONAL APPROACH

### HISTORICAL CONSIDERATIONS: HJ EYSENCK

The dimensional approach to psychological disorders can be almost entirely traced to the ideas of one man. Hans Eysenck, whose professional life spanned more than 50 years (he died as recently as 2000) was a writer of extraordinary research output and breadth of interest. These included many disparate areas of psychology – from astrology and parapsychology to psychosomatic medicine and behaviour genetics; indeed, almost any topic where a question about individual differences in behaviour could be raised (see Nyborg (1997) for a recent *Festschrift* appreciation of his ideas). However, the centrepiece of Eysenck's contribution – and that for which he will be mostly remembered – was his rigorously constructed theory of personality, which he continued to investigate and elaborate throughout his long career (Eysenck & Eysenck, 1985). Working in the psychometric tradition of individual differences psychology, Eysenck believed that it was possible to reduce personality to a series of continuously variable, quantitative traits, measurable at the descriptive level by questionnaire. Although there were eminent contemporaries (notably R.B. Cattell (1965)) who shared his views, Eysenck was unique, for two reasons. First, because he systematically pursued the idea that personality traits have a biological basis (Eysenck, 1967). Second, because his writings about personality made constant

16

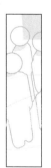

reference to the abnormal (Eysenck, 1960, 1973). Indeed, looked at from another point of view, Eysenck's proposals about the structure of normal personality may also be seen as a restatement, in dimensional terms, of the classification of psychological disorders. It is this aspect of his work and the ideas flowing from it that will concern us in the present chapter.

For deconstructing personality Eysenck's preference was to work, not at the trait level *per se*; trait characteristics were considered too narrow and the measurement of them unreliable. Instead, he favoured seeking a few broad, higher order dimensions, each of which was itself defined by groups of traits that correlate with one another. The method used to identify traits – and, at the higher level, dimensions – in a set of personality data is some form of *factor analysis* (see Cooper (1998) for a detailed account of the method). Briefly, factor analysis starts with a matrix of correlations among a set of items and then, on the basis of which items correlate with which, tries to discover the minimum number of factors or components necessary to account for the co-variation across all of the data. It is essentially an attempt to cluster the items, except that the 'clusters' here consist of continuously variable scales, each weighted on, and defined by, a particular subset of the items. 'Items', in the case of the higher order analysis of personality data leading to broad dimensions are, conceptually at least, traits which themselves have been identified by factor analysing behaviour at a lower level of personality organization.

In using factor analysis to discover the basic dimensions of *normal* personality Eysenck always had in mind the need also to describe and explain the *abnormal*. A continuity between the healthy and the pathological was therefore intrinsic to his theory. He considered that the various forms of psychological disorder recognized in psychiatry actually define the extremes of the personality dimensions he was describing; people with symptoms of the disorders were therefore seen to lie at the far ends of the dimensions. In effect, on the abnormal side, Eysenck set out to give a dimensional account of psychological disorders as these were portrayed earlier in Table 2.1 (Eysenck, 1957; Eysenck & Eysenck, 1976a, 1976b). The actual dimensions which he thought could best mirror this were Neuroticism (N), Psychoticism (P), and Introversion–Extraversion (I–E).

Neuroticism was intended to cover disorders on the left side, and Psychoticism to cover disorders on the right side, of the earlier Table 2.2 (p. 15). Thus, Eysenck considered N to be a general feature common to all people who suffered from non-psychotic disorders. Variations *within* this Neuroticism domain were explained by reference to differences in Introversion–Extraversion (see Figure 2.1). Individuals high on N who suffer from anxiety-related conditions were considered to be of the more *introverted* neurotic type. *Extraverted* neurotic types were judged to fall into a category of what in table we have referred to as 'impulse disorders', characterized by antisocial and acting-out behaviours. A comparable arrangement was suggested for psychosis and Psychoticism (see Figure 2.2).

17

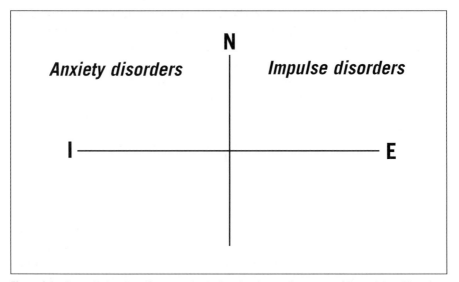

**Figure 2.1** Eysenck's location of non-psychotic disorders in two dimensions of Neuroticism (N) and Introversion–Extraversion (I–E).

Here, a similar way of differentiating types of psychotic disorder was suggested, again in terms of I–E. Schizophrenic individuals were regarded as people high in P and *introverted*; those suffering from serious mood disorder (for example manic-depression) were high in P and *extraverted*.

The thinking behind this dimensional classification of psychological

18

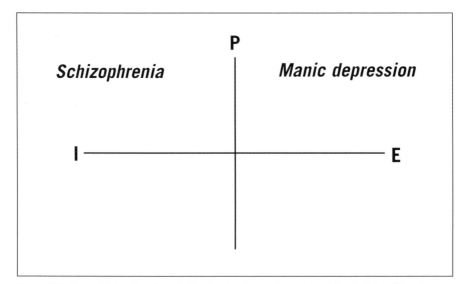

**Figure 2.2** Eysenck's location of psychotic disorders in two dimensions of Psychoticism (P) and Introversion–Extraversion (I–E).

disorders was Eysenck's view that the latter are not diseases in the medical sense. Instead, he argued, they are *behavioural* disturbances, exaggerated forms of the response patterns that characterize the personality dimensions or relevant configurations of them; for example, anxiety neurotics are the clinical counterparts of individuals who are introverted and high in neuroticism. The only concession Eysenck made to a medical viewpoint was his strong belief that psychological disorders are grounded in the biology of the organism. However, for Eysenck this meant something totally different from the disease process idea of the medical model. According to him, psychological disorders stemmed, not from a *neuropathology* of the brain, but from the individual's biological make-up, as an exaggerated form of it.

## COMMENTS ON EYSENCK'S THEORY

In keeping with Eysenck's notoriously radical, controversial style, his thinking about personality and psychological disorder contained some brilliant insights and some serious misjudgements. But one thing is clear. As we shall see at various points throughout this book, his writings have had a strong and continuing influence on others of a similar theoretical persuasion, either directly, through attempts to modify and update his theory, or indirectly, by helping to foster an alternative perspective on personality and illness. In the latter regard how does his dimensional model for psychological disorders stand up to modern scrutiny?

There are really two questions here. One concerns the particular dimensions that Eysenck proposed; the other is the general form of his version of a continuity between health and illness. At this point we shall confine ourselves to the second question, allowing answers about the actual details of his theory to emerge in later chapters.

Criticisms of Eysenck's dimensional description of psychological disorder actually began to be voiced even during the period in which he first proposed it, and are still valid. The most cogent arguments were those to be found in the early writings of Foulds (1965). Foulds made an important distinction that Eysenck always ignored, but which is vital to an understanding of how an alternative to the categorical description (and causal model) of mental illness would need to look, if it is to work. Foulds pointed out that 'personality' and 'illness' really represent two quite distinct areas of behaviour (or 'universes of discourse', as he put it). Each of these, he said, has its own uniquely different descriptive terminology.

As Foulds (1965) noted, the language for describing *personality* is couched in terms of *traits*. Traits have certain features, as follows:

- They are universal and commonly observed in the population.

- When measured, say, by questionnaire, scores tend to follow the bell-shaped curve of the normal distribution.

- They are ego-*syntonic*; viz. adapted to the healthy needs of the person.

*Illness*, on the other hand, is typically described by *signs* and *symptoms* ('Signs' refer to objective and 'symptoms' to more general, often subjectively reported, indicators of disease). Signs and symptoms have the following characteristics:

- They are relatively uncommon in the population.

- When measured by, say, rating scales or by questionnaire, scores are usually very skewed, with most people not showing the feature.

- They are ego-*dystonic*, viz. maladaptive and tending to interfere with the healthy functioning of the person.

So, although Eysenck was right to draw attention to the dimensional element in disorder, his own model was incomplete in failing to make the above distinctions. It is *not* the case, as he seemed to envisage, that clinical neurotic individuals are the same as healthy people who happen to be high in Neuroticism. Both share the *traits* of Neuroticism, but neurotic patients also have their *symptoms*; it is these that define them as ill and put them, even if only temporarily, in a different set or category from the healthy person.

Dimensions (continuity) and categories (discontinuity) are not therefore mutually exclusive ideas for describing the connection between personality and disorder; there are elements here of both. The real question is what the relative contribution of each is to disorder. And how one gives way to the other as the individual passes from disposition to illness itself. To understand this, it will be helpful to examine a dimensional view of disorder that goes beyond Eysenck's rather simple model.

## A DIMENSIONAL MODEL OF PSYCHOLOGICAL DISORDER

Figure 2.3 shows a model which takes account of both the personality and the illness aspect in disorder, as outlined in the previous section. The example we have chosen is anxiety but it will act as a useful template for understanding certain features of all of the disorders that we shall be discussing. The diagram is self-explanatory, but several points should be mentioned.

We first need to remind the reader of a crucial feature of the model. This concerns the *dual status* of those (trait) characteristics described at the personality level. By 'dual status' we mean that the dimension – in this case trait anxiety – defines two things: a continuum of personality, in the usual sense, and at the same time a varying *predisposition* to disorder – here anxiety disorder. It is this idea that helps to bridge the first gap between personality, as healthy individual variation, and illness as malfunction.

Second, the use of the term *state* in the model should be noted. Although not referred to previously here, this is an important additional construct that we require in order to give a complete account of psychological disorders. 'State' refers to some temporary fluctuation, usually in mood, relevant to and

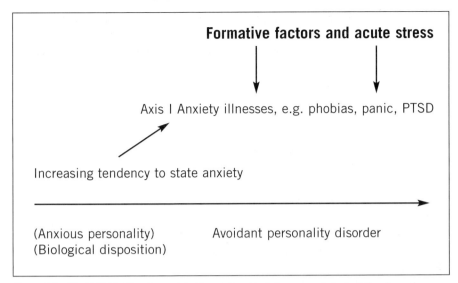

**Figure 2.3** Model illustrating, for anxiety, the relationship between psychological disorder and personality disposition (c.f. Figure 2.4).

stemming from an existing personality trait. Thus, anxiety as a trait describes a relatively fixed property of the person: the way he or she is generally, when averaged across many situations and as compared with other people. The *state* of anxiety, on the other hand, denotes the trait 'in action', how anxious the person is at this moment. The relationship between the two is such that the strength of the trait can also be defined as the upper limit of the state that the individual will reach when aroused. Some very unanxious people never become fazed, however powerful the stressful stimulus or situation; others, occupying the upper end of the trait, will be easily provoked into strong state anxiety. As a component of disorder, state may be viewed as one of the mediators between personality and illness, something that brings about symptoms to which the personality predisposes the individual.

Third, we should ask: How compatible is this dimensional account of psychological disorders with the medical view? And how valid, therefore, are the past and present criticisms of psychiatry for making so much use of the disease model? The fact is that there is no real incompatibility here and Eysenck was certainly wrong to reject outright what psychiatrists were saying about mental illness. For there is, in reality, no *one* medical model. Here, it is instructive to pursue the parallel with physical diseases.

Physical diseases differ widely in what causes them. Some are due to infections, some traceable to a single faulty gene, some the result of accident and so on. Nevertheless, despite their different origins and manifestations, these types of disease do have one thing in common. They all tend to have the distinctive appearance of failures of function; and they all fit what most people,

21

if asked, would probably think of as 'the medical model' (the neurological diseases referred to in a previous section fall into this category).

But there are some kinds of physical disease whose general form is not like that and which are more comparable to the psychological disorders than is often realized. We are referring to the so-called 'systemic' diseases. These are conditions which, as the name implies, occur because of some breakdown or failure of a vital bodily system – one that otherwise performs some perfectly healthy function in the body. Figure 2.4 illustrates this for one major class of systemic diseases: those associated with high blood pressure (essential hypertension).

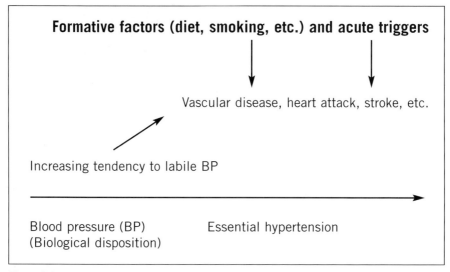

**Figure 2.4** Dimensional model of physical systemic disease, illustrated for blood pressure and hypertension (c.f. Figure 2.3).

A comparison with Figure 2.3 will show the similarity with psychological disorders. In the hypertension example (Figure 2.4), the equivalent of the 'personality trait' is blood pressure. This is a continuously variable characteristic, naturally higher in some people than in others, and something that forms part of normal bodily functioning: it meets all of the criteria for a trait described earlier. It also shows fluctuations; in that respect, therefore, it has the properties of a state. Then, at the illness level, the diseases associated with, and partly mediated by, hypertension – for example stroke and heart disease – are analogous to the disorders in the psychological sphere, as we have portrayed them here. That is to say, they are relatively uncommon, symptomatic conditions that undermine the healthy behaviour of the organism.

Lastly, we need to mention another, more subtle feature of the models portrayed in Figures 2.3 and 2.4. It concerns 'dimensionality' *within illness*. We

briefly touched upon this earlier when recalling that the symptoms of disease (whether physical or psychological) can occur with varying severity. This variability gives rise to the notion of *subclinical* disorder, where it may be hard to tell whether the person is simply high on the trait underlying the illness, or is showing minimal signs of the illness to which the trait is relevant. In the anxiety example the decision might simply lie with the sufferer, to decide whether his or her everyday life is being sufficiently interfered with to need to seek help. In the hypertension example the decision is also arbitrary, albeit in a different way. Although ultimately those with sustained high blood pressure will begin to show symptoms and objective signs, hypertension is mostly asymptomatic and the initial judgement 'ill or not ill' rests on the presence of a blood pressure reading that doctors have agreed is a clinically significant deviation from average.

## FROM CONTINUITY TO DISCONTINUITY

Thinking about the model for illness described above, there is still the question to be asked: How do we visualize the transition from disposition to illness, from dimensional, trait-like variation to symptomatic discontinuity of function? In the case of hypertension-related disease – used as our example of medical illness – the clue lies in understanding how the physicochemical mechanisms responsible for chronically raised blood pressure bring about changes in vascular structure and function, initially as barely detectable perturbations in the retina and kidney, but increasingly as major alterations that threaten vital life systems and the catastrophic failure associated with heart attack or stroke. In psychological disorders the process is more complexly psychobiological and in any case much of the detail is still missing. Nevertheless, the principle is the same and there are certain descriptive formulations (applicable to both physical and psychological disorder) that can help us to grasp the problem (Table 2.3). We shall look at these in turn.

**Table 2.3** Ways of conceptualizing how the continuity of personality is translated into the discontinuity of illness.

| |
|---|
| U-shaped functions |
| Positive feedback states |
| Kindling |
| Amplification theory |
| Two-hit theory |
| Catastrophe theory |

**Inverted-U functions** The simplest insight into how adaptive traits might become maladaptive symptoms is contained in the commonly quoted law in psychology, of the inverted-U function. In its most generally stated form this recognizes the frequently observed non-linear relationship between some index of efficiency or capability and a measure of the organismic state. For example, as sports people and other public performers know only too well, moderate levels of fear or anxiety are beneficial, motivating them to perform at the peak of their capacity. But, beyond that optimum, very strong negative emotion actually begins to interfere with adaptive responding. If the state persists or the experience is repeated too often, the symptoms of disorder will appear, manifesting as fear of public speaking or other social phobia. Mediating this transition is an upward shift in the person's *state* of anxiety, which is more likely to occur anyway in someone who is high on the dimension of *trait* anxiety. This introduces a certain element of positive feedback into the situation; state anxiety is more easily evoked in someone prone to it and, once triggered, exacerbates the maladaptive behaviour that it caused in the first place.

**Positive feedback states** The tendency for abnormality to feed upon itself, and so cause increasingly worsening effects, is another principle which has considerable generality in the understanding of both physical and mental disorder, helping to account for several features, including the drift into chronic illness. In psychology the idea has been applied – interestingly by cognitive psychologists – to several conditions. A good example is panic disorder (see Figure 2.5). There, some stimulus, either internal or external,

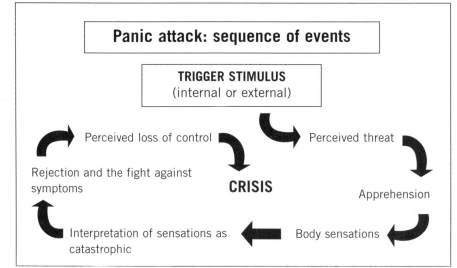

**Figure 2.5** Example of positive feedback effect in disorder. (Thanks are due to Dr Herbert Chapps for permission to use this figure)

24

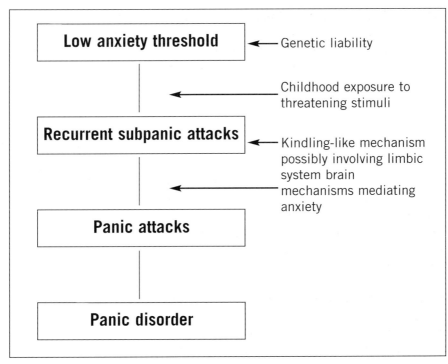

Figure 2.6   Illustration of panic disorder as an example of 'kindling'.

triggers off bodily sensations which the individual misinterprets as more serious than they really are, possibly even life-threatening. This elicits further anxiety, including the bodily reactions, creating a vicious cycle of cause and effect. A significant element is the individual's increasing sense of loss of control which further exacerbates the positive feedback process.

**Kindling** A rather similar idea is to be found in the notion of kindling, although there the application has been rather different. 'Kindling' has been used in a more developmental sense, over a longer time-scale, in the explanation of the possible mechanisms underlying the progression of disease. The concept originated in epilepsy research, to explain the 'lowered threshold effect', the fact that once an individual has had a seizure the likelihood of having another is increased (Post & Ballenger, 1981). This may be mirrored in experimental research on animals in which a repeated, initially subthreshold, electrical stimulus, which to begin with only produces a normal neuronal afterdischarge, eventually brings about full seizure activity. Although having a well-understood neurobiological grounding in the explanation of epilepsy, 'kindling' has been applied, more speculatively, to other disorders, including psychiatric illnesses such as manic-depression and panic disorder (Rosenberg, 1989). The latter is illustrated in Figure 2.6. The idea is that repeated subtraumatic experiences in childhood may 'kindle' the tendency of some individuals to react with panic in adult life. The mechanism is considered to be a predominantly biological one, mediated by (limbic) brain systems that control the physiology of fear and anxiety, and which are more susceptible to kindling in genetically predisposed individuals (see Chapter 3 for further discussion of the personality/vulnerability aspects of anxiety and Chapter 5 for an account of the biology of the anxiety disorders).

**Amplification theory** A similar idea to kindling, but stated in a more general, clinical form, is the theory of 'amplification' proposed by Paris (1994). This theory was developed mainly to account for the personality disorders and we shall come across it again in Chapter 4. It suggests that, although certain temperamental traits are associated with, and do strongly predispose to, particular clinical disorders of the personality, the latter are more than mere exaggerations of the normal personality. As shown in Figure 2.7, it is envisaged that a range of biological, psychological, and social factors will act upon the basic temperament in childhood so as to exaggerate an existing tendency to deviance and bring it out into open behaviour.

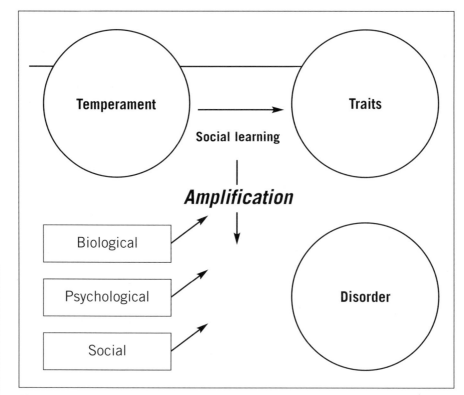

**Figure 2.7** Paris's model of 'amplification'.

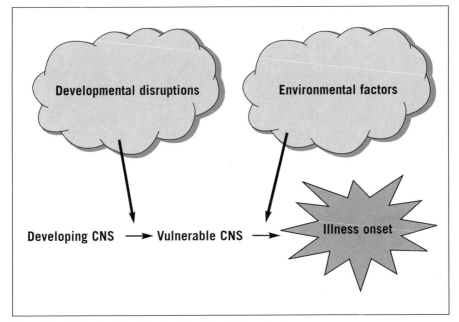

**Figure 2.8**  Illustration (for schizophrenia) of 'two-hit' hypothesis.

**Two-hit theory** Yet another idea that addresses the longitudinal progression from vulnerability to illness is the so-called 'two-hit' hypothesis. This originates in attempts to explain the aetiology of complex physical diseases, such as cancer, in which genetic predispositions may lie dormant or, alternatively, 'explode' into disease depending on the presence or absence of environmental triggers. In the psychiatric field the two-hit theory has so far mainly been applied to schizophrenia (see Figure 2.8). There, the biological approach is increasingly wedded to a neurodevelopmental view of schizophrenia as a disorder whose aetiology has a long trajectory, starting in processes that occur before birth and are partly of genetic origin. The illness itself is of much later onset (typically occurring in early adulthood) and the two-hit explanation would be that further environmental events are necessary for schizophrenic breakdown to occur; without these the otherwise vulnerable individual will be spared serious disorder (Maynard *et al.*, 2001).

**Catastrophe theory** Lastly, a formulation that has dealt most explicitly with the problem of how continuity gives rise to *dis*continuity is the mathematically highly sophisticated catastrophe theory. The brainchild of the French mathematician, René Thom (1975), catastrophe theory is a branch of topology which attempts to quantify the manner in which abrupt changes in phenomena may be associated with, and may be predicted from, determining

27

processes that are themselves continuously variable. Descriptively, its essential features have been stated as follows:

> Many processes yield graphs with obstinately ill-behaved curves: there are spikes, breaks, and regions where one value of $x$ corresponds to any of several values of $y$, and vice versa. The planets travel in stately Newtonian paths, but meanwhile winds wrap themselves into hurricanes, chickens alternate with eggs, and we change our minds. Discontinuity is as much the rule as the exception. To take a relatively simple example, the physical properties of water are discontinuous at the freezing and boiling points. A graph of its temperature versus the flow of heat energy shows large, abrupt thresholds at those points, and no simple equation can relate the two qualities (Woodcock & Davis, 1978; 6).

In its heyday, catastrophe theory attracted a good deal of attention because of its apparently promising application to the 'inexact' sciences, such as psychology and sociology, where discontinuities in behaviour are rather evident. These uses included several in psychopathology, most notably the attempt to explain the abrupt shifts between bingeing and starving seen in the eating disorders (Zeeman, 1976).

Unfortunately, catastrophe theory has so far rarely been able to specify exact, quantitative values for the parameters it proposes; this is especially true of the behavioural applications. The predictive value of the theory is therefore limited and its utility is mostly descriptive and conceptual. But for precisely that reason it does remain an extremely significant statement about natural phenomena in the present context, keeping in the forefront of our minds the very important issue of how continuity and discontinuity sit side by side in psychological disorders.

## SUMMARY AND CONCLUSIONS

In this chapter we have seen that, for various practical and historical reasons, psychological disorders have mostly been described and classified as categorical diseases, in the tradition of the medical model. This has given rise to psychiatric glossaries (the DSM and the ICD) which have proven practical usefulness. They allow easy communication between clinicians, help in deciding treatment, and for research purposes, facilitate the selection of clinical populations according to agreed criteria.

However, a major problem with this categorical approach is the overlap between different disorders. This leads to comorbidity, where an individual meets the diagnostic criteria for more than one disorder. Comorbidity may be observed on both of the 'axes' recognized in the DSM: Axis I (major mental illnesses) and the Axis II personality disorders. Furthermore, there are some clear connections *between* Axis I and Axis II disorders, even though these are kept separate in the DSM. Another problem with categorizing disorders is the difficulty of defining the boundary between health and illness, or adjustment and maladjustment.

Dimensional description tries to deal with these problems by proposing continuities in disorder, rather than distinct classes. Historically, the most important attempt at this was Eysenck's theory, which was also significant for two other reasons: it stressed biology and it attempted to relate psychological disorders to normal personality. For Eysenck, mental illnesses and personality disorders simply represented the end-points of normal personality dimensions and could be explained as exaggerated forms of the biology and behaviours associated with those dimensions (Neuroticism, Psychoticism, and Introversion–Extraversion).

Eysenck's theory was, however, *too* dimensional. He failed to recognize that there are some discontinuities in what he was trying to explain and that a distinction has to be drawn between 'personality' and 'illness'; one refers to continuously variable, adaptive traits, the other to quasi-dimensional signs and symptoms of malfunction.

Here a more accurate model was described, taking account of these distinctions, but preserving the idea that personality and disorder are nevertheless intimately related. Personality traits and dimensions were referred to as having dual status: they describe healthy individual variations between people *and* define dispositions to disorder. A typical example quoted was anxiety and anxiety disorder. Attention was also drawn to the role played by fluctuating *states* in mediating and defining the presence of disorder.

We have stressed that this dimensional analysis of psychological disorder is quite consistent with one version of the medical model; certain physical conditions – the so-called systemic diseases – may be viewed in a similar way. The example of physical illness we used was hypertension-related disorders, where we find the same elements as in the psychological disorders: a naturally varying trait that also acts as predisposition to illness (blood pressure) and a symptomatic state to which it can give rise.

The comparison we have drawn between the psychological disorders and the physical systemic diseases also brings into focus one further final point. Both illustrate a paradox which is, nevertheless, a central theme of this book: an apparent contradiction that many find difficult to reconcile. It is the puzzle of how perfectly normal, healthy features of the organism can, at the same time, be vehicles for illness, disease, and maladjustment. Or, put the other way round, how disorder can originate in healthy function, by a simple transformation of it. Many years ago, the eminent American physiologist, Walter B. Cannon – famous in psychology for his theory of emotion – confronted the same question (Cannon, 1953). He concluded as follows:

> There are many systems in the body which, because of misuse or misfortune, may have their services to the organism as a whole so altered as to be actually harmful. Thus vicious circles of causation become established which may lead to death ... The development of pathological functions in a system is quite consistent with its usual performance of normal functions. (Cannon, 1953; 16)

29

Cannon was, of course, referring to narrowly defined physiological functions that go wrong; indeed, the hypertension example we used here is a good example of what he was talking about. But his comment can be generalized beyond that, to a general principle that applies equally to the connections between the dimensions of normal personality and psychological disorders.

# CHAPTER 3

## PERSONALITY DIMENSIONS: DESCRIPTION AND BIOLOGY

In the previous chapter we outlined a general model for understanding how personality differences can connect to psychological disorders. In this chapter we examine the personality aspect in more detail. For the moment we shall mostly concentrate on those dispositional dimensions that relate to the *non-psychotic* disorders, as we have already broadly defined them. As a starting point, it is logical to pick up where we left off in Chapter 2, with the work of Eysenck, whose theory is the prototypical example of how normal personality has been linked to the abnormal. This will also allow us then to introduce contemporary themes from the more recent literature.

### HISTORICAL ANTECEDENTS AND EYSENCK'S THEORY

Just as we have tried to convey here, Eysenck always stressed the importance of knowing where ideas come from historically. In the case of his own theorizing about personality, he made frequent reference to its antecedents in the classic typology of the four temperaments (see Figure 3.1). This theory, which originated in Hippocratic medicine and was later extended by the Graeco–Roman physician, Galen, was one of the earliest attempts to describe human personality differences. What is remarkable, and indicative of the longstanding influence of the typology, is the fact that its terminology has survived into modern everyday usage; it is still employed as a handy description of our fellow human beings. We still speak of the carefree and optimistic as 'sanguine'; the gloomy and pessimistic as 'melancholic'; the angry as 'choleric'; the calm and unemotional as 'phlegmatic'. Furthermore, when using these terms we definitely mean to refer to the person's 'basic' temperament or ingrained outlook on life. So, our folklore belief and language have always contained some sense that people differ intrinsically from one another.

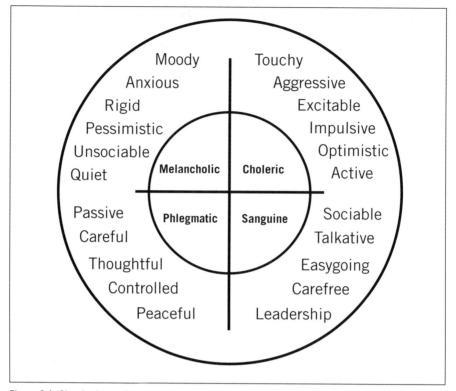

**Figure 3.1** Classic theory of temperaments.

The classic theory of temperaments is also significant for other reasons. Its medical origins emphasize an early attempt to relate normal to abnormal, especially physical disease (Phillips, 1987). This reflects the fact that in Greek medicine illnesses were thought to came about because of the influence of bodily fluids or 'humours', consisting of blood, phlegm, and bile (which came in two varieties, black and yellow). The eventual connection of these humours to temperaments – sanguine (blood), phlegmatic (phlegm), melancholic (black bile), choleric (yellow bile) – was therefore an early example of a biological theory of personality.

Another reason the classic theory of temperaments is of interest here is that it illustrates an important point about 'types' as mere shorthand, not meant to capture all the fine detail of description. We came across this issue in a different context in Chapter 2, when discussing categories in psychiatric classification and the part they play in diagnostic labelling. No one pretends that the psychiatric categories give a complete account of what they are attempting to describe. But they do provide a useful summary statement: in the case of psychiatric nosology about the typical form of illnesses and, in the diagnostic process, about what is wrong with a given person.

It is the same with personality 'types': they are handy labels. But it is inconceivable that the Greeks thought there really were only four kinds of people! In fact, in their medical use of their humoral theory the emphasis was very much on the *balance* of the humours and how the relative overproduction of one of them might cause an illness or set of illnesses. So again we encounter the notion of gradations or degrees of variation, of blending of characteristics, rather than sharp differences and discontinuities. In making this same point Eysenck was fond of drawing an analogy with the colour spectrum; that, although there are only three primary colours, mixing them in different proportions can result in an infinite number of hues (Eysenck, 1952).

In seeking the 'primary colours' of personality, differential psychology took a major step forward with the introduction of statistical methods, especially that of factor analysis, referred to in the previous chapter. This made it possible to search somewhat more objectively for personality traits and the broader dimensions that they defined. Here, Eysenck made a major contribution.

## THE EYSENCK DIMENSIONS

As we mentioned in Chapter 2, Eysenck proposed three statistically derived dimensions which he believed were fundamental in accounting for normal and abnormal personality differences. The two most important of these were Neuroticism (N) and Introversion–Extraversion (I–E); important, that is, if we judge by how well the dimensions he proposed mapped on to psychological disorders, in the way Eysenck had intended. (By comparison, his Psychoticism (P) dimension turned out to be something of an anomaly, a point we shall come back to later.) In the case of N and I–E, it may be recalled that he supposed that anxiety neurosis was the clinical counterpart of neurotic introversion; in contrast, disorders with an antisocial, or acting-out element were regarded as the clinical counterpart of neurotic extraversion.

It is easy to follow Eysenck's thinking in that regard if we examine the traits that define N and I–E (Figure 3.2). Neuroticism referred in the theory to *general emotionality* and was therefore something that should be high in all individuals – whatever their other personality characteristics – who are predisposed to suffer strong, changeable mood, and to overreact in emotional situations. Combine this with the social inhibitedness of the extreme introvert and we should have what Eysenck argued was the typical profile of the anxiety neurotic. Combine high N with extreme *extraversion*, on the other hand, and we have, he said, the sort of person who acts out their emotions, perhaps even in an antisocial way. Did the evidence confirm this?

Like all personality psychologists of the tradition in which he worked, Eysenck constructed self-report questionnaires to measure his dimensions. In his case they actually formed several generations of questionnaires of slightly different content, designed to measure Neuroticism, Introversion–Extraversion (and later Psychoticism) in both adults and children (Eysenck & Eysenck,

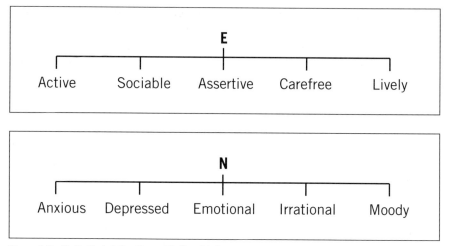

Figure 3.2    Traits that define Eysenck's N and I–E.

1976a, 1991). Administering these questionnaires to diagnosed psychiatric patients demonstrated quite convincingly that, as far as anxiety neurotics were concerned, Eysenck's theory was very strongly confirmed: such patients were indeed extremely introverted and very high on neuroticism. Effects were rather more ambiguous for patients expected to be highly extraverted: some were and some were not high in E. But some antisocial psychopaths did have extreme E scores, as well as being high in N. So, the theory worked well enough for it to look at that time as though Eysenck was along the right lines in attempting to relate the non-psychotic disorders to personality traits.

But Eysenck was not content simply to *describe* these relationships, as revealed in questionnaires scores. He was also interested – indeed this was the main thrust of his work – in trying to give what he called a '*causal*' account of his personality dimensions, in terms of their biology. Naturally, this was also intended to give an explanation of the disorders associated with the dimensions. The actual details of Eysenck's theorizing about the biology of personality are now mostly of historical interest. But some account will be helpful in explaining how here, too, he laid the foundation for more contemporary work.

## EYSENCK'S 'CAUSAL' THEORIES

The heading for this section is in the plural because Eysenck actually devised *two* theories to account for the biology of Neuroticism and Introversion-Extraversion. The first was published in the mid-1950s and was strongly influenced by the writings of the famous Russian physiologist, IP Pavlov (1928, 1955). Pavlov is mostly celebrated for his contribution to physiology and general experimental psychology, through his pioneering work on the phenomenon of the conditioned reflex. Even outside the academic world

Pavlov's experiments on dogs drooling to ringing bells are famously known. But equally groundbreaking were his observations on the *individual differences* that could be found among his animal subjects; Pavlov discovered that not all of his dogs acquired their conditioned reflexes, or lost them, at the same rate. He further noted that these differences seemed to be related behaviourally to the temperamental characteristics of the animals, whom he classified according to the classic theory of types outlined above.

Pavlov then went on to devise what came to be known as the *theory of nervous types*. This was the idea that individual differences in certain properties of the nervous system accounted for the differences observed in temperament and, therefore, in laboratory conditioning. By 'properties' Pavlov meant features like the ability of the nervous system to withstand very strong stimulation, its 'fatigability', and so on.

Pavlov's speculation about how the brain works was the first true conceptual nervous system – or at least one that placed such emphasis on individual variation. It chimed well with Eysenck's search for a biological explanation of personality; especially given that Pavlov himself eventually came to apply the theory of nervous types to human differences, including mental illness (see Gantt *et al.*, 1970). In developing his own first theory Eysenck (1957) therefore explicitly referred to Pavlov's writings. But we must emphasize that he did so in a very simplified way. Pavlov's theory of nervous types was conceptually very complicated. And it became even more so as Pavlov elaborated the theory during his lifetime, and as others developed it after his death (Nebylitsyn & Gray, 1972; see also Mangan, 1982).

Eysenck's very loose version of the theory connected the I–E personality dimension to the simple idea that nervous systems differ in the extent to which 'excitatory', as against 'inhibitory' or restraining, processes predominate in controlling brain functions. In practice, this translated into the even simpler notion that some people (introverts) have more 'excitable' brains than other people (extraverts). On the abnormal front, the theory allowed Eysenck to try to explain why introverts and extraverts developed different psychiatric symptoms. He argued that differences in central nervous excitability went along with differences in the ease with which people will form conditioned responses. Consequently, unstable extraverts become psychopaths because they fail to learn society's rules; emotionally hypersensitive introverts *over*condition, even learning some pointless, maladaptive responses, like phobic reactions.

Surprisingly, Eysenck here rather neglected the possible biological basis of Neuroticism, merely ascribing it to variations in the activity of the autonomic nervous system, the two divisions of which – sympathetic and parasympathetic – are involved in the physiology of emotional states. In proposing his second, later theory Eysenck (1967) tried to remedy this and also attempted to make his conceptual nervous system look more like the real thing. But the model was still very generally stated. What Eysenck now suggested was that central nervous system excitability – or arousability – depended upon two brain circuits, each of which showed functional variation across individuals. One is the limbic system or 'emotional brain'; the other is the ascending reticular activating system (ARAS) originating in the brain stem and a major part of the circuitry that modulates variations along the sleep–wakefulness continuum. Eysenck then went on to theorize that Neuroticism is due to differences in the responsivity of the limbic system, whereas the ARAS accounts for variations in Introversion–Extraversion. Interactions between the two biological systems therefore accounted for the different combinations of personality and mental illness to which the I–E and N dimensions could give rise.

Eysenck never really worked out how this limbic system/ARAS interaction worked in practice; at least not across the whole spectrum of disorders or their associated personality dimensions. However, there was one prediction from the theory that has stood the test of time experimentally. It concerns the biological status of individuals characterized by the high N/low E combination: in the clinical domain anxiety neurotics. According to Eysenck these people should have a double 'dose' of central nervous system arousability, originating from high activity in *both* the emotional brain *and* the brain stem systems. In theory, then, they should be the most extreme when tested with experimental procedures which reflect that; viz. physiological indices, such as electroencephalography (EEG) activity, or measures of the autonomic nervous system. The prediction turned out to be true, establishing early on a strong biological connection between personality and at least one major group of disorders, the anxiety disorders (Claridge, 1967). We will illustrate this with a single example, a research finding that also serves to introduce a further continuing theme in the study of the biology of personality. It, too, is a topic that Eysenck pioneered.

We are referring to the association between personality and the response to psychoactive or, as they are sometimes called, psychotropic drugs, viz. substances that have their primary effect on the central nervous system. As Eysenck was quick to point out, as long as we can assume that such drugs act on the same biological systems as those underlying personality, then individuals should differ in their reactions to them. In a broad sense this assumption is, of course, true. Indeed, it is the basis of drug treatment; after all, there is no point in giving anxiety neurotic individuals tranquillizers if these do not affect the systems that underlie anxiety!

The connection was exploited early on as a way of testing out Eysenck's biological theory, and many experiments were carried out examining how an individual's response to centrally acting drugs varied according to personality type and psychological disorder (Eysenck, 1963). A particularly powerful technique for doing this was through the use of a procedure called the *sedation*,

or *sleep threshold*. The principle of the test was straightforward. One of the barbiturate drugs – central nervous system depressants – was injected by continuous infusion until the subject either went to sleep or reached some specified level of drowsiness, defined behaviourally or physiologically. The amount of the drug required to reach that point (corrected for the body weight) was then a measure of the person's tolerance of sedation; or, put another way, of his or her degree of central nervous system 'arousal'.

Using this test it was repeatedly shown that extremely high drug tolerance (resistance to sedation) was to be found in anxiety neurotic individuals and in those non-clinical subjects who, according to Eysenck, were their healthy equivalents, viz. people rated as neurotic introverts on questionnaires (Shagass & Jones, 1958; Claridge & Herrington, 1960). Physiologically the results made sense because the barbiturate drugs used are known to have their action on the very brain areas – ARAS and limbic systems – which, the theory argued, were hyperactive in these personality 'types'. Also consistent was the finding that the converse – very *low* drug tolerance – could be observed in both highly neurotic extraverted normal subjects and individuals who, according to Eysenck, were their supposed clinical counterparts: psychopaths and individuals with so-called 'hysterical disorders'.

Although it is nearly half a century since those studies were carried out they still represent a valid observation about the biology and pharmacology of personality and psychological disorder. Together with many other experiments along similar lines they laid the groundwork for the later research and theorizing discussed below and in the following chapters.

## A NOTE ON THE STATUS OF PSYCHOTICISM (P)

In the neat nosological world envisaged by Eysenck we would not have occasion to mention his third dimension until the final chapter of this book, when we consider the psychotic disorders. However, compared with N and neurosis, Eysenck was less successful in mapping the P dimension onto psychosis. This is not to say that Psychoticism – as he defined it – has nothing to do with psychosis: the question is still open to debate, as we shall eventually discuss. But, whether it does or not, there is general agreement that the way Eysenck developed the dimension – and the traits he thought it covered – was rather idiosyncratic. To be precise, P seems more relevant to psychopathic and other antisocial behaviours than to conditions like schizophrenia. This is illustrated in Figure 3.3, which shows some of the defining features of P, as measured by the items contained in the Eysenck Personality Questionnaire (EPQ) (Eysenck & Eysenck, 1991).

The picture that emerges of the high scorer on the Psychoticism scale is of a rather aggressive, tough-minded, impulsive individual, a constellation of traits certainly descriptive of some forms of personality disorder. Where we encounter P in this book it will therefore often be in that context.

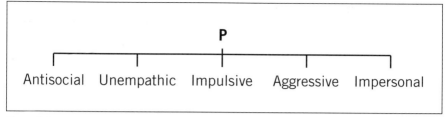

**Figure 3.3**  Some of the defining features of P.

There is another point to bear in mind about Eysenck's P dimension, especially important for the remainder of this chapter. It concerns the personality characteristic of *impulsivity*: this is significant in understanding how Eysenck extended his two-dimensional scheme in order to arrive at three dimensions, and how others have built upon his theory in developing their own models of personality. Historically, impulsivity has been handled by personality theorists as one of two components defining extraversion; the other is *sociability*. However, impulsivity was also one of several features eventually used by Eysenck to define his separate Psychoticism dimension (see Figure 3.3 above). Extraversion, in his theory, then effectively became synonymous with Sociability. Most contemporary writers in the field recognize this and, where they employ constructs like 'impulsivity' they tend, if they refer to Eysenck, to bundle parts of his P dimension along with it. To complicate matters further, another, apparently different, component of P is aggressiveness. Eysenck eventually came to see this as also a very important feature of P, which he sometimes labelled 'toughmindedness'.

## TEMPERAMENT AND PERSONALITY COMPARED

Before describing contemporary theories, it will be helpful to examine another issue that is highly relevant here, especially to how we interpret the connection between personality and psychological disorder. It concerns the distinction between 'temperament' and 'personality'. So far, we have used these terms interchangeably, and rather loosely. Early accounts of personality – notably the classic theory – have certainly come down to us as theories of *temperament*. But, in current parlance 'temperament' has a rather old-fashioned ring and, with a few exceptions, most modern personality psychologists have dropped the word from their vocabularies. Even Eysenck, who explicitly traced his own ideas to the classic typology, preferred to see his own theory as being about personality. Does this matter? We believe that it does, on the grounds that 'temperament' refers to something different from 'personality'; a fact that has important bearing on what we mean when we say that 'personality' differences predispose to psychological disorders. Table 3.1 lists some of the differences between the two constructs.

**Table 3.1**  Temperament and personality compared.

|  | Temperament | Personality |
|---|---|---|
| Refers to | Basic emotional reactions | Complex psychological traits |
| Seen | Clearly as normal variation in infancy | As development of individuality from childhood onwards |
| Reflects CNS differences | Directly | Indirectly |
| Heritability | Strong | Via underlying temperament |
| Environmental influences | Biological, e.g. brain damage | Family, social, cultural, individual experience |
| Example | 'Fearfulness' | 'Honesty' |

The most general distinction to be made between temperament and personality is that the former is the much narrower term, referring to rather basic, mostly emotional, constitutional characteristics of biological origin. Personality, on the other hand, is more elaborate, more socially constructed, and more the result of learned experience. Then there are two specific distinguishing features that deserve further comment. One concerns the fact that equivalents of human temperament may be seen in animal species; the other that quite early in life, and even in the absence of a fully formed personality, infants and young children show differences in emotional 'style' that seem to correspond to the temperamental variations found in adults. We shall return to this developmental perspective later in the chapter.

On observations about animal temperament, we noted previously that these were famously documented by Pavlov in his experimental dogs, a fact that led directly to theories about the biology of human personality, through the notion of nervous types. Since then, a huge amount of research has documented the differences in temperament that can be observed both within and between a wide range of species: from zebra fish and hedgehogs, through sheep and spotted hyenas, to baboons and chimpanzees. Differences have been demonstrated with respect to a variety of salient characteristics that connect to ideas about human temperament (Gosling, 2001). These include aggressiveness, nervousness, impulsivity, and curiosity. The following are two early examples that are especially pertinent here:

In a novel experiment combining naturalistic data collection and precise statistical analysis, Chamove *et al.* (1972) carried out observational ratings of the behaviour of a group of Rhesus monkeys studied under semi-captive conditions. Separated at birth from their mothers and reared in individual cages, the animals were later placed in peer group social situations. Factor analysis of the data collected demonstrated three components in the observed behaviour: affiliativeness, fearfulness, and hostility. The authors concluded that these factors corresponded exactly to the E, N, and P dimensions described in humans by Eysenck (one of the co-workers in the study).

A common and long used procedure for assessing stress response in the laboratory rat is the so-called 'open field test', in which the animal is placed in a brightly lit arena sometimes located under a source of loud noise. One part of the rat's reaction to this environment is defaecation, as a measure of fearfulness. However, it was discovered early on that rodents differ considerably in this characteristic, a fact leading to now famous genetic studies in which rats were selectively bred for degree of 'emotional reactivity' (Broadhurst, 1975).

This animal research underlines the reason why we need to be aware of the distinctions between temperament and personality, in the fuller sense. The two constructs are obviously very closely related and sometimes it is difficult – indeed, too limiting – to try to discuss one without the other. At other times, however, it is more helpful to keep them separate, in order to be clear on the point being made. This is especially so in the presence of those theories of individual differences on which we mostly concentrate here. Most of these theories, although purporting to be theories of *personality*, could more accurately be judged to be theories of *temperament*.

## CONTEMPORARY THEORISTS

### GRAY

Of the theories to be considered, Gray's is the most directly descended from Eysenck's own. Indeed, it originated as a revision of the Eysenckian two-dimensional personality framework of Introversion–Extraversion and Neuroticism (Gray, 1981) As an alternative, Gray proposed the scheme shown in Figure 3.4. This substituted two dimensions of *Anxiety* and *Impulsivity* for Eysenck's Introversion–Extraversion and Neuroticism dimensions. The result was effectively a 'fusing' of, on the one hand, Introversion and Neuroticism (Anxiety) and, on the other, Extraversion and Neuroticism (Impulsivity). Gray justified the modification on the grounds that his two new dimensions were likely to map more directly on to underlying biological mechanisms of personality than was the case with I–E and N. As we shall see, he was probably right; his formulation, and its derivatives, have certainly been more effective in providing a factually grounded conceptual nervous system for the temperamental characteristics previously referred to by Eysenck as E and N.

It is important to note, however, that Gray arrived at the picture shown in Figure 3.4, *not* via a factor analysis of personality items, but merely by drawing

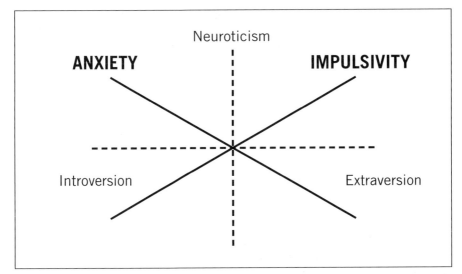

**Figure 3.4** Gray's revision of Eysenck's descriptive theory.

two diagonals across the Eysenck dimensions! In fact, interestingly, his approach to personality theorizing at that stage was quite the opposite of most other writers in this field, including Eysenck. Instead of starting by looking, at the descriptive level, for statistically valid personality dimensions and then seeking their biological correlates, Gray was more concerned with the latter, using his rough-and-ready, empirical dimensions as descriptive templates for exploring the underlying biology.

A further step in Gray's revision of Eysenck's model was to propose a motivational – or what he now calls a 'reinforcement sensitivity' – theory of Anxiety and Impulsivity (see Figure 3.5). The suggestion is that the two dimensions correspond to differences in the sensitivity to types of reinforcement. Individuals falling along the Anxiety dimension are judged to be highly sensitive to signals of *punishment*, whereas those high in Impulsivity are very sensitive to signals of *reward*. This distinction, which we shall come across frequently in later chapters, is regarded as very significant for understanding susceptibilities to disorders where one or other of these two motivational systems play a part in aetiology.

On the biological side, Gray's theory was, and still is, most highly developed for the Anxiety dimension, where much of the early effort was concentrated (Gray, 1982). The central idea is the notion of a *behavioural inhibition system* (BIS). The functional properties of this system (see Figure 3.6) are to act as a response modulator for certain inputs to which the anxious person is particularly sensitive. As shown in Figure 3.6, these include signals of punishment (and non-reward), novel stimuli, and fear-producing stimuli to which the organism is preprogrammed, during evolution, to respond. This

41

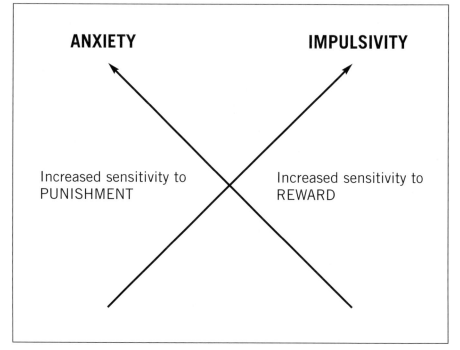

**ANXIETY**        **IMPULSIVITY**

Increased sensitivity to
PUNISHMENT

Increased sensitivity to
REWARD

**Figure 3.5** Gray's motivational theory of Anxiety and Impulsivity.

'biological preparedness', as it was once described (Seligman, 1971), has particular relevance to the understanding of certain kinds of unlearned phobia (see Chapter 5). The output of the BIS is, appropriately, an increase in central nervous system arousal and enhanced attention, as well as a 'freezing' of behaviour in anticipation of possible threat.

The current version of Gray's theory envisages twin *behavioural inhibition systems* (BIS) and *behavioural activation systems* (BAS) corresponding, respectively, to Anxiety and Impulsivity in the personality, or temperament, domain (Pickering & Gray, 1999). As illustrated in Figure 3.7, the BIS and BAS are considered to form two interacting, mutually inhibiting parts of a single system. For example, excitation of the BIS by signals of punishment (anxiety response) is thought to inhibit the BAS, and vice versa. Appetitive and fear-provoked behaviours are therefore regarded as being incompatible with each other. The neurobiology of the BAS is considered to be similar (if not identical) to that underlying reward-directed behaviour, viz. involving the same mesolimbic and mesocortical *dopaminergic* pathways as those found to be hyper-responsive in highly hedonic or pleasure-seeking individuals. We will discuss this in more detail in later chapters, in relation to disorders whose primary motivational aetiology appears to lie in enhanced reward sensitivity.

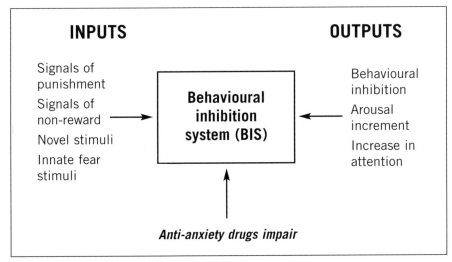

**Figure 3.6** Gray's behavioural inhibition system (BIS) model of Anxiety.

Gray's BIS/BAS theory has created interest among other workers, on several fronts. One has been in questionnaire measurement. Early attempts to assess BIS/BAS traits were not all that successful. This was because the inventories used were based on conventional personality questionnaires of extraversion, neuroticism, anxiety, and impulsivity, rather than trying to measure BIS/BAS

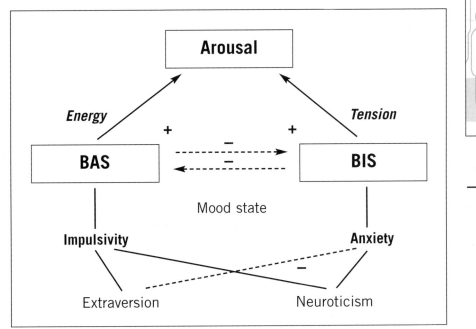

**Figure 3.7** Gray's BIS/BAS model of temperament.

43

directly. Of course, the two domains are connected (that is, part and parcel of the theory), but they are not synonymous. Anxiety is influenced by more than BIS sensitivity, whereas Impulsivity is a complex dimension of probably varied origins. Recently reported scales try to get closer to BIS/BAS itself and seem more promising (Carver & White, 1994; Torrubia *et al.*, 2001).

On the theoretical side, a number of writers have made use of Gray's ideas or developed similar formulations of anxiety and impulsivity. Tellegen and colleagues have especially considered the association between BIS/BAS and negative and positive mood states (Watson *et al.*, 1999), whereas others have elaborated on the neurobiology (Fowles, 1987; Depue and Collins, 1999).

## CLONINGER

Unlike Gray, Cloninger developed his theory from a clinical perspective, in an attempt to explain the personality features observed in varieties of psychological disorder. Cloninger is also the only writer among those discussed here to make an explicit distinction between temperament and other aspects of personality (Cloninger *et al.*, 1993). Thus, he refers to both *temperament* and *character* as forming two different parts of personality (Figure 3.8).

---

**Temperament** described as:

... biases in automatic responses to emotional stimuli that are moderately heritable and stable throughout life regardless of culture and social learning

**Character** described as:

... individual differences in self-object relationships, which develop as a result of interactions among temperament, family environment and individual life experience

---

**Figure 3.8** Cloninger's descriptions of temperament and character.

44

The theory consists of seven dimensions, three of character and four of temperament, measured with the Temperament and Character Inventory *(TCI)* (Cloninger *et al.*, 1994). These dimensions, together with their definitions, are listed in Table 3.2.

According to Cloninger, several differences between temperament and character need to be noted:

- Temperament accounts for variations in rather low level, automatic, unconscious responses of the organism, whereas character is more concerned with consciously organized thought and behaviours.

**Table 3.2** Cloninger's seven dimensions.

|  | High | Low |
|---|---|---|
| **Temperament** | | |
| Harm avoidance | Worrying, fearful | Relaxed, bold |
| Novelty seeking | Curious, impulsive | Indifferent, detached |
| Reward dependence | Warm, attached | Practical, independent |
| Persistence | Industrious, ambitious | Indolent, modest |
| **Character** | | |
| Self-directedness | Mature, resourceful | Unreliable, purposeless |
| Co-operativeness | Empathic, helpful | Opportunistic, critical |
| Self-transcendence | Wise, patient | Impatient, unimaginative |

- With respect to learning, temperament mediates differences of an associative conditioning type, whereas character variations are represented at a cognitive, conceptual level.

- The temperamental dimensions have as their focus, narrow motivational concerns; character, on the other hand, reflects differences in broad cognitive sets towards self and others.

On the face of it, Cloninger's character dimensions look a little arbitrary, 'plucked out of the air', as it were; certainly they have no obvious reference point in other prominent or contemporary trait theories. Nevertheless, Cloninger himself argues that they have proven utility in their clinical application, a claim we shall return to in the next chapter, when considering the personality disorders. Irrespective of the validity of this particular aspect of his theory, Cloninger's separation of temperament from character does make an important general point. It concerns the need to take account of *both* the more biologically based emotional tendencies that constitute temperament *and* the way these are shaped by experience to form personality in the complete sense. Using his own theory, Cloninger gives the example of an individual high in Novelty seeking and low in Harm avoidance who might develop an impulse disorder if low in both Self-directedness (immature) and Co-operativeness (opportunistic). A person of the same temperament, but *high* on those two character dimensions (mature and socially tolerant) might, he says, become a 'daring explorer, inquisitive scientist, or acquisitive business man' [*sic!*].

Compared with the descriptors for character, Cloninger's formulation of

45

temperament is more clearly grounded in mainstream theory and a prominent part of his research is trying to establish the biological basis of his temperament dimensions. This has entailed using a range of experimental procedures in human subjects, alongside his questionnaire scales (Cloninger, 1998). Methods have included:

- Psychological measures of performance, learning and cognition, from which differences in neural functioning may be inferred.

- EEG and neuroimaging techniques, especially positron emission tomography (PET), to examine regional brain activity.

- Neurochemical procedures, including drug challenge tests and measures of neurotransmitter levels in body fluids.

The conclusions reached by Cloninger from these studies are summarized in Table 3.3. In essence he argues that his four temperament dimensions represent what he considers to be four 'dissociable' brain circuits, each responsive to a different class of stimuli, and each modulated by a different neurotransmitter system. A notable feature – and possibly the strongest part – of Cloninger's theory is the proposed association between his Novelty seeking dimension and the dopamine-mediated brain reward system. Persistence, on the other hand, seems to be a more dubious facet of temperament.

**Table 3.3**   Biology of temperament (Cloninger).

| Temperament dimension | Brain system | Neurotransmitter system(s) |
|---|---|---|
| Novelty seeking | Behavioural activation | Dopamine |
| Harm avoidance | Behavioural inhibition | Serotonin GABA |
| Reward dependence | Social attachment | Noradrenaline Serotonin |
| Persistence | Partial reinforcement? | Glutamate? |

## ZUCKERMAN

As a third prominent contender in this field, Zuckerman's theory had different origins again from those of Gray and Cloninger, although his work has influenced and been influenced by both of them. Zuckerman started by concentrating on a single construct, that of *sensation seeking*. The thinking behind this was that individuals differ in the extent to which they try to maintain an optimum level of central nervous arousal: some individuals who have difficulty doing that are therefore prone constantly to seek out stimulation in order to maintain a comfortable brain state. Sensation seeking was originally investigated in the context of sensory deprivation experiments, where subjects were exposed to periods of sensory isolation. The prediction was that self-confessed sensation seekers would show reduced tolerance of the sensory deprivation experience. This actually turned out to be an oversimplified hypothesis; in some cases the opposite was true. Even a *lack* of sensation is a sensation for some sensation seekers!

Zuckerman's most recent definition of sensation seeking is as follows:

'The seeking of novel, intense, and complex forms of sensation and experience and the willingness to take risks for the sake of such experience.' (Zuckerman, 1994; 5)

The trait has been most commonly measured with Zuckerman's *Sensation Seeking Scale (SSS)*, which consists of four (correlated) subscales, measuring different aspects (Figure 3.9).

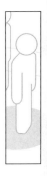

---

- *Thrill and adventure seeking* (*TAS*): engaging in physically risky sports or other activities

- *Experience seeking* (*ES*): expanding the mind through music, art, travel and a nonconforming lifestyle

- *Disinhibition* (*Dis*): seeking sensation through social intercourse, drinking and varied sexual partners

- *Boredom susceptibility* (*BS*): avoiding sameness in activities and friends and getting restless in the absence of novelty

---

**Figure 3.9**  Zuckerman's *Sensation Seeking Scale* (SSS).

Although sensation seeking continues to form the centrepiece of Zuckerman's work he has elaborated on the concept in a number of ways, as well as extending his theorizing into other areas of personality. One development has been Zuckerman's search for *rapprochement* with other personality theories, including that of Eysenck – and, by extrapolation, the Gray modification. Factor analysing a broad domain of questionnaire items he has arrived at a five-dimensional description of personality, as shown in Table 3.4. The main point to note there is the appearance, yet again, of two dimensions which, in a slightly different guise, we have already come across, viz. Neuroticism–Anxiety and Impulsive–Sensation seeking (a modified version of Zuckerman's original sensation seeking construct).

**Table 3.4** Zuckerman's five dimensions.

- Impulsive sensation seeking*
- Neuroticism–anxiety
- Aggression–hostility
- Activity
- Sociability

*Sometimes called 'P–Impulsive Unsocialized Sensation Seeking' to recognize overlap with Eysenck's 'Psychoticism'.

Zuckerman has also addressed the biological basis of personality in some detail, although his conclusions are difficult to summarize. This is partly because he insists on the idea of multiple interactions between what, even individually, are already known to be complex neural circuits (Zuckerman, 1994, 1996). Unlike Cloninger, for example, he does not believe it is possible to talk of separable neurobiological systems (or neurotransmitters) that can be mapped onto discrete temperamental dimensions. However, three main features capture the gist of Zuckerman's ideas, as follows:

- A *dopaminergic/approach system* feeding into sensation seeking, or what Zuckerman here calls P–Impulsive Unsocialized Sensation Seeking (P-ImpUSS).

- Additional, serotonergic, influences on P-ImpUSS, but apparently more on its aggressiveness component.

- N–Anxiety associated with arousal stemming from an interaction between *noradrenergic* and *GABA* systems.

## FIVE-FACTOR THEORY (COSTA & McCRAE)

48

Five-factor theory actually refers to a class of personality theories that have their roots in attempts to seek dimensions of personality in the natural language of personality description (John, 1990). It originated with Cattell and in the application of factor analysis to lists of common adjectives used to characterize personality traits. The development of this approach then formed the basis for establishing what is claimed by adherents of such theories to be the five 'fundamental' dimensions of personality. Currently, the most prominent exponents of Five-factor theory (or the 'Big Five', as it is sometimes grandiosely called) are Costa and McCrae (1992). The five factors in question – sometimes summarized under the acronym OCEAN – are listed in Table 3.5.

**Table 3.5** Five-factor theory.

| | |
|---|---|
| **O**penness | Culture |
| | Intellect |
| **C**onscientiousness | Conformity |
| **E**xtraversion | Surgery |
| | Dominance |
| **A**greeableness | Likeability |
| | Friendliness |
| **N**euroticism | Emotional instability |

Five-factor theory has stimulated sometimes acrimonious arguments about what indeed *are* the fundamental dimensions of personality and about the optimum number required for a complete description of individual differences. Is it three (according to Eysenck), five (according to Costa & McCrae and other Five-factor theorists), five (according to Zuckerman), seven (according to Cloninger), 16 (according to Cattell), or what? The debate has been mostly futile and raises questions that are unlikely to be solved to everyone's satisfaction, at least using present methodology. The number of dimensions claimed in any given study, for example, and how these are labelled will depend on several influences, including the kind of factor analysis used and the data being analysed. Or, to paraphrase a cynical but soberingly true maxim of the factor analytic procedure: 'what you get out is what you put in'. Different writers might therefore arrive at different solutions according to the vicissitudes of their chosen methodology rather than having come nearer to the 'truth'.

There is also the question of what is meant by dimensions that are more 'fundamental', introducing again the temperament/personality issue. In a more reductionist sense 'fundamental' could reasonably be taken to mean lower order, biological, or 'causal' – what we have seen is signified by the term 'temperament'. If so, Five-factor theorists are not in much of a position to enter the debate since the models they have constructed are weak in this regard. They are mostly concerned with personality description and structure, as revealed through factor analysis and there has not been much attempt to examine mechanisms or causes of personality, biological or otherwise. However, things are changing in that regard. There is interest in the possible genetic influences on the five factors (Loehlin, 1992). And recently, some attempts have been made to pursue their biology through animal models, in chimpanzees (King & Figueredo, 1997) and in horses (Morris *et al.*, 2002). The latter study assessed ten horses on the OCEAN dimensions and claimed it was possible to recognize the equine equivalents of the 'Big Five', indicating some convergence with more biologically grounded theories of personality. Although this seems convincing for some of the factors – for example Neuroticism and Agreeableness – the mind slightly boggles at the authors' accounts of their subjects' Conscientiousness ('keeps a neat and clean stable') or Openness to Experience ('has day dreams … spends much time speculating about the nature of the universe'). But perhaps horse-loving readers of this book will find some face validity in the descriptions!

Despite some criticisms, Five-factor theory does deserve attention here because of efforts that have been made to relate its dimensions to psychological disorders. But, rather than evaluating it as an *alternative* personality theory, it is more profitable to try to judge its relative merits, including its points of contact with the other models already discussed. The following points are worth noting:

- The appearance of Extraversion and Neuroticism in Five-factor theory is obviously consistent with most other analyses of personality traits, firmly establishing these as valid, easily replicable broad dimensions.

- Although not identical, the *negative* pole of Five-factor Agreeableness is similar to Eysenck's P dimension, with its overtones of aggressiveness, impulsiveness, and general 'nastiness'.

- Openness to Experience seems to correspond to little or nothing in the sphere of temperament, and suggestions that it reflects intelligence are probably wrong. More likely, it represents some higher level 'cognitive' trait, for example similar to Cloninger's self-transcendence factor, or some aspect of creativity.

## AN INTEGRATED VIEW OF THE THEORIES

At first glance, two, somewhat conflicting, conclusions may be drawn from the review of theories in the previous section. On the one hand, there is a remarkable uniformity in the findings by workers reporting from quite varied theoretical perspectives. But in other respects the picture is rather ragged, with some features being tantalizingly similar but not exactly alike. Contributing to the confusion is the terminology: writers sometimes use a different label for evidently the same characteristic; or, alternatively, the same label for what may be different traits. All of this is exacerbated by the 'bridge too far' propensity. We are referring to the tendency for personality theorists (perhaps theorizers in general) to start off with a single, strong explanatory construct, but then to elaborate it beyond its powers; or, on the basis of a simple model to attempt overextensive theories that, frankly, cannot be sustained by the evidence.

Lastly, there is the problem that, apart from Cloninger, the writers discussed make little or no distinction between personality and temperament. A

consequence of this is that traits subsumed under 'personality' would be better ascribed to 'temperament'. Indeed, the regularities that can be identified in what we have reviewed may probably be best discussed under those two headings.

At the level of higher order dimensions, the most convincing finding is the universal appearance of Neuroticism and Introversion–Extraversion; this alone justifies the continuing search for connections between normal personality and abnormal states – and vindicates Eysenck's pioneering work in that direction. There is a downside to the regularity, however. These dimensions might actually be *too* high order and, because of that, not explanatory enough, in the detail required. After all, it was this that caused Gray to abandon them.

Neuroticism also has its particular problems as a dimension that is too non-specific for explanatory purposes. Elsewhere we have examined this problem in detail (Claridge & Davis, 2001). Briefly, our argument has been that high Neuroticism is a universal feature of *all* forms of abnormality and deviance (physical as well as psychological); so much so that, by itself, it explains nothing. Gray's modification of Eysenck underscores this point, in recognizing introverted and extraverted forms of neuroticism (and neurotic disorder), which are quite different – indeed, entirely opposite from each other. Unfortunately, this ambiguity about N is perpetuated in the continuing tendency to equate it, at least terminologically, with anxiety, as for example in Zuckerman's label 'Neuroticism–Anxiety' (N–Anx) for one of his five dimensions. Of the theorists discussed, only Cloninger makes a similar observation to our own about the overgenerality of N, which was why he was led to invent character dimensions of a quite different kind to explain various forms of psychological disorder.

The picture becomes more coherent if 'temperament' is adopted as the reference point. Here, there is strong convergence across theories, at least with respect to certain dimensions (see Table 3.6). Everyone agrees that there is

Table 3.6 Temperament models compared.

| | 'Anxiety' | 'Impulsivity' (hedonic capacity) | 'Sociability' | 'Aggression' |
|---|---|---|---|---|
| **Gray** | Sensitivity to punishment | Sensitivity to reward | | P-related traits |
| **Cloninger** | Harm avoidance | Novelty seeking | Reward dependence | High NS/ Low HA |
| **Zuckerman** | N–Anxiety | Sensation seeking | Sociability | P–Imp–USS |

something for which the simplest description is *Anxiety* – or, in other terminology, *Harm avoidance* (Cloninger), *N-Anx* (Zuckerman), or *Sensitivity to punishment* (Gray). There seems nothing to choose between these, all of which point towards a source of individual variation – and its underlying mechanisms – which defines the predisposition to, and driving force for, anxiety-related disorders. But – reiterating an earlier point – we do need to remember that this Anxiety component of temperament forms only a *subcomponent* of what personality theorists generally mean when they refer to Neuroticism. The latter is a broader construct that refers to negative affect, or lack of emotional stability in general.

The second major construct we can recognise is captured in Cloninger's *Novelty seeking* , Zuckerman's *Sensation seeking*, and in *Impulsivity* as described by Gray. A single label for this component is difficult to find. But it appears to involve, as Gray claims, a strong element of 'sensitivity to reward', the motivational drive to seek and find pleasure in sensory and other forms of stimulation. As we shall see, it is a common element in several types of aberrant behaviour. (We need to be careful here not confuse 'reward sensitivity' with Cloninger's similarly sounding dimension of 'reward dependence', which refers to something different).

A third evident component of temperament is *Aggressiveness*. This certainly has ecological (real-life) validity though, interestingly, in none of the models described does it appear very clearly. A problem seems to be that of differentiating aggressiveness from impulsivity, with which it undoubtedly shares some features. This is most obvious in Zuckerman's *P–Imp–USS* dimension which tries to capture both sensation seeking and hostility. Cloninger deals with the problem in a comparable manner by connecting aggressiveness to high *Novelty seeking*, though only, it seems, in the presence of low *Harm avoidance*. Here, Cloninger is stating an important generalization: that, although temperament dimensions are theoretically (for example, statistically) independent, the behaviours that issue from them result from individuals having different weightings on them.

Of the remaining sources of individual variation that might be 'reduced' to temperamental status, one is *Sociability*. This regularly appears as a cluster of traits in most analyses of personality, either on its own (for example, as one of Zuckerman's 'alternative five' factors) or as a component of Extraversion (Eysenck; the 'Five-factor' theory). But, in Cloninger's model it forms a major temperament dimension – as *Reward dependence*, which, at its high end, is mostly defined in terms of sociability or social sensitivity.

Lastly, Cloninger seems alone in postulating his fourth temperament of *Persistence*. Originally part of *Reward dependence*, it was later hived off from it. Only time will tell whether Cloninger's claim is correct: that *Persistence* corresponds to the phlegmatic type in the classic theory of temperaments, so neatly filling the fourth slot in that ancient model.

# GENETIC CONSIDERATIONS

## BEHAVIOUR GENETICS

All of the theories discussed here assume that heredity significantly determines the individual differences described; this is true whether they are formulated as models of personality or of temperament. Much of the evidence collected to date supporting that claim has come from traditional *behaviour genetics*, involving the administration of (mostly) questionnaires to family members of different kinship, especially twins. Before looking at that evidence, we should digress to explain some of the methodology and terminology involved.

The standard, and simplest, method in behaviour genetics is to compare a sample of monozygotic (MZ) and a sample of dizygotic (DZ) twins on a trait of interest. The correlation (or concordance) between MZ and DZ twins then provides a rough measure of the 'heritability' (in the population sampled) of the trait in question. 'Heritability' here refers to a figure calculated as twice the difference between the MZ and the DZ correlations, representing the proportion of the trait variance due, in theory, to heredity. For a perfectly inherited characteristic this would work out as: $2 \times 1.0 \, (\text{MZ}) - 0.5 \, \text{DZ} = 1.0$ (or, expressed in percentage terms, 100 per cent). However, this is never achieved in practice, even for physical traits known to be highly heritable. For psychological characteristics, figures around 50 per cent would be regarded as very reasonable.

The estimate of heritable influence, as defined above, is very crude and tells us little beyond the fact that genetics seem to play a part in the trait studied. Its major flaw is that it takes no account of the environment, for example that the greater concordance of MZ twins might be due to them having a more similar environment than DZ twins (most of the reported twin research is done on unseparated pairs). Behaviour geneticists therefore try to take the exercise further by applying sophisticated statistical model-fitting techniques to the data. Here, conventional twin data are still mostly used, although that information can be, and is, supplemented by results obtained using other research designs, viz. studies of families, adopted individuals, and separated twins.

53

The model-fitting procedure essentially enables the behaviour geneticist to take the trait correlations observed in twins (or other kinships) and to partition the variance these represent into their different components. When defining a model to be tested assumptions are stated about effects that might be at work in the data; the model is then tested for statistical fit. In the simplest models the main effects sought are, of course, the estimated influence of genes. The others concern two kinds of environmental influence: one due to the *shared* and the other due to the *unshared* environment. Shared environment is to do with the effect on a trait arising from, say, experiences within a family that are common to its members: for example twins are alike partly because they are subject to the same environmental influences. Non-shared environment is what is unique to each individual, even within the same family.

Behaviour genetic modelling can, and usually does, get more complicated than this. Tests are often made for other influences that can account for trait differences. Although we shall not refer to these again, the reader should be aware of them, as follows:

- *Type of gene effect*: most genetic influences on continuous traits are assumed to be *additive*, that is, the similarity between individuals is linearly related to the proportion of genes they share. But sometimes that is not true and the genetics involve *dominant* gene effects. These will distort estimates of trait similarity in, say, twin comparisons.

- So-called *epitasis*: this refers to the fact that trait differences are due to an interaction between multiple genes – discoverable, if we could locate the genes themselves, at different sites across different chromosomes.

- *Assortative mating* or the tendency in partner selection for like to attract like.

- *Genotype–environment relationships*: this refers to the tendency for individuals of different genetic make-up either to be exposed to different environments or to respond to the same environment in different ways.

The model-fitting procedures described above clearly require an act of faith that actual genetic effects can be revealed in statistical data. Critics of this approach to explanations of personality could therefore be forgiven for concluding that the methods represent something of a 'black art'. They are certainly advised to be sceptical of the sillier claims made by some behaviour geneticists about the influence of heredity; for example that genes strongly determine political allegiance! The balanced view is that behaviour genetics is as much about determining environmental, as genetic, effects; though it is naturally the latter that mostly interests them. Our advice, therefore, is that claims about heritable effects on personality should be evaluated conservatively. They should be given credence only when the data seem overwhelmingly in favour of there being a genetic influence. In practice, this may be judged by the consistency of findings across studies.

Adopting that criterion for the major personality characteristics we have referred to here, there is strong support across many studies for there being a significant heritable component (Loehlin, 1992; see also Matthews & Deary

(1998) for a review of the evidence). There is, however, another, more interesting, fact to emerge from some of these analyses. This has been noted for some time (Plomin, 1986), but is now attracting a great deal of attention among behaviour geneticists. It concerns the surprising, but frequently made, observation that the *shared* environment often appears to have little or no effect on individual differences, across a wide range of personality traits. The environmental influences – which nevertheless are substantial – mostly come from *non-shared* sources, from experiences unique to the person. That may have considerable implications for our understanding of how, in a given individual, personality dispositions and life events interact to produce psychological disorder.

Supplementing the research already mentioned, two other kinds of behaviour genetics evidence are relevant here. One comes from twin studies of narrower *temperamental* traits. Some of the effects observed there are, of course, enclosed in those described above for the larger personality dimensions. But separate evidence has been reported about the heritability of temperament, as measured by the Cloninger scales (Cloninger *et al.*, 1994).

Twin research of a quite different kind provides a final set of evidence here. This consists of studies, not of self-report scales, but of more objective laboratory measures which have themselves sometimes been used to examine the biological correlates (and therefore possible underlying mechanisms) of personality. We set out the rationale for this earlier in the chapter when explaining Eysenck's theory and his distinction between 'descriptive' and 'causal' levels of personality analysis. The example we gave there of a 'causal' measure was the sedation threshold, as a test of drug tolerance related to anxiety. But there are numerous other psychophysiological measures, such as EEG, indices of autonomic nervous system function and so on, that have been examined under this rubric.

A logical next step is to examine such measures in twins, a research strategy which, in principle, should provide more certain evidence about the heritability of personality than that gained from self-report scales. It should, as it were, take us nearer to the genotype. The downside is that, because of the technical nature of the experimental procedures involved, it is more trouble to carry out, and far less data can be collected than with questionnaires. Nevertheless, a body of evidence about twins does exist, using this strategy to examine genetic factors in personality (Claridge & Mangan, 1983). Results are, if anything, more impressive than those obtained with questionnaires – as indeed one would expect them to be, given the more objective nature of the procedures. Many psychophysiological measures that correlate with personality show marked MX/DZ twin differences, suggesting significant heritability for the 'marker' in question. To quote the example of drug sensitivity we have already referred to, several measures of this have been found to be under strong genetic control.

## MOLECULAR GENETICS

The findings from behaviour genetics that there are heritable influences in personality has provided an obvious stimulus for the search for actual genes. Progress so far has followed a predictable course, typical of all new endeavours: extravagant claims are made, which later research fails to replicate. Studies on the genetics of personality are no exception. Nevertheless, there are some interesting trends that we should mention. First, a brief word about some technical aspects.

The rationale behind molecular genetic analysis is that phenotypic characteristics (for example, observable behaviours) can be found to be associated with a particular sequence of DNA at a given locus on a certain chromosome. However, a DNA sequence can show variability, known as *polymorphisms*. It is this variation that can be expressed phenotypically as a certain behaviour. Identifying these connections is (relatively speaking) straightforward for recognizable, easily definable 'big effects' – like well-known diseases. It is much more difficult for the kinds of phenotype found in personality research. This is partly because the core features that need explaining may not be all that obvious or agreed; and partly because, even if they are, they do not represent such huge differences between people that these will be discoverable above 'the noise' in the system. Nevertheless, two claims have been made for a connection between a gene variation and temperament (or personality).

The first is an observation by Cloninger (2000) that his *Novelty seeking* dimension is strongly associated with variations at the D4 dopamine receptor gene. This finding is seen as consistent with other evidence that activity in the brain dopaminergic systems mediates novelty seeking behaviours. However, Cloninger admits that this genetic association has not always been replicated, as a recent further failure to do so confirms (Burt *et al.*, 2002). The need for caution about these claims is further illustrated by the second example, viz. a supposed association between Neuroticism and/or Anxiety and the transporter gene (5-HTTL-PR) regulating the uptake of the neurotransmitter, serotonin (Goldman, 1996). Unfortunately, at least six other studies have been unable to replicate that finding.

The Neuroticism results are a good example of the dilemma of trying to match behaviour genetics to real genetics. As we have seen, N is a strong construct in personality theory. It appears without fail in factor analyses of personality traits and its 'heritability' (in the statistical, behaviour genetics sense) seems beyond doubt. High neuroticism is also an almost universal feature of abnormal states: it accompanies virtually every form of psychological disorder. That, perhaps, is the problem: N is *too* general, the combined result of many genetic influences. It is perhaps a classic case of epistasis, where many genes will be found to contribute to the variation. This is even likely to be true of the narrower temperament dimensions, such as those described by

Cloninger. Although they are more specific and have an intuitively more biological 'feel', they still represent fairly complex behaviours, distant from the gene or genes that contribute to their variation.

A related issue about the complexity of genetic effects is the dimensional nature of personality characteristics. These differ markedly from discontinuous or nearly discontinuous phenotypes, where discovery of a single gene or manageably small group of genes is feasible. The realization that this is almost certainly not true for personality dimensions has led to a new branch of molecular genetics, called quantitative trait loci (QTL) genetics, which assumes that multiple genes will prove to be responsible for many forms of psychological variation seen in psychology (Plomin *et al.*, 1994). It is probably QTL that will yield many of the real discoveries that help to provide a biological reality for the statistical speculations of behaviour genetics. Indeed, the convergence of the two is an interesting full turn of the circle in the study of the genetics of human variation. For behaviour genetics itself – as 'quantitative genetics' – was established, some 80 years ago, as a method for adapting classical Mendelian single-gene principles so as to deal with continuous characteristics.

In this respect, it would almost certainly help if questions about genetic influences in temperament were framed in a more sophisticated way, as a recent study of the Cloninger dimensions illustrates (Berman *et al.*, 2002). The authors, who were interested in the known joint contributions of Novelty seeking and Harm avoidance to substance abuse, examined variations in the dopamine receptor (D2D2) gene among a group of adolescent boys. They found that the association between the two Cloninger dimensions was opposite in sign according to which form (allele) of the gene a person possessed. It was concluded that there are really two kinds of novelty seeking behaviour and that it is those individuals whose genotype results in a positive association between Novelty seeking and Harm avoidance who are likely to be most at risk for substance abuse. Otherwise, it was argued, novelty seeking will be observed as a benign, positively rewarding activity.

## THE DEVELOPMENTAL PERSPECTIVE

Virtually all of the ideas presented so far in this chapter stem from studies of, and theories about, adult personality. Although it is true that Eysenck produced junior versions of his personality scales, none of the writers discussed has shown a serious interest in how the dimensions they describe shape up in children. Are the dimensions even recognizable in children? And, if so, in what form? These questions bear on a number of issues, including the validity of the adult dimensions, as well as their interpretation as indicators of later behaviour or, in the present context, vulnerabilities to adult psychological disorder.

The developmental perspective is also relevant because it addresses naturally the temperament/personality distinction on which we have placed so much emphasis here. For, if adult personality characteristics are present in early life, these are most likely to be observed in some primordial form, as *temperamental* features. Indeed, referring back to Table 3.1 (p. 39) will remind us that this is one of the criteria defining the difference between personality and temperament. Furthermore, it is interesting to note that, compared to the adult literature, the term 'temperament' is more often used to describe personality variations among children. A representative body of work that illustrates this, and which connects well to the ideas discussed here, is that reported by Buss & Plomin (1984).

Building upon previous studies of childhood temperament, these authors address similar issues to those discussed in adult research, against a not dissimilar theoretical background to that adopted here. But they do so from a developmental point of view and within an explicit agenda: that temperament refers to *constitutionally* based early signs of adult personality. For them temperament is, by definition, largely hereditary in origin. Constrained in this way, they arrived at three dimensions of temperament, based on analyses of data from parental and teacher ratings.

The dimensions in question are *Emotionality*, *Activity*, and *Sociability*. Two of these – Emotionality and Sociability – map clearly onto adult equivalents of Neuroticism and Extraversion (Shafer, 2001). Not so clear is Activity. It has been suggested that this is because, although manifestly a feature of early behaviour, it is rarely assessed in adulthood. Perhaps it becomes absorbed into behaviours which by then are recognized as something else. This might also just help to explain another fact – the loss of *Impulsivity* from what was originally a four-dimensional scheme, known under the convenient acronym, EASI. According to the originators, Impulsivity as an early measured trait failed to meet the criterion of being strongly heritable. It was therefore dropped from the child studies, though it still appears in adult research.

Attempting to map early temperamental traits onto adult personality dimensions of course involves much more than simply finding parallels between cross-sectional analyses of data at two points in time. It also entails looking longitudinally at trajectories of change and behavioural continuities (or lack of them) across infancy, childhood, and adult life. The EAS scheme, complemented by other approaches to childhood temperament, has formed the basis of substantial research examining these effects (Plomin, 1986; Plomin & Dunn, 1986; Schmitz *et al.*, 1996). The results strongly confirm the idea that certain psychobiological traits, partially of genetic origin, do remain with us into adulthood. Sometimes these characteristics take on extreme forms, perhaps even being observed as disorder in childhood. Where they do so, they undoubtedly lay the groundwork for later similar psychopathology; anxiety and anxiety disorders are potent examples (Eley & Gregory, in press).

## SUMMARY AND CONCLUSIONS

In this chapter we have outlined the main theories of personality that can identify dispositions to the psychological disorders discussed in subsequent chapters. Unsurprisingly, the picture is not entirely neat. There are several reasons for this. One is simply lack of knowledge in a highly complicated field. But many stem from the fact that personality theorists have different agendas for what they choose to study, how they phrase what they say, or try to persuade others of what they believe. There is a chronic problem of terminology. Despite that, there are some definite themes and some recognizable communalities across different approaches to the topic.

One theme to which we kept returning in this chapter is the difference between temperament and personality. Not all writers recognize the distinction, but it is difficult to avoid the necessity of making it. Having said that, the actual dimensions of temperament (and personality) that enter into disorder are sometimes difficult to name unequivocally. But some of the constructs used by different writers do show substantial overlap – and occasionally they look identical.

The convergent development of these ideas in normal personality research and abnormal psychology strengthens the idea of temperament as disposition to disorder. It is surely intuitively obvious, for example, that people at the upper extreme of Cloninger's Harm avoidance temperament dimension are likely to be at greater than average risk of developing an anxiety disorder; or, put another way, if they do become ill, they are likely to suffer from primary anxiety symptoms.

Of course, for any given individual, other factors will be very influential in promoting, or protecting from, psychological breakdown. Indeed, one of the most striking recent observations in behaviour genetics is the influence of unique (as distinct from shared) experience on personality. It is an intriguing idea that individuality – including the experience, or otherwise, of psychological disorder – results from a fatalistic combination of one's inherited temperament and the chance vicissitudes of life!

# C H A P T E R 4

## PERSONALITY DISORDERS

### SOME BASIC FEATURES

Personality disorders provide the most obvious link between the two halves of this book and the clearest example of the dimensionality between normal and abnormal. Personality disorders represent aberrations of behaviour which, superficially at least, seem to be continuous with features that in the normal range describe healthy individuality. In other words, they seem for the most part to be exaggerations of normal personality or temperamental variation. The directness of this association contrasts somewhat with the dimensionality found within the disorders to be discussed in later chapters. In those cases personality differences act more as underlying vulnerabilities to symptom-based illnesses and, where they play a part in aetiology, do so by interacting with other, precipitating factors. The connection to personality disposition is therefore more concealed than it appears to be in the personality disorders, where causation and natural individuality coincide to a greater degree. Later in the chapter we shall see that the picture is not quite as simple as that, but for the moment it suffices to emphasize the distinction between personality disorders and other forms of abnormality.

Although the general nature of personality disorder is fairly self-evident, classifying its various forms – and finding a consistent, scientific basis for doing so – has not always been easy for psychiatry. One reason for this is that writers have come to the question from many different points of view, ranging from the psychoanalytic to the neurological. It is therefore not surprising that finding a consensus on personality disorders has not been easy. There is then another, by no means trivial, reason why the personality disorder concept has always been problematic – one that needs to be mentioned right at the outset, because it pervades the whole topic.

The psychiatric label 'personality disorder' has always had negative overtones, a fact that has got seriously in the way of studying it objectively. It is not a neutral description of a person, or one that implies sympathy for others' suffering – as would be the case, for example, of someone with a disabling anxiety neurosis. On the contrary, calling someone 'personality disordered' generally elicits annoyance, fear, distaste, condemnation, or other derogatory sentiments. This is partly because the label is frequently bracketed with 'criminal' or 'antisocial' and, among the general public at least, is often first encountered in a legal or semi-legal context. But that is not the complete explanation. There are other negative associations to disordered personality that do not have a criminal connotation, yet the attitude towards the person is still unfavourable. It is as though anything suggesting that behaviour is due to some inherent personality defect is simply regarded by others as a not very nice description of someone. Or perhaps we are just not very tolerant of any behaviour that sits outside normal limits, which is essentially how personality disorders are defined. Whatever the reason, alarmingly, this prejudice towards the temperamentally deviant is not confined to the so-called 'lay' person, as the study described below illustrates.

As recently as 1988 a paper appeared in the *British Journal of Psychiatry* entitled 'Personality disorder: the patients psychiatrists dislike' (Lewis & Appleby, 1988). In it the authors reported a study in which psychiatrists were asked to evaluate an hypothetical case history, the basic form of which was as follows:

> … a 35-year-old man complains of feeling depressed and crying alone at home. He is worried about having a nervous breakdown and requesting hospital admission. He has thought of suicide by overdosing, having done that previously. At that time he saw a psychiatrist who gave a diagnosis of personality disorder. He has recently gone into debt and is concerned about how to repay the money.

In some forms of the case history the investigators varied the reference to the previous diagnosis given to the patient; in some versions it was stated as 'depression' and in others as 'no diagnosis'. The evaluating clinicians were then presented with a series of statements asking which of these they would apply to the 'patient'. Strikingly, when 'personality disorder' was the previous diagnosis many more negative statements were endorsed. These included:

- Manipulating.

- Unlikely to arouse sympathy.

- The drug overdose was attention seeking.

- Not a suicide risk.

- Condition not severe.

- Person not mentally ill.

- Difficult management problem.

- Would not want in clinic.

- A waste of NHS time.

There is an interesting corollary to the above study. In addition to changing the previous diagnosis, the investigators also altered other identifying features. In some permutations of the case history the person was referred to as a lawyer and in others as a woman, rather than a man. Generally, the evaluations were less negative if the patient was perceived to have the social status of a lawyer, but they were particularly *negative* if she was a woman! So, women who are not lawyers, with a diagnosis of personality disorder, are likely to have a hard time, even from their clinicians.

## PERSONALITY DISORDERS IN DSM-IV

Currently, the most commonly cited classification of the personality disorders is that contained in the DSM. This recognizes two different expressions of abnormality – symptom-based illness and disordered personality – which the DSM separates by distinguishing between Axis I and Axis II conditions. The personality disorders included under Axis II in DSM-IV are defined as referring to:

> ... an enduring pattern of inner experiences and behaviour that deviates markedly from the expectations of the individual's culture, is pervasive and inflexible, has an onset in adolescence or early adulthood, is stable over time, and leads to distress or impairment.

Table 4.1 shows the DSM classification of personality disorders, with a brief definition of each type. One point to note is the grouping of the disorders into three classes, clusters A, B, and C – colloquially known as the 'Mad, the Bad and the Sad'! Two of these clusters reflect important themes in the characterization of the personality disorders. One (represented by Cluster B) is the strong dissocial, acting-out, or otherwise unlikeable, element which they undoubtedly do contain and which, as we have just seen, is often allowed to generalize to the personality disorders as a whole.

The other theme – summarized in Cluster A – is the connection that can be found to *psychotic disorders*. We shall touch upon this many times; at this point it needs comment because of the existence in personality theory of constructs like 'psychoticism', already encountered in the previous chapter. Although originated (by Eysenck) as a dimension to explain psychotic illnesses, psychoticism – in the sense in which Eysenck came to define and measure it (and as elaborated by Zuckerman) – is more often currently applied to certain

Table 4.1  The DSM Axis II personality disorders.

| | |
|---|---|
| **Cluster A – Odd/eccentric ('mad')** | |
| *Schizoid* | Distrust of others |
| *Paranoid* | Detachment from social relationships |
| *Schizotypal* | Cognitive disturbance & eccentricity |
| **Cluster B – Dramatic/emotional ('bad')** | |
| *Antisocial* | Disregard & violation of others' rights |
| *Borderline* | Interpersonal & emotional instability |
| *Histrionic* | Attention seeking & extreme emotionality |
| *Narcissistic* | Grandiosity & need for admiration |
| **Cluster C – Anxious/fearful ('sad')** | |
| *Avoidant* | Social inhibition & anxiety |
| *Dependent* | Submissiveness & clinging behaviour |
| *Obsessive–Compulsive* | Perfectionism & control |
| *Plus*: 'Not otherwise specified', for example, Passive–Aggressive | |

forms of personality disorder. This itself raises an interesting question about a possible genuine overlap between the 'mad' and the 'bad'. This is brought to our attention by the rather arbitrary nature of the DSM Axis II classification, portrayed in Table 4.1. Thus, 'Borderline Personality Disorder' – because of its own suspected connections to psychotic illness – could equally well belong in Cluster A. Again, we shall say more about that later.

The individual labels shown in Table 4.1 are in general chosen rather haphazardly and are not founded on any common, coherent theory of personality disorder. Where some theoretical basis for a particular label may be discerned, this tends to be different for different disorders, and is sometimes quite narrowly focused. The reason for this is that the various personality disorder 'types' arose from different clinical and scientific origins. Thus, some of the personality disorders are consciously anchored in one or other of the Axis I illnesses. Good examples are Schizoid and Schizotypal Personality Disorder (both in schizophrenia), and 'Obsessive Compulsive Personality Disorder' (in Axis I Obsessive Compulsive Disorder). Other Axis II disorders, however, have no reference in Axis I. Narcissistic Personality Disorder is a case in point. It derives from one of several personality constructs – mostly found in psychoanalytic theory – that are used to describe certain features of personality dynamics and personality development. But there is, as such, no symptom-based narcissistic *illness*.

Another feature to note is that even the DSM in its most recent edition does not quite avoid the negative connotations of personality disorder labelling,

63

including occasional sexist overtones. In some cases, for example Antisocial Personality Disorder, this is unavoidable: most criminals, whether personality disordered or not, actually are not very congenial. As for gender bias, this continues to be a tricky issue. On the face of it there do seem to be genuine sex differences: for example Borderline Personality Disorder is more common in women and Antisocial Personality Disorder more common in men (Becker, 1997). Of course, this could be because clinicians simply have a lower threshold for applying such diagnoses to women (or men). There is evidence that actually that is not the case, at least for the 'female' disorders (Funtowicz & Widiger, 1995). But there are bound to be lingering doubts about the gender neutrality of personality disorder labels, given their generally poor image.

Certainly, some of the Axis II terminology is unfortunate. It is surprising, for example, that the descriptor 'histrionic' – as in Histrionic Personality Disorder – was allowed into the DSM-IV. 'Histrionic' – together with its effective synonym 'hysterical' – has a long and chequered history in psychiatric nosology and theory, as well as in everyday usage (Roy, 1982). The heyday of 'hysteria' was the late nineteenth and early twentieth centuries when the diagnosis was frequently and increasingly applied, mostly to women. Indeed, as the feminist writer, Elaine Showalter (1987) points out, during that time 'hysteria' became the prevailing icon of the 'madness that is woman', and a readily available label for early female protests against the prevailing social order. But the term goes back much further than that – its Greek origin in 'the wandering womb' gives the game away – and 'hysteria' has never really thrown off its gender bias. Ironically, 'histrionic' has a quite different etymology – it comes from the Latin for 'actor' – but it sounds too similar and, in any case, it has absorbed some of the meaning of 'hysterical', so assuming the same derogatory connotation.

A further complication with 'hysteria' should be mentioned. In its nineteenth-century usage hysteria came to refer, not just to hysterical *personality* but also to a symptomatic illness known as *conversion hysteria*. Here, the individual develops a complete or partial loss of some sensory or motor function, for which there is no neurological explanation. He or she becomes blind or deaf, or paralysed, or loses sensation in a limb. Sometimes the 'conversion' of emotional distress (for that is what it is claimed to be) takes the form of amnesia, or a fugue state in which the individual wanders off and forgets his or her identity.

Traditionally, therefore, there have been two usages of 'hysteria', one referring to an *illness* element and the other to a *personality/personality disorder* element. The latter, as mentioned above, finds its nearest modern equivalent in the DSM Axis II label, Histrionic Personality Disorder. As for the illness component (in Axis I), this is confusingly spread across two different categories. The very global forms of 'conversion' (amnesia, fugue states, etc.) are put under the heading of 'Dissociative Disorders'. More localized conversion reactions are bundled under 'Somatoform Disorders', together with

other syndromes in which distress is channelled into bodily symptomatology: pain reactions, body dysmorphic disorder, and hypochondriasis. This splitting of the older, larger category of conversion hysterias is unfortunate in some ways, as the global and more localized reactions probably do share some similar underlying causal mechanism, in the form of a psychophysiological dissociation from anxiety not found in other bodily expressions of emotional distress, such as pain. (Incidentally, the ICD-10, recognizing this, does keep both local and generalized dissociative reactions under one heading.)

How do the two elements in 'hysteria' – personality and illness – relate to each other? There is some early work, carried out within Eysenck's theory and referred to briefly in Chapter 2, which suggests that they are not unconnected biologically, and that people prone to dissociative disorders are more likely to show 'hysterical', or equivalent personality traits (Claridge, 1967). This particular question has not been researched much in recent years. But it does illustrate what in general *is* a hotly debated general point, viz. how we are to visualize the connection between Axis I and Axis II disorders. If, that is, there *is* a connection: by putting the two kinds of abnormality on separate axes, the DSM half implies that there might not be.

This relationship, if it does exist, is naturally of most interest for those personality disorders that appear to have an anchor point in Axis I and there are two ways in which we might examine the question. One procedure – by now self-evident to the reader – is to look at the presence of certain personality traits in individuals with symptom-based illnesses, in order to determine whether such characteristics are necessary precursors, or accompaniments, of the condition. Alternatively, we could go about it by studying the *comorbidity* between the illness and a relevant Axis II disorder. These methods are to an extent complementary, but they do not necessarily give the same answer and therefore need to be distinguished. Consider an example.

Suppose we want to find out whether individuals suffering from the Axis I illness of Obsessive–Compulsive Disorder (OCD) are basically obsessional people. We could do this by seeing whether they score highly in obsessional traits on a questionnaire drawn from normal personality psychology. Or we could examine a group of OCD patients to see how many may also be diagnosed as having Obsessive–Compulsive Personality Disorder (OCPD). Either way we will be led to draw certain conclusions about the characteristic personality style found in OCD. But it is important to note that, of the two methods, comorbidity analysis is the blunter strategy and, taken by itself, can lead to misleading conclusions. This is because it is much more difficult for someone to meet the criteria for a clinical disorder than to achieve high scores on a personality questionnaire. So, in our OCD example, lack of comorbidity with OCPD could cause us to conclude, wrongly, that there is no association with obsessional traits. In fact, only results from personality assessments can properly address that question.

# PERSONALITY DISORDERS AND MODELS OF THE ABNORMAL

In Chapter 2 we spent some time explaining different meanings of 'dimensionality' and how these can inform our understanding of the medical model. Here, it may be helpful to reiterate some crucial points from that discussion, as a preamble to considering the possible dimensional status of the personality disorders.

It will be recalled that we distinguished two forms of dimensionality. One is the familiar trait continuity on which normal personality structure is based. It is this that describes the healthy dimensions of personality and/or temperament and, at the same time, the corresponding predispositions to clinical states. A second form of dimensionality we described is continuity within disorder itself – and here, for the moment, we are referring to symptom-based, Axis I type, conditions. Using anxiety disorder as our example, we explained that, because illnesses can occur with different degrees of severity, symptoms themselves might form a quasi-dimension or spectrum. At the lower end of this clinical continuum, mild symptoms (for example, transient phobic reactions) might merge with, and be indistinguishable from, personality trait features (for example, chronic worrying); the boundary between these two expressions of deviation from the normal then starts to look conceptually rather blurred. So what about the personality disorders? Where do they fit into the picture?

There are two possibilities. One is that the personality disorders really *are* simply exaggerations of normal variation; in other words, they lie at the far end of a number of genuinely continuous personality dimensions, as extreme examples of traits. The other is that they represent attenuated forms of symptom-based illnesses and just happen to look like extreme personality variation because, as we have seen in the case of our anxiety example, mild symptoms can sometimes look like traits. Either way, phenomenologically, personality disorders seem to fall somewhere between the normal range of personality variation and symptom-based illness, showing some qualities that look like traits and some that look like symptoms. Foulds, whose pioneering ideas we quoted in Chapter 2 as one of the few writers to have made a clear distinction between 'symptoms' and 'traits', realized the dilemma. He admitted that personality-disordered individuals do pose a special problem. Such people do not seem to be 'ill' in the ordinary sense, but, if their behaviour *is* on a continuum with normal, it seems almost too extreme to be comfortable with. To deal with this ambiguity Foulds (1971) coined the idea of 'deviant traits'.

But are we not splitting unnecessary hairs here? Does it really matter which of the above two dimensional explanations of personality disorders is correct? It does in the sense that it will influence where we look for underlying causes. If personality disorders are mild illnesses, it is by studying the aetiology of Axis I conditions that we will gain an understanding of corresponding Axis II

equivalents. On the other hand, if they represent extremes of normal function then we need to study the determinants of healthy personality and then extrapolate from that into the abnormal domain. These are two different research strategies: one, the former, is more medically based, the other more personality based.

In practice, neither alternative is likely to prove universally true for all forms of personality disorder. As noted above, if we follow the DSM, in some instances there *is* no Axis I illness of which the personality disorder could be a mild form: we cited Narcissistic Personality Disorder as an example. But in other instances we quoted, for example Schizotypal Personality Disorder, there is; indeed, in that case there is an ongoing very vigorous, sometimes bitter, debate about which form of dimensionality applies to that particular form of personality disorder (see Chapter 9).

For any given personality disorder even the same behaviours occurring in different individuals will also differ in the way in which they can be explained. In one individual the disordered personality might be just a gross exaggeration of some otherwise healthy temperamental trait. In another person – or on closer medical examination – the same behaviour could prove to be due to clearly demonstrable brain pathology. Cases in point are the disinhibited behaviour that can follow damage to the frontal lobes and the impulsive anger sometimes associated with temporal lobe epilepsy. Here, it is no coincidence that the same brain systems are likely to be implicated in the 'natural' variant as in the 'neurological' form. Indeed, evidence collected on the latter is often used in support of theories about the biology of temperaments and, by extrapolation, their deviant forms.

## APPROACHES TO THE EXPLANATION OF PERSONALITY DISORDERS

There have been many attempts to characterize and explain disorders of the personality, from very disparate points of view. Here we shall mention just some of them, mostly those that draw upon or connect to the ideas we have already presented. Even so, finding an orderly way of presenting the material is not easy, but the, albeit arbitrary, arrangement to be adopted is probably as useful as any. When reading through subsequent sections it may be helpful to bear in mind the following themes that run through the literature on personality disorders and around which we have loosely organized our discussion of them.

First, there are those – mostly North American – researchers who take the DSM Axis II classification at its face value and attempt in some way to go beyond it. They do so either by trying to refine the description of the personality disorders listed in the DSM and/or by offering an explanation of them. Then, there are writers who have concentrated more on a single form of personality disorder, sometimes using the DSM nomenclature and sometimes not; instead – either for theoretical or historical reasons – they have stepped outside Axis II to use another label. Lastly, some observations on the topic have come, not directly from the clinical end, but made by personality theorists extrapolating from their ideas about normal individuality. Cutting across these various approaches, explanations have differed widely, from the biological to the cognitive and taking in genetic, as well as more environmental, perspectives.

## FIVE-FACTOR THEORY AND AXIS II

A prominent part of the current literature on personality and personality disorders (as portrayed in the DSM) concerns the application of the Five-factor theory outlined in the previous chapter. Indeed, the contribution of Five-factor theorists to abnormal psychology has mostly been confined to that group of disorders. This fact has been recognized by the authors of the DSM-IV, who go as far as to cite the work as an example of attempts to identify fundamental dimensions of personality that could account for the Axis II conditions. They do so in a short section devoted to the issue raised earlier, of whether the personality disorders are best viewed as dimensional with normal personality or dimensional with Axis I illnesses. They rather sit on a conservative fence in the matter, merely saying that dimensional models are 'under investigation'.

A variety of approaches have been taken to the topic. Some research has used factor analysis to see how accurately the dimensions in Five-factor theory map onto clinical features of the Axis II disorders, assessed independently by another set of scales. The authors of one such study concluded that there was very good correspondence between the two systems (Schroeder *et al.*, 1992). Although such findings are statistically convincing, they seem less satisfying when one examines the Axis II disorders individually, in terms of the profiles they show across the dimensions of Five-factor theory. Figure 4.1 summarizes the findings for three representative personality disorders – Schizoid, Borderline, and Avoidant – belonging, respectively, to clusters A, B, and C in the DSM-IV (Widiger & Costa, 1994).

It is clear from the diagram that some differences are to be observed between the three personality disorders shown there. Particularly interesting is the rather *low* Neuroticism of the Schizoid group. This is an exception to the usually very high Neuroticism found in clinical conditions of almost any kind, including the other two personality disorders shown in the figure. But it does fit in with the absence of emotional responsiveness found in schizoid individuals who tend, overtly at least, to seem rather unfeeling. In other respects, however, it has to be said that profiles of this kind tell us little that we do not already know. For example, it is not too surprising that both schizoid and avoidant forms of personality disorder are found in highly introverted personalities. Or that people with Borderline Personality Disorder are low on Agreeableness; we saw earlier that some individuals with extreme personality traits are occasionally not very nice.

At least it may be said that Five-factor research establishes some validity for

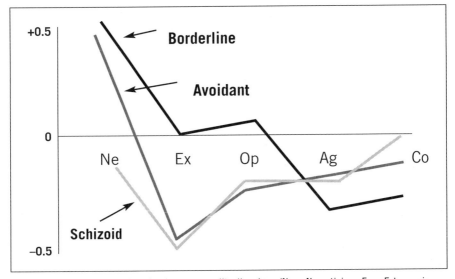

**Figure 4.1**   Five-factor profiles for three personality disorders. (Ne = Neuroticism; Ex = Extraversion; Op = Openness; Ag = Agreeableness; Co = Conscienciousness.)

the Axis II classification of personality disorders, by pointing to understandable differences on major personality dimensions that have been established independently of the DSM. Unfortunately, as noted in Chapter 3, Five-factor theory is weak on the 'causal' side of things, not having a well-worked out account of the underlying determinants, for example biology, of its dimensions. Mostly, the question of aetiology is referred to in discussions about the possible genetic influences on the Five-factor dimensions. This is fine in its own way but it offers nothing unique that other approaches are not also addressing.

Also, research on healthy subjects of the heritability of normal personality traits (whether or not Five-factor theory inspired) is only one strategy for trying to unravel the complex genetics of personality disorders. Other methods involve direct study of personality disordered individuals, or trying to extrapolate from what is known about the genetics of related Axis I disorders. Taking all this information into account, the findings to date are rather mixed (Nigg & Goldsmith, 1994). Some Axis II disorders – mostly in Cluster A – do seem to have strong heritability. The evidence for others, including – surprisingly perhaps – Obsessive–Compulsive Personality Disorder, is more equivocal.

Some of the ambiguity here stems partly from weaknesses in the definition and delineation of the personality disorders themselves. Because of the high comorbidity between certain Axis II diagnoses, it is unlikely that very specific genetic effects will be found for some disorders; that is, effects that cannot be assigned to some common set of personality traits, or temperament dimension.

An example is Histrionic Personality Disorder which overlaps considerably with Borderline Personality Disorder and which might share with it a strongly inherited element of, say, impulsivity.

## CLONINGER REVISITED

Like the Five-factor theorists, Cloninger has also proposed a comprehensive account of normal personality. And, in the clinical sphere, he too has applied his ideas especially to personality disorders. However, compared with Five-factor theory, Cloninger's account is altogether more searching, in two respects. First, it makes the important distinction between temperament and character, each being broken down into several dimensions, which it is claimed interact to produce differences in healthy and unhealthy personality structure and functioning. Second, Cloninger offers a well-defined, albeit speculative, biological (including genetic) explanation for the temperamental differences, along lines that chime with other mainstream personality theories of a similar type.

Applying his theory to Axis II, Cloninger argues that the basic tendencies towards the various personality disorders lie in differences among the four, substantially inherited, temperament dimensions: *novelty seeking*, *harm avoidance*, *reward dependency*, and *persistence*. The expression of these dispositions can be, and usually is, healthy; but where the temperamental traits are extreme, or circumstances conspire to distort them, a personality disorder will result. This outcome is seen to depend on the three character dispositions of *self-directedness*, *co-operativeness*, and *self-transcendence* (Svrakic *et al.*, 1993).

Cloninger established profiles for all of the Axis II personality disorders by use of his Temperament and Character Inventory (TCI) (Cloninger *et al.*, 1994). Four examples are illustrated in Table 4.1: the three shown earlier in Figure 4.1 – Avoidant, Borderline, and Schizoid – to which we have added, for interest, Antisocial Personality Disorder (Table 4.2). Three points are worth noting.

The first concerns scores on Cloninger's three character dimensions. All four of the disorders shown in Table 4.2 are virtually identical on these factors and

70

**Table 4.2** Profiles for four personality disorders (Cloninger).

|  | Novelty seeking | Harm avoidance | Reward dependency | Persistence | Self-directedness | Cooperativeness | Self-transcendence |
|---|---|---|---|---|---|---|---|
| Antisocial | + |  | − |  | − | − |  |
| Borderline | + | + |  |  | − | − |  |
| Avoidant | − |  |  |  | − |  |  |
| Schizoid |  |  | − |  | − | − |  |

fairly equally deviant on two of them: *self-directedness* and *co-operativeness*. Indeed, looking at Cloninger's full set of profiles it is evident that all of the Axis II disorders are very similar on the character dimensions. What this signifies is that people with personality disorders tend, in general, to be rather unco-operative and to lack self-directedness or, as Cloninger himself puts it: '...have difficulty accepting responsibility, setting meaningful goals, resourcefully meeting challenges, accepting limitations, and disciplining their habits to be congruent with their goals and values'. This combination of traits probably helps to explain why most people with personality disorders are not very well-liked.

The second point to note about Table 4.2 concerns the variation on the temperament dimensions. It is evident that antisocials are very high in 'novelty seeking', as befits their impulsive behaviour and constant seeking of positive reinforcers. In contrast, avoidants are very low in this, but especially high in 'harm avoidance', consistent with their high anxiety. One other interesting feature is the profile of schizoid subjects, whose main temperamental feature is low 'reward dependency'; appropriately, they find little satisfaction in social stimulation. Taken together with the unusually low Neuroticism found in the Five-factor profile, this suggests that schizoid individuals are, as always thought, a bit odd – they do not even conform to the norms of disordered personality!

The conclusion from Cloninger's work, then, is that the factors determining which personality disorder an individual shows are almost entirely *temperamental* in nature, owing to differences in basic biological drives or tendencies of the kind outlined in the previous chapter. To the extent that these characteristics are inherited it may therefore be said that the deviant behaviours normally descriptive of personality disorder are under some genetic control. But, if we follow Cloninger, the actual expression of these dispositions will be shaped by what he refers to as his character dimensions. These, according to his analysis, are flawed in a very similar way and to a similar degree, across different disorders.

## THE WORK OF MILLON

A writer whom we have not mentioned before but one who has made a major contribution to the literature on personality disorders is Millon (Millon & Davis, 2000). In the context of this book Millon is unusual for two reasons. First, his ideas about normal personality have been very much driven by his attempts to account for its disorders rather than vice versa. And, second, his theorizing has been rather outside the mainstream thinking that we are mostly drawing upon here. Despite the fact that Millon's work has not had great impact in general personality psychology, it has had considerable influence on clinicians in the field of personality disorders. Among other things, Millon is the originator of a widely used psychometric procedure for assessing personality disorder features in clinical and community samples: the *Millon Clinical Multiaxial Inventory* (*MCMI-III*) (Millon *et al.*, 1996).

Millon's stance on the relationship between normal and abnormal personality consists of what he calls a 'biosocial learning approach'. In its very basic form this extrapolates from a classification of normal personality patterns to dysfunctional forms that constitute the Axis II disorders. The essential features of the theory are shown in Table 4.3. According to Millon normal personality differences are accounted for, or reflected in, two influences: an individual's preferred source of reinforcement, and an instrumental behaviour pattern in relation to that. Thus, individuals may be proactive or passive in their behaviour and find satisfying reinforcement in one of four ways: *independent*, *dependent*, *ambivalent*, and *detached from others*. This matrix gives rise to a series of personality patterns which, in their abnormal form, are seen in the various Axis II disorders (see Table 4.3).

**Table 4.3** Personality disorders: Millon's theory.

| Behaviour pattern | Source of reinforcement | | | |
|---|---|---|---|---|
| | Independent | Dependent | Ambivalent | Detached |
| Proactive | Antisocial | Histrionic | Passive-Aggressive | Avoidant |
| Passive | Narcissistic | Dependent | Obsessive–Compulsive | Schizoid |

One further feature of Millon's analysis to be noted is that it proposes a continuum of severity *within* the personality disorders. Thus, apart from Schizoid, the Cluster A conditions – Borderline, Schizotypal, and Paranoid – are perceived to be more severe expressions of the same normal personality patterns responsible for milder forms. Although Millon provides no experimental evidence for his theory – his ideas are largely based on clinical observation – the implied dimensionality between personality disorders and psychotic illness does chime with a theme in this topic already mentioned several times, and to which we shall return.

## BECK'S COGNITIVE APPROACH

Beck is most celebrated for his writings on depression. Less well-known are his clinical speculations about personality disorders (Beck *et al.*, 1990). As with depression, Beck concentrates on the cognitive approach, inspired by an interest in applying cognitive behaviour therapy to Axis II disorders. His view of the latter is that they represent deviant personality patterns defined by abnormalities in three areas of function: cognition, emotion, and motivation.

The resulting mental schemata to which these abnormalities give rise differ across the various disorders and may be observed clinically in four ways:

- The view of the self.

- The view of others.

- The predominant belief system.

- The main strategy for dealing with the world.

Table 4.4 summarizes how, according to Beck, the main Axis II disorders differ in these four respects. The features shown are fairly self-evident when compared with the DSM and other clinical descriptions of the personality disorders. But they do help to supplement these and are meant to provide a focus for therapeutic efforts to bring about change in clients with personality disorders.

**Table 4.4**  Cognitive biases in personality disorders (Beck).

| | |
|---|---|
| *Paranoid* | Motives are suspect; be on guard; do not trust |
| *Schizoid* | Others are unrewarding, relationships undesirable |
| *Antisocial* | Entitled to break rules; others are wimps |
| *Histrionic* | People are there to serve and admire me |
| *Narcissistic* | I am special and deserve special rules |
| *Avoidant–dependent* | If people know the real me they will reject me; need people to survive and be happy |
| *Obsessive–compulsive* | I know what is best; details are crucial |

In his discussion of personality disorders Beck raises the inevitable question of where dysfunctional belief systems of the kind shown in Table 4.4 come from. Unfortunately, he fails to address the issue beyond vague statements about 'nature–nurture interaction' and individuals being predisposed 'by nature' to overreact in childhood to certain negative life events that could lead to the distorted cognitions and behaviours associated with the various personality disorders. Beyond this, no attempt is made to specify, for example, particular biological tendencies or mechanisms that could account for the different disorders. Nevertheless, his insightful descriptions of these could provide a useful starting-point, at the clinical end, for trying to integrate psychological and biological approaches to the personality disorders.

## PARTICULAR PERSONALITY DISORDERS

The disorders we have introduced in this chapter differ in importance from one another in several respects: their status as significant stand-alone forms of abnormal behaviour; their relatedness to symptom-based illnesses; and the extent to which studying them may contribute to our understanding of psychological disorders in general. Some have received comparatively little attention. Histrionic Personality Disorder is a case in point. Most of what is known about Histrionic Personality Disorder comes from its overlap with other disorders in the same Axis II cluster or via its historical association with hysteria and hysterical personality. A rather different example is Narcissistic Personality Disorder. A great deal is still written about narcissism, but most research on it is not very empirical; this, coupled with a lack of connection to any specific Axis I illness, leaves it rather stranded from mainstream theory in psychiatry and abnormal psychology. In contrast, four personality disorders stand out as being sufficiently different from the remainder to have become the focus for more substantial research and the collecting point for some important ideas in the field.

Obsessive–Compulsive Personality Disorder (OCPD) is unusual in showing relatively low comorbidity with other Axis II disorders. Its relationship, or not, to Axis I Obsessive–Compulsive Disorder (OCD) also raises interesting questions. How far do OCD and OCPD share common underlying personality traits? If not, is this because OCD is itself a heterogeneous condition? What light can the study of OCPD, including its genetics, throw on this matter?

Schizotypal Personality Disorder (SPD) – and its associated personality dimensions – have an even more strategic role in shaping our understanding of Axis I illnesses, notably schizophrenia, but others as well. The research effort there has been considerable and is one of the best examples of the convergence of ideas stemming from studies of normal personality, personality disorder, and symptom-based illness.

Antisocial Personality Disorder (APD) is important, not least because it sits at the traditional centre of the personality disorder construct, representing that part – the dislikeable criminal element – with which most people associate the label. Unfortunate though that is, by being generalized to personality disorders as a whole, it is obviously highly relevant to the understanding of APD itself. APD has inspired a considerable amount of research, although, as explained below, much of the definitive research has been carried out under a different label.

Fourth, Borderline Personality Disorder (BPD) is, in a sense, the archetype of 'disordered personality', encompassing most of the defining features of the latter. These include chaotic personality dynamics, a probable association to psychotic illness, unlikeability, and yet, despite these things, a recognizable dimensionality with normal behaviour. The term 'borderline' also has a fascinating history, appearing in several guises in psychiatry. For that reason it has attracted a wide range of explanations from very different research perspectives.

In the rest of this chapter we shall consider only two of the personality disorders just mentioned: APD and BPD. The other two – OCPD and SPD – are best considered in the chapters devoted to the corresponding Axis I disorders: OCD in Chapter 6 and schizophrenia in Chapter 9, respectively.

## ANTISOCIAL PERSONALITY DISORDER (PSYCHOPATHY)

Antisocial behaviour stems from many causes, both individual and situational, both biological and cultural. People transgress the moral or written rules for all sorts of reasons. At the more trivial end of the spectrum a momentary impulsive need may tempt a perfectly average citizen to steal his neighbour's pen, and most of the population drives some of the time some miles per hour above the speed limit. As for more serious law-breaking, much of this can be traced to poverty, social deprivation, unemployment, poor education, or merely living in a criminal subculture: if theft or violence is the everyday norm, unsurprisingly, people learn to steal and hit each other.

However, here we are more concerned with the personality and clinical features which – over and above those other causes – contribute to some kinds of antisocial behaviour; in other words, characteristics that can supposedly be found in people who are regarded as inherently antisocial individuals. In the current DSM Axis II terminology this cluster of traits is labelled Antisocial Personality Disorder. However, for the purpose of our discussion here, we shall abandon the DSM and the APD construct, in favour of 'psychopathy' and 'psychopathic personality'. The reason for doing this is that the most systematic research has been done, and the most coherent set of ideas has been developed, around the concept of 'psychopathy', rather than APD. Yet, having said that, we also need to define our terms even more precisely.

The label 'psychopath' itself has suffered greatly in the hands of psychiatrists and psychologists, who over the years have defined and re-defined and subcategorized it in various ways. The main division that we need to be concerned about here is the distinction between *primary* and *secondary* psychopathy. As the name implies, the latter refers to antisocial behaviours that are consequent upon or can be accounted for by some other event or feature of the individual. This could include subcultural factors, immediate or remote life events or, on the personal front, associated mental illness that triggers or potentiates the antisocial act. In contrast, primary psychopathy refers to the idea that there are some individuals whose criminality, or other antisocial behaviour, can be very largely explained by their personality or temperamental make-up.

**Cleckley's clinical description** The best clinically based accounts of the psychopathic personality are to be found in Cleckley's classic book, *The Mask of Sanity* (Cleckley, 1976). In some of the most colourful prose in the psychiatric literature, and with detailed case histories, Cleckley paints a composite picture of the psychopath which, for those who have come face to face with such individuals, will be instantly recognizable. He (most, although not all, psychopaths are male) is the sort of egocentric person who, whilst sometimes superficially charming and plausible, is devious, unreliable and insincere; who lacks guilt, shame and empathy for others; who constantly seeks to relieve boredom; and whose poor judgement is coupled with a chronic failure to learn from experience. It is difficult to do justice to the richness of Cleckley's characterizations, but the following extract captures some of the quality of his text and of the psychopathic individuals he is describing:

> In a world where tedium demands that the situation be enlivened by pranks that bring censure, nagging, nights in the local jail, and irritating duns about unpaid bills, it can well be imagined that the psychopath finds causes for vexation and impulses towards reprisal. Few, if any, of the scruples that in the ordinary man might oppose and control such impulses seem to influence him. Unable to realize what it meant to his wife when he was discovered in the cellar *in flagrante delicto* with the cook, he is likely to be put out considerably by her reactions to this ... His father, from the patient's point of view, lacks humor and does not understand things. The old man could easily take a different attitude about having had to make good those last three little old cheques written by the son. Nor is there any sense in raising so much hell because he took that dilapidated old Chevrolet for this trip to Memphis. What if he did forget to tell the old man he was going to take it? It wouldn't hurt him to go to the office on the bus for a few days. How was he (the patient) to know the fellows were going to clean him out at stud or that the bitch of a waitress at the Frolic Spot would get so nasty about money? What else could he do but sell the antiquated buggy? If the old man weren't so parsimonious he'd want to get a new car anyway! (Cleckley, 1976; 390)

Cleckley's insight into the psychology of the psychopath led him to several interesting conclusions. For one thing Cleckley was not very convinced by the idea that the primary psychopath's behaviour could be traced, in any significant degree, to experiences within the family. He noted that a very large percentage of the psychopaths he saw came from backgrounds that appeared conducive to happy development and good adjustment. And, by the same token, where early incidents could be identified that might have explained the later antisocial behaviour, similar experiences could frequently be demonstrated in the backgrounds of many perfectly happy, successful adults. Cleckley's preference was for a constitutional explanation, a strong argument in favour being the 'black sheep' phenomenon, viz. the sharp contrast in behaviour that could be observed between the psychopath and the other healthy, adjusted members of his family.

Second, addressing the cognitive functioning of psychopaths, Cleckley noticed that a lack of intelligence, in the ordinary sense, did not appear to be the problem; on the contrary, many of the patients he saw were quite bright. The difficulty was more subtle. It consisted, he said, of some flaw in semantic processing whereby elaboration of the meaning, especially the emotional

76

meaning, of words is poorly developed. As Cleckley put it, the psychopath:

> ... cannot be taught awareness of significance which he fails to feel. He can learn to use the ordinary words and, if he is very clever, even extraordinarily vivid and eloquent words which signify these matters to other people. He will also learn to reproduce appropriately all the pantomime of feeling; but, as Sherrington said of the decerebrate animal, the feeling itself does not come to pass. (Cleckley, 1976; 374)

The same point was made elsewhere in the now famous description of the psychopath as someone who '... knows the words, but not the music' (Johns & Quay, 1962).

A third, fascinating, insight by Cleckley concerned the manifestation of psychopathic traits in everyday life, outside a criminal or overtly antisocial context. He devotes several sections of his book to 'The psychopath as businessman ... as man of the world ... as gentleman ... and as scientist, physician – and psychiatrist'. The dimensional message is plain and should not surprise us. Like other personality characteristics that have the potential for disorder, given the opportunity those found in the psychopath can and do lead to success, often in high places!

**The work of Hare** Cleckley's writings provided the inspiration for a long, systematic programme of studying the primary psychopath by Hare and colleagues (Hare, 1986, 1993; Cooke *et al.*, 1998). This work has had two strands of research, developed partly in parallel.

**Table 4.5** Psychopathy checklist (Hare).

| |
|---|
| **Factor 1: Personal & emotional traits** |
|     Glibness/superficial charm |
|     Grandiose sense of self-worth |
|     Pathological lying |
|     Manipulative/conning |
|     Lack of remorse or guilt |
|     Lack of empathy |
|     Shallow affect |
| **Factor 2: Lifestyle** |
|     Need for stimulation |
|     Parasitic lifestyle |
|     Early behavioural problems |
|     Lack of realistic goals |
|     Impulsive behaviour |
|     Poor probation or parole risk |

The first involved the construction of an instrument for measuring psychopathic features, largely based on Cleckley's description. This – in its current form the *Revised Psychopathy Checklist (PCL-R)* – is listed in Table 4.5. A point to note about the checklist is that factor analysis revealed two different types of item (Hare *et al.*, 1990). One concerns psychopathic *personality traits*; the other *lifestyle habits*. Although the two factors are highly correlated, Hare considers it desirable to retain the distinction between them because, according to him, they relate differently to other variables. Most important to note here is that the Axis II diagnosis of APD correlates only with the second, lifestyle, factor, showing no relationship to the personality traits measured by Factor I. Hare is probably right, therefore, to suggest that one needs to take *both* aspects into account, in order to assess psychopathy properly.

The other strand in Hare's research programme has been experimental studies of criminals, examining various theories of psychopathic behaviour. The standard methodology has been to compare primary psychopaths, selected by one or other version of the Hare checklist, with non-psychopathic criminals. The research has spanned several decades. Consequently, a wide range of experimental paradigms has been tested over the years, from behavioural to neurocognitive (see Table 4.6). When evaluating these different explanations it is important to note that all of them, including the early ones, have a place in accounting for some facet of psychopathic behaviour.

**Table 4.6**   Primary psychopathy: possible explanations (Hare).

| |
|---|
| **Physiological arousal** |
|     Arousal deficiency |
|     Low anxiety |
|     Poor anticipation of punishment |
| **Sensory modulation** |
|     Efficient sensory gating |
|     'Tuning out' of threat |
| **Neurocognitive functioning** |
|     Weak lateralization for language |
|     Failure to connect to affective significance of language |

The earliest formulations made use of the idea that psychopaths apparently fail to avoid punishment when tested in an aversive conditioning situation. This seemed to be related to the fact that psychopaths have a steep temporal gradient of fear arousal. That is to say, they do not readily anticipate the onset of an impending punishment; as measured in the laboratory by their autonomic (skin conductance) response to an expected electric shock. A middle phase of Hare's research shifted to a more 'cognitive' explanation, when it was noticed that, contrary to prediction, primary psychopaths showed an unusual pattern of physiological response to stress. Although in general physiologically rather unresponsive, their heart rates tended, paradoxically, to go *up* when stressed. Hare argued, in line with some current thinking about the interpretation of such effects, that psychopaths have an efficient attentional gating mechanism when under threat. In other words, when faced with something that is potentially disturbing, their brains are quick to react with: 'I don't like the look of that; I'll just ignore it, not think about it'. This 'dissociation' from stress – which is indeed known to cause the heart rate to go up – might also explain why psychopaths do not learn from experiences that involve punishment. Most of the time they are not even paying attention.

Hare's later explanations of psychopathy have been more thoroughly neurocognitive and picked up on the 'know the words but not the music' theme referred to earlier. In one study, testing this idea, EEG responses to emotional and non-emotional words were measured in primary psychopaths and non-psychopathic criminals. It was predicted that because psychopaths would make inefficient use of the affective information contained in some of the words, there would be *less difference* in their EEG reactions to the two kind of stimuli, compared with control subjects. This proved to be the case (Williamson *et al.*, 1991). Then, in their most recent study of this same emotional processing deficit, functional magnetic resonance imaging (fMRI) was used to study the brain activity of psychopaths whilst performing an affective memory task. It was found that, compared with control subjects, psychopaths showed reduced activity in the limbic structures (amygdala, hippocampus, cingulate gyrus) presumed necessary for the processing of emotional stimuli (Kiehl *et al.*, 2001).

**The work of Blair** Research that follows almost directly from that by Hare and his colleagues is the recent elaboration of the neurocognitive perspective on primary psychopathy by Blair. Blair's theory attempts to provide a neurological explanation of two related aspects of the psychopath's behaviour: his deficiency in emotional processing (empathy) and his poor control over aggression (Blair, 1995).

The core idea in Blair's thinking is the notion of a Violence Inhibition Mechanism (VIM). This draws upon the work of ethologists and the suggestion that social animals possess mechanisms that suppress attack responses in the presence of cues of submission from their foe; for example an aggressive dog ceases to fight if its opponent bares its throat. Blair's proposal is that a similar mechanism exists in the human, but is absent or functions poorly in the primary psychopath. Blair reports two kinds of experiment – both conducted with adult psychopaths selected on the basis of the Hare checklist – which he claims support his theory:

- It was argued that if psychopaths have a weak VIM, they should be abnormal in their processing of others' emotions. This was tested by asking psychopaths (and non-psychopathic control subjects) to attribute emotions to characters in stories displaying various positive or negative affects. It was found that, in response to 'guilt stories', psychopaths were significantly less likely to state guilt as the dominant theme; the emotion tended, instead, to be happiness or indifference (Blair *et al.*, 1995).

- Along the same lines, it was predicted that psychopaths should show a reduced physiological reaction to signs of, specifically, distress in others. This was tested by comparing psychopaths and non-psychopaths in their skin conductance responses to slides illustrating scenes eliciting different emotional cues. Although not differing for threatening and neutral stimuli, psychopaths showed significant reduced response to cues of distress (Blair *et al.*, 1997)

In other experiments, similar effects, using the same methodology, were found in children selected for psychopathic tendencies on the basis of another of the Hare screening procedures (Blair, 1999).

Blair's conclusions from these studies are that a frail **VIM** could be an inherent biological feature of the antisocial individual, influencing moral development from an early age. Further speculating on the possible neurology of this mechanism, he proposes that the amygdala might play a central role, given its known function in emotion, especially the processing of facial affect. Once more, therefore, some deficiency in limbic system functioning seems to emerge as a crucial feature of the biology of those forms of antisocial behaviour where the deviation may be ascribed to personality differences.

## BORDERLINE PERSONALITY DISORDER (BPD)

**The 'borderline' construct** The history of BPD is as confused as those suffering from the disorder itself. The first point to note is that 'borderline' (and the terminology surrounding it) is almost exclusively of American origin, stemming from certain trends of thought in mid-twentieth century North American psychiatry. 'Borderline' emerged there partly as a way of articulating the dimensionality of psychotic disorders, in particular schizophrenia. Not, we should add, dimensionality in precisely the way we are presenting that idea here; rather, more to reflect the very broad, socio-psychological view of schizophrenia that prevailed in the USA through the 1950s and 1960s. During that period clinical labels were in use which expressed this borderline view, such as 'latent schizophrenia', 'pseudoneurotic schizophrenia', and indeed 'borderline schizophrenia'.

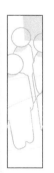

An important influence there – stronger than in the European psychiatry of the time – was psychoanalysis and, in some usages of the term, 'borderline' was occasionally defined therapeutically. Borderline patients came to be seen as individuals who, although not manifestly psychotic, were too ill to respond well to conventional forms of psychoanalytic psychotherapy. Furthermore, in some writings, discussion of 'borderline' became detached from formal issues about connections to psychosis. There was, instead, a shift towards trying to characterize the clinical features and underlying dynamics of this peculiar, pervasively chaotic psychological disorder. It was this trend in the study of 'borderline' that brought the topic more into the personality disorders domain; running by this time in parallel with debates elsewhere about the dimensionality of psychosis and the schizophrenia spectrum (Claridge, 1995).

**'Borderline' in the DSM** It was not until the 1980s – with the first major revision of the DSM – that a degree of order was brought into the clinical and diagnostic confusion surrounding the 'borderline' construct. With only minor revisions in subsequent editions, DSM-III recognized two usages of 'borderline', now enshrined in Schizotypal Personality Disorder (SPD) and Borderline Personality Disorder (BPD). Although the two forms show considerable overlap, this dichotomy kept separate the dual themes in the history of the construct: the personality disorder aspect and the connection to psychosis. One rather artificial consequence of this division, as noted earlier, is that SPD and BPD are assigned to different Axis II clusters.

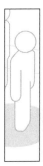

Table 4.7 summarizes the current criteria for BPD, as defined in the DSM-IV. The notable features, which help us to understand the difficulties – in more than one sense – of the disorder, are to be found in the characteristic combination of outrageous behaviours, erratic social interactions, and unregulated emotion which cause the sufferer to veer constantly out of control, yet mostly, and remarkably, not quite enough to break down into frank psychosis. All of this adds up to a picture of chronic derangement neatly captured in one classic description of borderline patients: that they are 'stable in their instability'!

**Table 4.7**   Borderline Personality Disorder – the DSM criteria.

Frantic efforts to avoid abandonment
Unstable and intense interpersonal relationships
Unstable self-image
Impulsivity (in, for example, sex, spending, substance abuse)
Suicidal and/or self-mutilating behaviour
Marked reactivity and instability of mood
Chronic feelings of emptiness
Inappropriate intense anger
Dissociative symptoms

Before considering attempts to explain BPD, it is worth drawing attention to some prevailing themes in the literature on the disorder, especially to compare it with its twin disorder, SPD. As we shall see in Chapter 9, the latter has been the subject of considerable experimental research. This has not been so of BPD where, until quite recently, the focus for research has been somewhat different. Perhaps reflecting the way the BPD form of 'borderline' evolved, the emphasis has tended to be on more clinical concerns. Two topics in particular have been of interest.

The first is the comorbidity of BPD with other psychological disorders, especially those to which borderline traits and borderline personality dynamics might be expected to make an individual susceptible. Obvious candidates here are depression, drug abuse, and eating disorders of the bulimic type. Although personality disorders in general are frequently comorbid with these Axis I illnesses, the association is especially strong for BPD (Oldham *et al.*, 1995; Hudziak, *et al.*, 1996).

A second focus in BPD research has been on the role of sexual abuse in its aetiology. This has been extensively studied and there is indeed evidence that sexual abuse can make a significant contribution to the aetiology of the disorder (Zanarini *et al.*, 1997). Having said that, to place sole emphasis on *sexual* abuse is too limiting. Sexual abuse almost always occurs in the context of more general neglect, which in any case is common in most forms of psychological disorder, both Axis II and Axis I (Wexler *et al.*, 1997). As with every other disorder, the actual outcome for the individual will result from an interaction between the traumatic experience and those personality and temperamental traits that influence how he or she reacts to it. One writer who has been prominent in trying to bring these various sources together for BPD is Paris (1994).

**Paris' biopsychosocial model of BPD** The reader should be wary of multi-stemmed adjectives, such as 'biopsychosocial' (and its several variants), since they generally serve to gloss over a failure to understand the constituent parts or the interactions between them. However, Paris' model for BPD is an exception. At the very least, it provides a useful framework for visualizing how the different influences on BPD might work together to produce the disorder. It is also a good illustration of how, as a matter of general principle, psychological disorders mostly come about.

The model is reproduced in Figure 4.2. At the biological level, Paris identifies two features which it is generally agreed are major risk factors for BPD, viz. *impulsivity* and *instability of mood*. He argues – again from some existing evidence – that certain, otherwise healthy, temperamental traits may be precursors for these risk factors.

Referring to the *EAS* typology described in the previous chapter, Paris suggests that potential borderlines are likely to be high in sociability, activity,

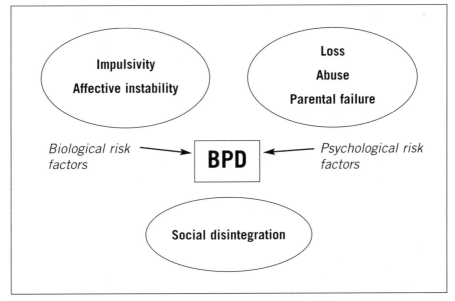

**Figure 4.2** Paris's amplification model of Borderline Personality Disorder.

and emotionality. Normally, he notes, such people will be engaging, socially active, if slightly demanding, people who like doing things on the spur of the moment. But, he goes on:

> In the presence of psychological risk factors, such as trauma, loss, and parental failure, these characteristics could become amplified. Emotional reactions could become labile and dysphoric. If activity were used inappropriately to cope with dyphoria, it could become impulsive acting out. Substances, sexual activity, or chaotic interpersonal relationships could be used to damp down dysphoria. Dysphoria and impulsive action would reinforce each other, and a feedback loop would develop. The pattern would begin to resemble *BPD*. (Paris, 1994; 95)

A significant point here is Paris' use of the notion of *amplification*, introduced in Chapter 2, the idea that stress will exaggerate pre-existing traits into a pathological form. This provides a useful way of envisaging the interface between predisposition and environment, and the way they interact along a developmental trajectory. Paris makes two other important points arising from his model.

The first concerns the role of what in Figure 4.2 Paris calls 'psychological risk factors'. Here, he notes that the psychological stressors that amplify predisposing traits into clinical risk may not be all that specific. Notwithstanding the fact that childhood abuse, as we have mentioned, does seem to be quite frequent in BPD, a range of traumatic events could act along several pathways towards a final common outcome of disorder.

83

Paris' second point harks back to an observation in the previous chapter, that individuals to some extent create their own environments; or, in the language of genetics, that much of the early environmental influence on personality is of the within-family variety, unique to the individual. Paris takes up this theme in commenting that the abnormal traits thought to predispose to BPD might elicit negative responses from parents. Thus, very impulsive, affectively labile children might be seen as 'difficult' and therefore be more likely to face parental rejection and abuse. A further layer to this interaction could come from the presence of psychopathology in parents themselves, acting in a synergistic fashion to enhance the child's clinical risk for later disorder. Illustrating this effect is a retrospective study of the psychiatric status of the parents of borderline patients during the formative years of their children. Evidence was found that the parents of future borderline individuals showed a high incidence of several psychiatric conditions, especially depression and anxiety, but also substance abuse and even psychotic disorder. Not surprisingly, personality disorder was also common in the parents (Shachnow *et al.*, 1997).

**Susceptibility to BPD** In the model of BPD just described, Paris quite rightly draws attention to the interacting contribution of many factors, to both susceptibility and clinical presentation. In this he emphasizes the crucial importance of the underlying personality as a probably necessary precursor in most cases. He notes, for example, that given the same psychological and social stresses, individuals of different temperament would react differently, leading to a different personality disorder:

> 'An introverted child, in contrast, when faced with loss, trauma, or neglect, will withdraw ... Amplify this process still further and the behaviours will begin to correspond to the criteria for personality disorders of the dependent and avoidant types.'

So, what more can we say about the nature and determinants of the inherent traits that help to steer the individual towards BPD, rather than some other personality disorder? On the genetics front, the evidence is actually rather mixed when the BPD diagnosis has been used as the phenotype for investigation (Nigg & Goldsmith, 1994). But there is some support for a familial connection; the fact that it is not stronger might be yet another example of the bluntness of this methodology as a research strategy. A more convincing database to draw upon is that on normal temperament, reviewed in the previous chapter; there we saw that genetic influences can play a major rôle in some traits that might be significant precursors of BPD. Although the evidence on impulsivity – strongly backed by Paris – seems ambiguous, rough equivalents, such as Cloninger's novelty seeking, fare better. Borderline individuals certainly score highly on that dimension, as we can see by looking

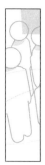

back at Table 4.2 (page 70). Curiously, however, borderline individuals also rated highly on harm avoidance, which seems to be the opposite of novelty seeking. In this important respect they differed from antisocial individuals, with whom they are frequently compared.

This dual weighting of BPD on two temperament dimensions that are normally regarded as incompatible – harm avoidance and novelty seeking – could merely reflect the heterogeneity of the diagnostic category. Or, it could be a genuine sign of the contradictory – literally ambivalent – emotional style of borderline individuals. This would connect to another theme in the borderline literature: the close similarity between Borderline Personality Disorder and Post-Traumatic Stress Disorder (PTSD). Diagnostically, PTSD is a different condition, classified in the DSM among the anxiety disorders on Axis I. But it has been argued that, where trauma plays a part in the aetiology of BPD, there may be an element of anxiety in common with PTSD. One proposal, pursuing the neurochemistry of this idea, is that both disorders share noradrenergically mediated hypersensitivity to stimulation – trauma induced, but in PTSD also partly due to pre-existing temperamental disposition. Borderline individuals differ, it is suggested, in their serotonin-mediated impulsivity which causes them to deal with their dysphoria by indulging in aggressive, self-damaging or otherwise risky acts (Figueroa & Silk, 1997). (c.f. here the recent evidence quoted earlier (page 57) on the possible genetics of Novelty seeking and Harm avoidance.)

Experimental research, for example neuropsychological, that might help to illuminate some of these issues, and help to define the borderline personality more precisely, is still in its relative infancy, There is, however, one small group of studies worth noting, examining emotional processing in borderline personality, a behaviour clearly of considerable relevance to the understanding of the disorder. (Interest in the same topic in relation to primary psychopathy is no coincidence, given the suggestion that BPD represents its female equivalent.)

The studies in question mostly use a similar methodology. This consists of measuring the accuracy and/or speed with which subjects recognize emotions in pictures of faces presented to them; here, particular interest is paid to negative emotions, especially anger, which is so prominent in BPD. Almost all the studies report that borderline personalities differ from control subjects on this task, in some cases not just for anger but for negative emotions as a whole. But, interestingly, the direction of difference observed varies across experiments. In some cases borderline individuals have been found to be *less* responsive in processing emotional information (Herperz *et al.*, 1999); in other cases the *opposite* has been shown to be true (Wagner & Linehan, 1999).

The contradiction in these studies might be partly explained by differences in sampling or task demands – or a combination of both. There is an interesting parallel here with observations on anxiety (Williams *et al.*, 1997).

85

We know that anxious individuals are abnormally sensitive to signals of threat. But whether this shows up as a faster, or a slower response to fearful stimuli depends on the nature of the task. If the test requires an orientation to the stimulus the reaction is faster, but if the natural response is avoidance, or screening out of the stimulus, the opposite occurs.

Another possible reason for the conflicting findings on BPD is that the experimental paradigm was simply not capable of capturing the subtleties of borderline pathology. In another, more clinically focused, study several facets of affect regulation were examined. There, borderline individuals showed what amounted to a mixture of hypersensitivity and ineffectualness. Compared with non-borderline subjects, they had lower levels of emotional awareness and were poor at both recognizing facial expression and dealing with mixed valence feelings; but they showed much more intense responses to negative emotions (Levine *et al.*, 1997).

## SUMMARY AND CONCLUSIONS

The personality disorders provide the most obvious bridge between normal individual differences and abnormal functioning. Nevertheless, although conceptually fairly straightforward, the detail, as we have shown, is not always easy to fill in. Definitions of personality disorders still leave something to be desired. Certainly, Axis II of the DSM – the most influential contemporary system of classification – is rather flawed; there is little consistent, rational basis for the 'types' of personality disorder it lists; nor, in psychiatry at least, is the issue of true dimensionality with normal personality fully resolved. Furthermore, there is considerable comorbidity among the Axis II disorders, as acknowledged in the three clusters proposed in the DSM.

Trying to go beyond Axis II to normal personality has attracted several different approaches. One is to seek to 'profile' the different disorders, in terms of familiar personality dimensions, such as those proposed in Five-factor theory. Although descriptively interesting, this tells us little else about the disorders themselves. Alternatively, the cognitive approach elaborates on possible psychological styles involved in each of the disorders, but fails to address two crucial questions: why this personality disorder rather than that? And: why a personality disorder at all? What might be termed 'vulnerability theory' concentrates especially on these issues, arguing that the predisposition to personality disorders is shaped by certain temperamental factors. These dispositions are assumed to have neuropsychological, genetic, and other biological correlates. Then, over and above temperamental susceptibility, there are (as Borderline Personality Disorder illustrates rather well) life course processes, as well as acute stressors, such as trauma, which may push emotionally sensitive individuals across a threshold where they are likely to develop dysfunctional behaviours appropriate to their underlying temperament. This would constitute Paris' biopsychosocial model; applied by

him to BPD, but generalizable to other personality disorders.

Lastly, the strong comorbidity and clustering of many of the Axis II disorders suggests that, at the level of temperamental vulnerability, the classification could be hugely simplified. Take, as an example, the Cluster B collection of borderline, antisocial, histrionic, and narcissistic disorders. It is probable that some common set of traits, for example impulsivity, sensation seeking, reward dependency or whatever, is shared by them all. The main question then is what other factors – environmental and constitutional (including gender) – determine which type of personality disorder the individual manifests.

# CHAPTER 5

## MOOD AND ANXIETY DISORDERS

### INTRODUCTION

In several significant ways, mood and anxiety disorders stand apart from the other psychiatric conditions we discuss in this book. Perhaps the most obvious is that their base rate occurrence in the population is substantially higher. For example, in Western countries, about one in five people experience clinically significant symptoms of anxiety or depression at some point during their lives, whereas most other disorders have much lower prevalence rates – of the order of one to three per cent. The symptoms that define these disorders are also much more continuous with the personality traits that give rise to them than we can claim for other Axis I conditions. Generalized Anxiety Disorder represents a particularly intuitive example of the continuity from normal personality to pathology since it describes, in large part, the extreme end of a dimension of trait anxiety, similar to the way that hypertension, as a medical condition, is simply the pathological elevation of normal blood pressure.

As we explained in Chapter 2, it is our intention, when framing the link between personality and disorder, to follow the diagnostic classification system imposed by the DSM. However, in the case of mood and anxiety disorders, we decided that it was more appropriate to integrate the two conditions in a single chapter. While several factors influenced our decision, perhaps the most compelling is their substantial symptom overlap. In the past, the term 'neurosis' was often used to reflect the great similarity between these disorders, but this terms has rather fallen out of favour and been replaced by 'distress disorder' to cover both conditions (Clark et al., 1994). There are also stable vulnerability factors that are common to both types of disorder. For example, in a large-scale study of female twin pairs, Kendler and colleagues (1992) found that the same genetic factors appear to influence both Major Depressive

Disorder and Generalized Anxiety Disorder, suggesting that environmental experiences largely determine whether 'at risk' individuals develop anxiousness or other depressive symptoms. In addition, although anxious and depressive 'cognitions' have a certain unique content, they share many more similarities, such as an habitual attention to negativity and threat. The common component between the two seems to be a state of general distress with the factors that differentiate them developing from that general base (Beck & Perkins, 2001; Hertel, 2002).

Also, highlighting the strong interrelationship between the two types of disorder is that some have proposed a new diagnostic category for the DSM, which they call Mixed Anxiety-Depression (MAD), because many patients with severe psychological impairment do not meet the full diagnostic criteria for either the anxiety disorders or depression; presenting instead with subclinical levels of both anxious and depressive symptoms (Barlow & Campbell, 2000). Even from a developmental perspective, we often find that parents have difficulty differentiating between symptoms of anxiety and depression in their children.

Another important factor that prompted our decision to discuss anxiety and depression in the same chapter is that *stress* is seen as a common factor in the aetiology of both disorders – as well as a consequence of them – suggesting that the three phenomena are strongly interrelated. Furthermore, as we shall see in the next section, the animal paradigms that have been developed to model anxiety and depression have considerable overlap and are, in many cases, based on exposure to stress.

Blurring of the diagnostic categories is especially clear in the case of Major Depressive Disorder where the heterogeneity of this condition has plagued clinical research for decades. In fact, the idea that 'depression' may actually comprise a cluster of loosely connected, discrete disorders has existed in some form since the early twentieth century (see Just *et al.*, 2001). One way this can be seen is by the diversity of response to psychological and pharmacological therapies in patients diagnosed with depression (Drevets, 1998). Furthermore, the different types of depression seem to have quite distinguishable and separate underlying neurophysiological mechanisms, as we shall see later in this chapter.

89

Although there are some common and recognizable features of all depressions, such as negativity, pessimism, and rumination, it is also clear that at least two, quite distinct, forms of the disorder exist. A pronounced deficit in the ability to find positive incentives pleasing and reinforcing – with associated symptoms of apathy, inactivity, and excessive sleeping – describes the severely depressed mood of some patients. Other depressed individuals display a more agitated form of the disorder, as seen by their difficulty in recovering from emotionally stressful events, and their obvious signs of anxiety and restlessness (Davidson *et al.*, 2002). Indeed, according to the DSM, as many as 80 to 90 per cent of depressed patients have symptoms associated with the anxiety disorders, such as poor concentration, sleep disturbances, loss of energy, irritability, excessive health concern, and panic attacks. Conversely, a frank 'depressed mood' is an associated feature of all anxiety disorders (see Table 5.1 for a brief list and description of the disorders that are subsumed under the general heading of Anxiety Disorders).

**Table 5.1** DSM-IV anxiety-related disorders.

### Panic disorder
The reoccurrence of panic attacks (that is, a constellation of symptoms, including increased heart rate, sweating, trembling, chest pain, choking sensation, feeling of losing control, and fear of dying) with anticipatory anxiety associated with the attack.

### Agoraphobia
Its literal definition suggests a fear of 'open spaces', though it is not a strictly accurate one. Individuals with this condition fear any place where they develop panicky feelings, such as crowded supermarkets, elevators, or standing in line. Some become 'housebound' as a result of this anxiety.

### Specific phobia
The excessive fear of some object (like snakes) or a situation (like being near the water) to the point that it is strenuously avoided, or endured with intense anxiety.

### Social phobia
The excessive fear of social situations, especially things like talking or eating in public, that usually involves the intense anxiety about feeling humiliated and blushing.

### Obsessive-compulsive disorder
See Chapter 6 for a detailed description.

### Post traumatic stress disorder
After a traumatic situation has occurred (such as a car accident) there is a re-experience of the event in the form of nightmares or flashbacks which results in extensive avoidant behaviour (in this case, driving in cars) or a numbing of general responsiveness which interferes with social and occupation activities.

### Generalized anxiety disorder
Chronic and excessive worry and anxiety associated with a variety of somatic symptoms, such as restlessness, impaired concentration, irritability, muscle tension, and insomnia.

# ANIMAL MODELS

As with many of the disorders we discuss in this book, animal models have provided us with some valuable insights, especially concerning the neurobiology and pathophysiology of the condition. Furthermore, because of the practical difficulties associated with the prospective study of mental illnesses (for example, their relatively low base rate in the population), animals can serve as useful proxies in research of this kind. However, certain features of a good animal model are necessary if this purpose is to be served adequately. For example, the paradigm should model a core symptom of the disorder and respond to the treatment drug for the condition it is alleged to mimic (for example, antidepressants for an animal model of depression and anxiolytic agents for models of anxiety). It should also use inducing conditions that are ecologically valid (Willner, 1997). In this regard, some animal models have been rather better than others in fulfilling these important validating criteria.

In certain senses, animal models of anxiety are more straightforward, and their validity easier to achieve, than those for depression. For instance, the defensive or fearful behaviours that we can induce in animals are closely analogous to anxiety-related behaviours in humans. Both can be seen as the excessive activation of our innate defence mechanisms arising from an exaggerated assessment of, or reaction to, danger. Second, since both share a common biological substrate, the animal response clearly has significance for human anxiety disorders (Palanza, 2001).

Probably the most frequently used rodent model of anxiety has been the 'open-field' test referred to in Chapter 3. This is a paradigm based on the assumption that novel environments elicit defensive reactions in rats and mice who tend, in their natural habitats, to avoid brightly lit and unfamiliar places. Other models of anxiety have assessed the animal's reactions to painful physical stimuli, such as a foot shock or an aversive noise. In most cases, researchers have measured the anxiety response of an animal in models such as these, either by drawing inferences from its behaviour – for example, increased locomotion in the open-field apparatus reflects higher levels of anxiety – and/or by assessing an animal's physiological response to a stressful event from biological markers, such as corticosterone (a stress hormone).

In recent years, however, there has been a significant paradigm shift in the area of animal models for mental health research since the emergence of technology to genetically engineer or modify the DNA of mice.

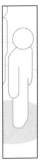

91

---

Transgenic mice

One of the most remarkable technical advances in biomedical research in recent years has been the development of transgenic mice. It has now become possible to genetically alter the mouse genome with nucleotide precision. These mouse models can be made by altering the animal's DNA in two specific ways. In one process, new DNA is injected into the zygote pronucleus of a fertilized egg so that the foreign DNA integrates into the mouse genome producing an animal which will 'over-express' a certain gene product. In another process a targeted gene is mutated producing a functional 'knock-out' of the gene. These models are especially effective for understanding how individual genes and environmental factors interact to affect human physical and mental health. To use an example from cancer biology, one gene being studied is a 'tumour-suppressor' gene whose functions seems to be the maintenance of genomic stability. Mice who have had this gene mutated are much more susceptible to lung cancer after treatment with a chemical carcinogen than animals who contain this gene.

In particular, a number of 'knock-out' mice models have been developed to study symptoms of anxiety and depression. For example, the 5-HT1AR knock-out strain (that is, mice lacking the gene that controls the expression of the serotonin 1A receptor) show increased anxiety-like behaviours in a variety of conflict tasks. This model has also been particularly useful in highlighting the role of environmental and early postnatal factors in promoting the proper expression of the 5-HT1A receptor gene and how it influences normal emotional behaviour later in life (Gross *et al.*, 2002).

Other transgenic mice have been developed to target aspects of the hypothalamic–pituitary–adrenal (HPA) axis since abnormal stress hormone regulation is believed to be one factor in the increased risk for depression (Holsboer, 2000). Although transgenic models are useful for the study of endogenous mechanisms underlying abnormal behaviour at the molecular level, so far – and this is unlikely to change – the deletion of a single gene has not provided any useful and comprehensive animal template for a particular psychological disorder. However, this is hardly surprising since complex human behaviours are far more likely to be caused by a concatenation of minor changes in so-called susceptibility genes, and even more likely by the interaction of these vulnerability genes with various environmental factors (Muller & Keck, 2002).

Animal models of depression have been somewhat more difficult to study because the primary symptom of this disorder is a change in mood. Researchers have therefore been forced to rely on observable responses of the animal that seem to parallel the behavioural parameters, such as withdrawal, problems in social functioning, and poor coping ability, that are seen in human depression. The 'stress hypothesis' of depression has led to a series of now classic putative models of depression which all have in common that the observed behaviour of the animal is triggered or caused by uncontrollable and aversive stimuli (Palanza, 2001). The most common of these are the *learned helplessness* and *chronic mild stress* models – the former being the most widely studied of all the animal models of depression.

In the mid 1960s, Seligman and colleagues discovered an interesting phenomenon while they were carrying out a Pavlovian classical conditioning experiment with dogs.

### Classical conditioning

The term 'Pavlovian Conditioning' derives from a series of famous experiments begun in 1889 by the Russian physiologist Ivan Pavlov, in which he demonstrated the potential for conditioned and unconditioned reflexes in dogs – that is, that a contingency could exist between environmental events and physiological responses. In these experiments, Pavlov rang a bell as he fed meat powder to his dogs. Each time the dogs heard the bell they knew that a meal was coming, and as a consequence, they began to salivate in anticipation. After a number of pairings of the bell and the food, Pavlov rang the bell without bringing food, and noticed that the dogs still salivated. They had been 'conditioned' to salivate at the sound of a bell. Pavlov believed that humans react to paired stimuli in much the same way.

From these original experiments the terminology of classical conditioning was born and may be directly related to the dogs, the salivation and the bell. The 'Unconditioned Stimulus' (UCS) is the event that triggers an automatic action which has been called the 'Unconditioned Response' (UCR) – the meat powder and the salivation respectively. Upon repeated pairing of a neutral stimulus – the bell – and the UCS, the former, called the 'Conditioned Stimulus' (CS), is reliably able to elicit the same response as the latter – the salivation – and has been called the 'Conditioned Response' (CR).

However, in this case, Seligman and colleagues paired the bell with an electrical shock instead of food while restraining the animal in a harness. After the dog was 'conditioned' to the bell by the inescapable shock, the experimenters put it into a box, which was divided into two compartments and had a low wall between the two over which the dog could jump to escape from either compartment. The experimenters fully expected that when they rang the bell (the CS), the dog would jump over the wall to escape, in the way that non-conditioned dogs did when they were shocked. Instead, to their great surprise, the animal didn't move! They concluded that the dog had 'learned' to be helpless. In other words, it had learned that attempts to escape were fruitless, and so it simply did not try. Employing a variety of learning tasks, this *helplessness* model was subsequently used to demonstrate that uncontrollable stress can produce significant performance deficits not found in normal animals.

Initially, the learned-helplessness model was adopted enthusiastically because it seemed to parallel the dynamics of human depression. However, its popularity soon began to wane when the experimental effects could not be reproduced in other animal species. People also began to question whether learned helplessness was really a behavioural process characterizing most depressed individuals (Palanza, 2001). For instance, many people fail to become depressed even when they experience traumatic life events, making it evident that the *predisposition* for depression is highly variable. In recent years, however, the learned helplessness paradigm has re-emerged as a good model of *vulnerability*. What was once its weakness – its unreliability – is now seen as one of its strengths in depression research. Because animals develop the helplessness syndrome to varying degrees, or not at all, researchers have used this natural variability in subsequent neurobiological studies to examine inherent risk factors for depression.

The *chronic mild stress* (CMS) paradigm is another popular animal model of depression whose validity is based on the rationale that it simulates *anhedonia* – that is, the loss of responsiveness to pleasurable or rewarding events – which is a core symptom of the melancholic form of depression. In a typical CMS experiment, animals are exposed sequentially to a variety of mild stressors, such as tail pinching, overnight illumination of their cage, periods of food deprivation, tilting of the cage, and change of cage mate. Over time, there is typically a decrease in the extent to which the animal will engage in previously rewarding behaviours, such as the consumption of, and/or preference for, palatable food and drink. Not only can these behavioural deficits be maintained for several months, but the animal's normal behaviour can also be restored quite reliably by treatment with a variety of commonly used antidepressant drugs. Another parallel with human depression is that antidepressant drugs only alter the behaviour of animals exposed to CMS, not that of non-stressed animals, similar to the way that antidepressants have no mood-enhancing effects on non-depressed individuals. The CMS model is especially appealing because, in addition to its anhedonic effects, it also causes the appearance of other symptoms of depression, such as diminished sexual behaviour, decreased locomotion, and increased aggression, without triggering symptoms of anxiety (Willner, 1997).

Despite their enormous utility in many aspects of anxiety and depression research, it would be misleading to suggest that animal models are without problems. In depression, for example, studies have shown that when animals are tested in more than one paradigm, there is often low convergent validity across the methods. This suggests that different models may be mediated by separate biological processes, thereby tapping into different aspects of the condition. There is also the questionable ecological validity of many animal models. For instance, animal studies have mostly relied on physical stressors, such as electric shock, tail pinching, or restraint, to produce depressive or anxious responses, even though we know that the main sources of human stress are *social* in nature. Therefore, a more appropriate animal analogue of the human stress reaction would be an experimentally induced social stressor, such as overcrowding. Another highly problematic issue in animal research is response differences across species and between genders. One poignant illustration is that although prevalence rates of depression are consistently higher among women than men, in many rodent models of depression, the females are actually less susceptible to the syndrome induction than the males. We also see a pronounced discrepancy in the workable methods of inducing

94

social stress in males and females – and regrettably, the majority of animal studies have only used male animals. For example, when female animals are housed alone, they tend to produce higher levels of corticosterone and display behavioural changes such as withdrawal and reduced exploration, which resemble symptoms of human depressive disorders. Male animals, on the other hand, do not show these changes when housed alone; instead they produce higher corticosterone levels when they are caged with other animals. In other words, crowding induces social stress in male animals, whereas solitude has that effect on females. These findings point to the ecological importance of developing models of social stress that take account of gender- and species-specific differences in the behavioural strategies each uses to cope with its social environment.

## COMMON SYMPTOMS OF MOOD AND ANXIETY DISORDERS

Given the considerable diagnostic overlap across the various anxiety and mood disorders, as well as the changes in how they have been defined in the various versions of the DSM, it seems more appropriate to discuss the primary symptoms that cut across these disorders rather than trying to fathom the unique aetiology – if there is one – of each disorder separately.

Like all the psychiatric conditions we address in this book, clues to their biology come from a variety of sources, including responses to drug treatment, markers of neurotransmitter status or activation, pharmacological and behavioural challenges, and neuroimaging procedures. Therefore, the greatest difficulty in trying to present a digestible account of their physical origins is the sheer number of neurochemical, neuroendocrine, neurophysiologic and neuroanatomical factors that have been investigated, and for which some evidence seems to exist. For that reason, we have had to be selective in our descriptions, and extend a caveat to our readers that we are only highlighting and touching upon themes for which there is the most consensus. Even when deciding which symptoms to address, we have had to be selective, eventually deciding only to include *fearfulness*, *anxiousness* and *melancholy*. However, by limiting our discussion to these three dimensions, we are aware that other common symptoms of mood and anxiety disorders, such as irritability, poor concentration, and abnormal fatigue, may have their own biological substrates.

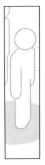

Before proceeding, it is also important to touch briefly on our rationale for treating *fearfulness* and *anxiousness* as separate constructs. Historically, and even in some current writing, the terms *fear* and *anxiety* are more or less interchangeable and have frequently been conceptualized as a single dimension of personality. More recently, however, the evidence favours the view that they are distinctly different emotional systems. White and Depue (1999) have provided an excellent summary of the evidence that *fearful* responses are generated by an emotional system that is sensitive to both the unconditioned and conditioned stimuli of physical punishment or harm. Initially, these responses tend to inhibit behaviour, but if necessary will result in active escape behaviours. *Anxiousness*, on the other hand, is a state of high emotional arousal fostered by situations of uncertainty and social comparison, the possibility of the negative evaluation of one's worth, and the threat of personal failure; in other words, it is fundamentally tied to social interactions. The responses to anxiety-provoking stimuli can range from worry and feelings of agitated distress to catastrophic ruminations.

However, some of the strongest evidence of the distinctness of the two emotional systems comes from psychometric studies. As we have seen in Chapter 3, all major trait theories, and every factor-analytic approach to personality, identifies a superfactor called variously neuroticism, negative emotionality, or negative affectivity, which taps into the anxiety domain. The correlations between these scales and specific fear scales are typically very close to zero. Other research has similarly found no correlation between neuroticism and questionnaire measures of constraint (which is viewed as a marker of inhibited behaviour).

Lastly, in an elegant series of experiments, White and Depue (1999) used pupil diameter as a non-invasive measure to test the association between fear and anxiety – a highly suitable paradigm since the pupil of the eye is rapidly enlarged during emotional activation (in order to maximize visual sensory input) and since two different processes affect dilation of the pupil. One is responsive to acute stimuli and is believed to relate to the response to fearful stimuli, whereas the second reflects a more tonic and stable function associated with individual differences in anxious reactivity. Their data led to the strong conclusion that the dissociation between the neural systems of fear and anxiety is, in fact, much greater than has traditionally been appreciated.

## FEARFULNESS

Fear is one of the most basic and normal of all human and animal reactions. Indeed, because of its fundamental role in promoting safety and security, it is fair to say that organisms would not survive for long without the ability to experience fear. However, in addition to our inherent capacity for *feeling* fearful – and our ability to respond appropriately – we are also able to recognize the environmental events that warn or predict of forthcoming threats. Psychologists have called this type of learning, *fear conditioning* because it seems to occur in the manner of classical Pavlovian associative conditioning – through the temporal pairing of relatively neutral stimuli with those that are aversive or dangerous. The study of fear conditioning has attracted great interest in the past decade because of its apparent role in the development of various fear-related disorders. For example, the 'fear network' in the brain is almost certainly involved in the aetiology of phobias, and in Panic Disorder.

From an evolutionary perspective, it is clearly adaptive for us to learn the appropriate associations between environmentally relevant stimuli and the threat

of danger. However, many of the things that people now learn to fear are not necessarily biologically relevant to our survival, but are learned through experience with the stresses and strains of life – like the fear of flying in aeroplanes. How fears can develop to inherently neutral events is aptly demonstrated in Watson's famous 1920 experiment with the baby, Albert, who became greatly frightened by the sight of a white rat after a loud aversive noise was sounded every time the animal was shown to the child. Before the experiment, Albert showed no fear, but after the conditioning trials he startled violently and began to cry whenever he saw the white rat. It is now generally agreed that fear conditioning involves more than the simple conditioned-stimulus responding seen in the experiment with Albert. In most cases, it seems to involve the learning of more complex hierarchical relationships between a threatening event and the various stimuli and contextual cues that predict it (Maren, 2001).

With the use of newer and better animal models and more advanced brain-imaging technology, the neurobiology of fear is now reasonably well-understood. Most authorities agree (for example, M. Davis, 1997; LeDoux, 1998; Maren, 2001) that the *amygdala*, which is a small walnut-sized structure deep inside the limbic brain area, is central to the regulation and conditioning of fear via its activation of various neurotransmitters and hormones. The primary function of the amygdala seems to be as a 'protection device' to evaluate environmental stimuli, and to disseminate information to a number of interconnected structures that co-ordinate autonomic and behavioural responses on the basis of this evaluation (Amaral, 2002).

Our first understanding of the importance of the amygdala came over a century ago, from observations of the effects of brain damage on emotional behaviour. Since that time, numerous other clinical and experimental studies have confirmed a notable loss of fear in people and animals with temporal lobe lesions. We have also seen that damage to this area has dramatic effects on one's capacity to learn about stimuli that warn of danger. For example, rats lose their fear of cats, and people lose their ability to recognize that certain stimuli, such as the smell of smoke, signal an impending threat. In other words, not only does temporal lobe damage disrupt primary fears, but, under some conditions, it inhibits learned fears. More advanced research has revealed that the loss of fear accompanying temporal lobe lesions stems specifically from damage to the amygdala. Other studies have also shown that heightened fear may be induced by electrical stimulation to the amygdala.

Basically, our capacity to evaluate the risk or safety of stimuli in our environment is moderated by a complex and highly integrated circuit which is first activated by sensory information – the things we see, hear, smell or touch. All sensory neurons send projections to the amygdala, which in turn sends projections to various brain stem structures whose task is to ready us for action. For example, activation of the locus cereleus causes an increase in norepinephrine release which contributes to the increase in blood pressure,

97

heart rate, and other behavioural responses that accompany fearfulness. This area also controls the level of attention to environmental events and the degree to which the individual is vigilant to signals of danger (Maren, 2001). Other amygdaloid projections to the hypothalamus stimulate the release of corticotrophin-releasing factor or hormone (CRF or CRH) which triggers the cascade of neurochemical reactions, known collectively as the 'stress response'. The prime purpose of all these actions and reactions is to activate the sympathetic nervous system and to initiate the shipment of glucose to the brain and muscles to mobilize the organism in readiness for 'flight or fight'.

Many now also believe that CRF is the master brain neurochemical regulator and integrator of the fear response because its cell bodies and receptors are found in abundance throughout the brain. For example, if CRF is infused in the brain of animals, they display a range of behaviours that is analogous to fear reactions in people, including elevations of heart rate and blood pressure. Moreover, when CRF is injected directly into the amygdaloid area, there is a prolongation of the fear reaction. Other studies have also shown that the density of CRF receptors is positively associated with the level of fear that experimental animals show to a novel situation.

Recent research has demonstrated the remarkable plasticity within the neural systems that mediate the fear response, and how environmental factors play a crucial role in determining whether or not we develop normal fear reactions. For instance, animal pups who have had *good mothering* (which has been defined in mice as frequent licking and grooming) show *decreased* behavioural fearfulness, and have *increased* benzodiazepine receptor densities in the amygdala and locus cereleus and *decreased* CRF receptor densities in the latter when they become adults (Caldji *et al.*, 1998). These maternal influences are not simply due to genetics – that is, that fearful mothers simply pass on 'fearful' genes to their offspring – because mice pups from an inherently fearful strain showed less fear as adults when they were reared by an adoptive mother that groomed and licked them more frequently, compared to a control group of pups from the same strain.

In summary, there is now good evidence that CRF plays a central role in fear reactions, that the amygdala is a prominent structure in the brain's fear circuit, and that one's early environment is also crucial in regulating the normal development of these biological processes.

Efforts to understand the brain circuits and neural mechanisms of the fear system have also relied heavily on the study of *fear conditioning*. Some research has implicated the hippocampus, and its primary role in memory, in the conditioning to contextual cues, whereas other studies have shown that damage to the prefrontal cortex inhibits the extinction of conditioned responses. How these processes work is clearly relevant to our understanding of clinically significant fears such as we see in those with panic disorder and phobias. It is also interesting to note that stress impairs the function of the

hippocampus and the prefrontal cortex, and that in many cases stressful life events (particularly in childhood) contribute to the onset of both panic and phobias (LeDoux, 1998).

**Panic Attack** Some hold the view that a panic attack is physiologically and behaviourally similar to a conditioned fear stimulus – albeit in an extreme and exaggerated form – and therefore that the same 'fear network' is activated. Elaborating on this view, Gorman and his colleagues (2000) proposed that a neurocognitive deficit in the cortical processing pathways results in a misinterpretation of bodily experiences, such as increased heart rate, via 'upstream' neural activation from the brain stem to the cortex, which then results in inappropriate 'downstream' activation of the fear network – in other words, misguided activation of the amygdala. Also, the fact that a whole host of agents/drugs with dissimilar biological properties are equally capable of inducing panic attacks in patients with Panic Disorder suggests that the onset of a panic attack may occur via several different triggers, but that whenever a trigger is present, the entire fear network is activated, not simply one pathway. Over time – or as a result of individual vulnerabilities – projections from the amygdala to the various brain stem sites, such as the locus cereleus, may become weaker or stronger, thereby accounting for the considerable variation in autonomic and neuroendocrine responses within an individual patient with panic disorder, or across the range of patients with this disorder.

Explained from a psychological viewpoint, several cognitive theorists have speculated on the factors that influence or initiate the vicious cycle of events that eventually culminates in a panic attack. The most popular model was proposed by Clark (1986) who argued that panic results primarily from the catastrophic misinterpretation of physical and mental sensations. In other words, some people tend to interpret the common symptoms of fear, like a racing heart beat, dizziness, or the shortness of breath, as much more dangerous than they really are. This, in turn, increases anxiety and apprehension producing even more pronounced bodily sensations which are then interpreted in an even more catastrophic manner and eventually the chain of synergistic events becomes a full-blown panic attack. Others have expanded on Clark's (1986) model by proposing that the development of panic involves the fusion of a temperamental vulnerability and a congruent trigger (Moore & Zebb, 1999). The overarching vulnerability is a set of harm-avoidant and/or anxiety traits. However, more specific vulnerabilities, such as hypochondriacal health beliefs about certain bodily symptoms also play a role. Central to cognitive theories of panic is the phenomenon of *selective attention* since patients with this disorder seem especially hypervigilant to their own bodily sensations, and are highly prone to mentally scanning their bodies for signs of danger which then increases the likelihood that certain feared sensations are noticed and overinterpreted (Kroeze & van den Hout, 2000).

**Phobias** The study of fear is also fundamental to our understanding of how we come to acquire phobic reactions. Perhaps the most widespread and popular view – expressed in *conditioning theories* – is that phobias arise from, or are the consequence of, a previous traumatic experience, and that conditioning can occur in a variety of ways:

- From direct or personal trauma.
- From the observation of trauma in others.
- From observing the phobic reaction of others (see Kendler *et al.*, 2002).

Although there is strong support for the notion that some phobias are acquired this way, for example, dental phobia (Poulton *et al.*, 1997), this approach has failed to explain the development of all clinical phobias since only a minority of them can be attributed to Pavlovian conditioning events (see Poulton *et al.*, 1998). One explanation why some people are apparently buffered whilst others are not has evoked the concept of *latent inhibition* and suggests that individuals who experience an aversive conditioning event later in life – without developing a phobic reaction – may have been 'rescued' because they had non-threatening exposures to the event (or something similar) early in life.

An alternative view is that the predisposition to develop most common phobias, such as the fear of heights, blood, water, and reptiles, is innate, mostly universal, and that what we actually *learn* as we go through life is how to overcome those fears (Rachman, 1978). In other words, *non-associative* or Darwinian models of fear acquisition suggest that most phobias occur without the involvement of learning or conditioning, and that the liability to phobias has arisen from evolutionary selection (Kendler *et al.*, 2002). One interesting study found that falls resulting in head injury in childhood (before the age of nine years) had occurred more frequently in those *without* a fear of height at age 18 – a finding opposite to the predictions arising from conditioning theories of phobia, but consistent with the innate or non-associative theories of fear acquisition (Poulton *et al.*, 1998).

On the other hand, *non-associative* theories may also be criticized since relatively few people suffer from clinically significant specific phobias, and because a large number of people have no reaction at all to these putatively innate fears. One explanation is that the ability to habituate to natural fear-arousing stimuli in the environment is influenced by individual differences in the tendency to arouse quickly and habituate slowly – ascribable to 'neuroticism', 'stress reactivity', or 'negative affectivity' in the prominent theories of personality we described in Chapter 3. Poulton and colleagues (2001) found that limited exposure to height stimuli in childhood (defined as time spent playing on swings and bars, and climbing trees and fences) – and therefore presumably less opportunity for habituation – was associated with a higher incidence of fear of heights during adolescence. Also, levels of neuroticism in childhood were higher among those who were height phobic in late adolescence compared to those who were dental phobic or had no fears. The authors concluded that some people do not overcome their innate fear of heights either because of limited opportunities to do so and/or because they are at the higher end of a continuum of emotional reactivity and therefore fail to habituate.

The Stress-Diathesis model of phobias extends the interaction model of vulnerability by proposing that a combination of environmental adversity and individual vulnerability gives rise to the condition, but importantly, that an inverse relationship exists between the two. In other words, individuals whose disorder was associated with severe environmental stress should, on average, have lower levels of personal vulnerability than those whose disorder was not associated with environmental stress. However, in a recent test of this model, Kendler *et al.* (2002) found no support for traditional associative theories, such as the Stress-Diathesis model, which assume environmental conditioning. Instead, their results were more compatible with Darwinian theories and individual vulnerability models. First of all, while neuroticism strongly predicted the risk of all phobias, it was not higher in phobias with no memory of an environmental trauma, nor was it lower in those who associated the onset of their phobia with a personal trauma. In all aspects, Kendler's study is in accord with the growing body of research suggesting that the development of many phobias is non-associative and that personal vulnerability is the key predictor.

Perhaps the most parsimonious and intuitive way to integrate associative and non-associative approaches to phobia is to take the position that *conditioning* processes are more salient in the development of fears and phobias that are 'evolutionary-neutral', such as dental fear, that inherent biological processes are the primary determinants for 'evolutionary-relevant' fears, such as the fear of height, and that personality factors contribute to the onset of both types of phobia (Poulton *et al.*, 2001).

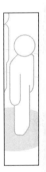

## ANXIOUSNESS

101

Over the years, and with each new version of the DSM, the number of categories subsumed under the heading of *anxiety disorders* has increased – from three in the first version to 12 in the current edition. Some have expressed concern that efforts at diagnostic precision may have come at the expense of a better understanding of the shared and overlapping features of these disorders. Perhaps the set of symptoms that define Generalized Anxiety Disorder – a state of chronic worry, apprehension, and hypervigilance which is usually accompanied by somatic symptoms, such as muscle tension – best captures what most of us understand by the term *anxiousness* and how it differs from, though is obviously related to, the concept of fearfulness. Generalized Anxiety

Disorder is probably the most basic emotional disorder because it comprises features that are present in varying degrees in all other mood and anxiety disorders, and because it reflects the principal personality dimensions of risk for these syndromes; factors such as neuroticism and negative affect. In fact, there is a debate about whether Generalized Anxiety Disorder is better conceptualized as the extreme of a trait that confers non-specific risk to a number of disorders, rather than as a distinct Axis I construct that is influenced, along with other anxiety and mood disorders (albeit to a greater extent), by the higher-order personality factors referred to above (Brown *et al.*, 1998). That neuroticism is a risk in the development of anxiety disorders is hardly surprising because, by definition, it is a trait that predicts people's susceptibility to anxious states. However, both Eysenck's and Gray's theories also predict that anxiousness is inversely correlated with the extraversion dimension. Although much research has focused on the additive effects of these two trait dimensions, some studies have found an interactive and synergistic effect of neuroticism and introversion on the risk for anxiety (see Jorm *et al.*, 2000, for a review). In other words, in these studies neuroticism was only associated with heightened anxiety in the presence of introversion.

There is also considerable evidence that cognitive factors play a role in the development and maintenance of anxiety disorders. For example, theorists such as Beck (1986) and Clark (1986) have emphasized the increased risk amongst those whose information-processing style tends to overinterpret the threat or danger associated with physical and psychosocial events in their environment. Other research has focused on attentional biases. Either because of biological factors or simply habit, some individuals selectively attend to certain stimuli in their environment; then again, because of habit or self-control, their attention is either sustained or it shifts to other events. We have learnt that people with anxious orientations tend to shift their attention frequently, being finely tuned to, and often scanning for, sources of threat in their environment. They also have a heightened tendency to perceive threat in ambiguous events. For example, a strange and unfamiliar noise is more likely to be viewed as anxiety-provoking than as something unimportant and worth ignoring. Another key characteristic of anxiousness is that it is quintessentially about 'worry' and therefore it is future-oriented. In other words, prospective judgements tend to have a more negative tone in anxious states, compared to melancholic states which are focused on past events, as we shall see in the next section (Hertel, 2002).

Consistent with cognitive theories is the concept of *anxiety sensitivity* which is viewed as a relatively stable cognitive individual difference variable that basically describes the 'fear of fear'. Those high in this trait tend to fear the overt bodily sensations, such as trembling, a racing heart rate, dizziness, and blushing, that are related to high physiological arousal. Usually this fear is generated by a belief that their anxiety symptoms are a portent of some forthcoming catastrophic physical event like a heart attack, that they signal a

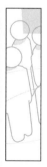

loss of cognitive control (as seen in some serious mental disturbance), or because of social concerns, such as the embarrassment and humiliation they might cause (Stewart & Kushner, 2001).

There has also been some seemingly unnecessary debate about the degree to which *anxiety sensitivity* is related to, or distinct from, *trait anxiety*. We say 'unnecessary' because it would be wholly surprising and counterintuitive if the two constructs were not associated. Indeed, in most studies they are moderately correlated, in the order of 0.4–0.5. The most obvious view is that anxiety sensitivity is a lower-order factor of trait anxiety which can accelerate anxiousness in those with high trait anxiety, or even foster it among those with low levels of anxiety. On the other hand, a measure of their distinctiveness is that there is not much more than about 20 per cent shared variance between their respective measures.

Like so many other symptoms and disorders we discuss in this book, the neurobiology of anxiousness has been related to potential abnormalities in a range of neurochemical, neuroendocrine, and neuroanatomical processes. Perhaps the strongest evidence – in part, because it has been the most studied – has implicated overactivity of brain 5-HT. This was a serendipitous finding first brought to light in the 1980s when it was discovered that a drug developed to treat psychotic patients was also useful for treating anxiety disorders (Snyder, 2002). Since then we have learnt that when post-synaptic 5-HT$_2$ receptors are activated in the limbic region there is an increase in anxiety and avoidance behaviour (Connor & Davidson, 1998). It has also been confirmed that 5-HT activation has a dual role in the regulation of defence. Relevant to generalized anxiousness is the fact that 5-HT enhances learnt responses to potential threats in the environment through its action in the forebrain (Graeff, 2002). It is also known that specific agonists of the 5-HT$_{1A}$ autoreceptors in the forebrain have anxiolytic properties in both humans and animals, and that increased anxious behaviours are seen in 5-HT$_{1A}$ receptor 'knock-out' mice (Ramboz *et al.*, 1998). Some very recent research has also demonstrated the crucial role of the early post-natal period in the subsequent development of normal anxious reactions in adulthood. Specifically, it appears that appropriate stimulation of the 5-HT$_{1A}$ receptor during this period is necessary to set in motion the long-lasting changes in the brain that are essential for normal anxiety behaviours (Gross *et al.*, 2002).

**Social Anxiety** In the remainder of this section, we shall look at two other relatively common disorders whose primary feature is the extreme expression of anxiousness. Social Anxiety Disorder (sometimes called 'social phobia') is a relatively common condition – indeed, the most common of the anxiety disorders, and the third most common psychiatric disorder following major depression and alcohol dependence – with a lifetime prevalence of about 15 per cent. Yet, many feel that it is still relatively underdiagnosed, undertreated, and one of the least understood of all psychiatric illnesses (Brunello *et al.*, 2000; Li *et al.*, 2001). The quintessential feature of this disorder is the extreme anxiety that is experienced in social situations, and most acutely when the individual has to perform in public or be exposed to the scrutiny of others, such as during a job interview or a class presentation. Typically, sufferers fear that while they are being watched by others they may be evaluated negatively, and/or that the signs of their anxiousness, such as blushing, shaking and sweating, will cause them great embarrassment. The *non-generalized* or stereotypical version of social anxiety is mostly confined to a single, or no more than a few, performance situations, such as speaking in front of an audience, whereas the *generalized* form involves the excessive fear of a broader array of social situations (Stein, 1998). Although social anxiety generally starts in early childhood or adolescence, it seldom occurs in isolation – being more frequently comorbid with a range of other disorders, including depression, other anxiety disorders, substance abuse, and eating disorders. What is interesting, however, is that social anxiety is usually primary to this 'cascade of comorbidity', suggesting that it may serve a causal role in these related forms of psychopathology (Brunello *et al.*, 2000).

The DSM classification of social anxiety has caused a certain amount of debate, and some cynicism, because its diagnosis seems to be largely a quantitative issue and a matter of clinical judgement based on the level of associated impairment. Indeed, some have strongly criticized the very existence of social anxiety as a 'disorder' claiming it to be nothing more than the 'medicalization' of shyness (for example, Talbot, 2000). However, this sort of criticism may aptly be applied to many other mental and physical illnesses whose symptoms, although they cause considerable distress to the individual, are simply the extreme end of a continuum of normal behaviour. Since we are, by nature, a species that typically finds pleasure in social interaction, there is little doubt that some level of pathology exists when one's social experience becomes a source of distress instead of comfort (Insel, 2002). An important question that arises is how social anxiousness is different from other forms of anxiousness? One answer lies in the fact that *social* information seems to be processed in our brains in a different way from other sorts of information. In other words, specific brain pathways seem to have evolved for the sole purpose of processing social stimuli (Young, 2002).

Most aetiological models of social anxiety propose an interaction of psychobiological risk factors that are exacerbated by negative thoughts and avoidance behaviours (Kashdan & Herbert, 2001). An easily identifiable temperamental style, which Kagan (1989) called *behavioural inhibition*, and which is already apparent in infancy, is a strong predictor of the later onset of social anxiety (and other anxiety disorders). Children with this disposition withdraw from novel social settings, are irritable and sleepless as babies, and become shy and socially inhibited as they get older. It is easy to see how certain life experiences, laid over this temperamental foundation, could contribute to

104

excessive social anxiety. For example, some research has implicated certain kinds of parent–child interactions, such as harsh maternal criticism, overprotection and overcontrol, and the modelling of anxiety (Coupland, 2001).

Early biological research on social anxiety focused primarily on the noradrenaline system because the symptoms of this disorder, such as blushing, sweating, and palpitations, are all characteristic of autonomic overactivity. However, more recently there has been a focus on the serotonergic and dopaminergic pathways. Although there is little evidence to suggest that current 5-HT models of anxiety are directly informative about *social* anxiety, we do know that the traits that correlate with this condition, such as submissiveness and social interaction, are regulated by 5-HT function, as are other characteristics of more generalized anxiousness (Li *et al.*, 2001).

A more informative line of neurobiological research has linked social anxiety with diminished dopamine transmission in the mesolimbic reward pathway, as seen by lower D2 receptor binding potential in patients with this disorder, and by the observation that neuroleptic drugs (dopamine blockers) tend to increase social anxiety. There are interesting parallels in primates of subordinate social status, and in a strain of particularly timid mice, both of whom show lower striatal dopamine (see Schneier *et al.*, 2000; Stein *et al.*, 2002 for reviews). Low striatal dopamine has also been implicated in other aspects of personality, such as avoidant, schizoid, and detachment traits (Li *et al.*, 2001). And, social anxiety is increased in Parkinson's disease in which there is a pronounced deficit of striatal dopamine. Stein (1998) presents a particularly interesting integration of the two primary neurotransmitter pathways discussed above by proposing an imbalance between risk assessment (probably modulated at the level of the amygdala) and the capacity for experiencing reward, so that the 'risk' of engaging in social interaction far outweighs any 'reward' that it could offer.

**Post Traumatic Stress Disorder** Post Traumatic Stress Disorder (PTSD) is alleged to afflict between 10 per cent and 15 per cent of the population sometime in their life, with its prevalence twice as frequent in women as in men. Although this condition is, by definition, linked to a traumatic, fearful event, patients with PTSD typically show quite normal fear reactions, although their anxiety reactions are elevated (M. Davis, 1998). Almost all individuals who experience a greatly frightening or traumatic event develop some psychological symptoms of anxiety in its aftermath. However, in most individuals, and over the space of time, these symptoms begin to abate. In only a subset of trauma survivors do clinically significant PTSD symptoms become chronic. In recent years, the factors that influence why some are buffered while others succumb to the distress of lingering PTSD symptoms have generated considerable research interest. One of the most salient predictors of PTSD seems to be the nature of the traumatic event, with human violence, such as torture or victimization, producing a substantially higher prevalence than natural disasters, such as earthquakes and floods (Yehuda *et al.*, 1998).

Although more than half of those who develop PTSD meet the diagnostic criteria for other mood and anxiety disorders – indicating once again the substantial overlap in the symptoms of all these disorders – PTSD seems to have a neurobiology rather distinct from other mood and anxiety disorders. The evidence points to a process whereby the initial traumatic experience becomes transduced into an anxiety reaction because of a disruption in the normal cascade of biological events that form the fear response and, more particularly, its resolution (Yehuda *et al.*, 1998). For example, different from what is typically observed in cases of depression, patients with PTSD are characterized by *decreased* levels of circulating cortisol and an increased sensitivity of the HPA negative feedback inhibition. In other words, it appears that the HPA axis is hypersensitive to inhibition feedback because of an increase in the number and the sensitivity of glucocorticoid receptors. An animal model of PTSD has also shown that although the basal cortisol levels in these animals were no different from control animals, after the stress challenge they consistently exhibited HPA hyporesponsivity to subsequent major stressors (King *et al.*, 2001). Based on available data, Yehuda and colleagues proposed that due to certain – as yet not fully understood – risk factors some individuals, in response to a traumatic event, may not release sufficient levels of cortisol to shut down the sympathetic nervous system (SNS) response. In turn, a prolonged and heightened SNS response tends to disrupt the normal processing of memory and sustains distress by causing repeated re-experiencing and reprocessing of the event.

It also appears that pre-traumatic vulnerability factors may contribute to the cause of this disrupted process. For instance, studies have found that psychological disturbance identified before the trauma, and a disruption of social support networks, consistently emerged as strong predictors of psychopathology following exposure to trauma (Pine & Cohen, 2002). Not surprisingly, neuroticism has also been positively associated with PTSD both in retrospective and prospective studies (see Holeva & Tarrier, 2001). Perhaps the risk is conferred because those with high levels of this trait show a propensity to become aroused and conditioned more easily. However, since neuroticism correlates with almost all aspects of psychopathology, this sort of information is not particularly helpful. Nevertheless, it is consistent with the accumulating evidence that the response to trauma and the likelihood of developing PTSD have a genetic basis (King *et al.*, 2001)

## MELANCHOLY

At the beginning of this chapter we emphasized that, despite some obvious common ground, depression is a very heterogeneous clinical condition with at

106

least two, quite distinct, subtypes, the first having symptoms that overlap greatly with those of the anxiety disorders. Therefore, in this section, we shall concentrate our discussion on the core symptom of the *melancholic* type of depression, characteriseed by a profound *anhedonia* and an almost total inability to experience pleasure, which has been explained in biological terms by an under-activation of the brain circuits that regulate reward and reinforcement.

Research over the past several decades has improved our understanding of two higher-order motivational systems. One is related to *approach*, and often called Positive Activation (or Affectivity), and the other to *withdrawal* and called Negative Activation (or Affectivity). These two dimensions represent the subjective or experiential components of more general biobehavioural systems that mediate activities directed towards the acquisition of positive goals, and those that are designed to avoid negative events. Although these systems have been given a variety of names, *behavioural inhibition* and *behavioural activation* are perhaps the most commonly used (as we have seen in Chapter 3). Not surprisingly, they tend to correlate strongly and systematically with measures of neuroticism and extraversion, respectively (Watson *et al.*, 1999). As we have seen in the previous section, high Negative Activation relates strongly to symptoms of fear and anxiety. On the other hand, low Positive Activation is the defining feature of *melancholy*.

The longest standing, and most persistent, biological theory of depression derives from the *monoamine hypothesis* which proposes that a central nervous system depletion of serotonin, norepinephrine and/or dopamine underlies the melancholic symptoms of this disorder. By far the most studied of these neurotransmitters is 5-HT. However, the supporting evidence is largely based on working backwards from the known mechanisms of drugs which either induce depression, or can successfully alleviate its symptoms. A key player in the formulation of this hypothesis was the discovery, half a century ago, that depression was a common side-effect of one of the first effective hypertensive medications (reserpine) – the link being made because it was also known that reserpine depleted brain 5-HT stores (Hirshfeld, 2000). Since then, the neurobiological study of depression has been inextricably linked to the mechanism of action of effective antidepressants, the newer of which (like the serotonin reuptake inhibitors (SRIs)) elevate brain levels of 5-HT. A brief description of the SRIs is given below.

---

Serotonin reuptake inhibitor drugs (SRIs)

SRIs, such as fluoxetine (the most familiar of these is marketed as Prozac), have a well-established antidepressant and antiobsessional effect, making them a highly popular treatment option for many patients with OCD and depressive disorders. The pharmacological mechanism of these drugs is to inhibit the removal of 5-HT from the synaptic cleft, back into the releasing neuron, by blocking the transporter or uptake pump that executes this function. In theory, the result of this blocking action is that more 5-HT is available in the synapse, and therefore able to bind to postsynaptic receptors. However, an important question, that has puzzled researchers since the introduction of these drugs, is why there is a delayed reaction of several weeks in their effectiveness for symptom improvement.

One convincing explanation is that although the initial use of these drugs serves to flood the synapse with 5-HT when the uptake pump is blocked, this action causes rapid sensitization of the 5-HT inhibitory autoreceptors located on the cell body and terminals of the serotonergic neurons. This serves to slow down the firing rate of the neuron. The net result is a small, but insignificant, enhancement of 5-HT. However, it is believed that over time, chronic use of SRI drugs helps to desensitize the overreactive 5-HT autoreceptors. In other words, with long-term use, 5-HT availability is eventually increased because of enhanced release from the neuron and diminished reuptake of 5-HT.

Despite the appeal of pharmacokinetics explanations, the action of these drugs is still only partially understood. And because their precise mechanism continues to defy a clear explanation, neurochemical experts often resort to a rather evasive explanation by saying that the action of the SRIs is not simply to increase or decrease 5-HT, but rather to make this neurotransmitter system work more precisely in modulating mood and impulse control. It has also been suggested that the SRI drugs cause a shift in the balance of tone in the indirect versus the direct orbitofrontal-subcortical pathways, decreasing activity in the overall circuit (Saxena et al., 1998).

Over the years, a wealth of indirect evidence has also supported the role of 5-HT in melancholy. For example, concentrations of a certain 5-HT metabolite are lower in patients with depression, and low concentrations in the central spinal fluid and cortex have been found in those who commit violent suicide. However, the difficulty with this sort of research is that no specific biochemical lesion has been successfully and consistently implicated, although certain candidates appear more likely than others. For instance, depleted 5-HT could be the result of defective synthesis in the cell body, reduced release from the cell, enhanced activity of the inhibitory autoreceptors, and impaired post-synaptic function (Leonard, 2000).

Recently, a more direct test of the monoamine hypothesis has been achieved with 5-HT depletion studies – the underlying rationale being that if melancholy is caused by a deficiency of this neurotransmitter, an experimentally induced depletion in normal subjects should foster the depressive symptoms seen in patients with this disorder. However, results from such studies have not been supportive since depletion of 5-HT and norepinephrine does not usually cause depressive symptoms in healthy volunteers. Nor does it worsen symptoms in unmedicated depressed patients (Delgado, 2000).

Another important line of neurobiological research has linked hemispheric asymmetry in the prefrontal cortex to melancholy. In a review of the data that has accumulated in this area, Tomarken and Keener (1998) concluded that resting levels of *left* prefrontal activation primarily reflect individual differences in the motivation to approach rewarding stimuli and the degree of responsiveness to pleasurable environmental events. Conversely, resting levels of *right* prefrontal activation reflect individual differences in withdrawal from stimuli that are potentially threatening (describing a system that is clearly relevant to our earlier discussions of fearfulness and anxiousness). Depression studies have shown that decreased activation in the left prefrontal cortex relative to the right (as measured, for example, by electroencephalographic (EEG) activity), is consistently correlated with measures of anhedonia, whereas happy and cheerful people tend to have higher resting activation in the left prefrontal cortex (Henriques & Davidson, 2000). Studies have also examined frontal asymmetry in the infants and children of depressed mothers and found left frontal hypoactivation compared to children of non-depressed mothers, further suggesting that frontal asymmetry may be a genetically based marker of risk for depression. However, asymmetry could also be the result of socio-environmental influences since we know that patterns of stimulation at critical periods of a child's development can produce changes in cortical connectivity. Therefore, it is possible that depressed mothers may show decreased signs of pleasure to their infant offspring, which may then retard the child's development of essential cortical connections (Tomarken & Keener, 1998). Most probable, however, is that transmitted risk is a function both of genetic and of environmental factors.

Patterns complementary to the cortical activity described above are also seen at the subcortical level. The brain's *mesolimbic dopamine reward pathway* is fundamentally implicated in melancholy since the level of functioning of this circuitry underlies individual differences in the capacity to experience pleasure, and the motivation to approach pleasurable stimuli. An extensive body of research – much of it conducted in the context of addiction research (see Chapter 7) – has confirmed the role of this neurotransmitter pathway in approach-related behaviours. Depue and colleagues have also shown positive correlations between dopamine availability and human variability in personality traits characterized by positive affect, such as extraversion (Depue & Collins, 1999). Relevant to the research on cortical asymmetry is the fact that projections from the mesolimbic region to the cortex tend to be concentrated in the *left* hemisphere (Watson *et al.*, 1999).

The high comorbidity between Major Depressive Disorder and drug abuse has also drawn attention to similarities in the neurobiology of the two conditions, with suggestions that the two disorders are different symptomatic expressions of the same pre-existing biological abnormalities, or that the effects of chronic drug exposure lead to biochemical changes which have some common elements with the biological events that mediate depression. We also know that stressful environmental factors mimic the brain's reaction to drug use (Markou *et al.*, 1998).

Perhaps the best demonstration of the role of mesolimbic dopamine in both melancholy (and addiction) is seen in the *chronic mild stress* (CMS) model where it is clearly established that the anhedonic effects of CMS are mediated by a downregulation of certain dopamine receptors in the nucleus accumbens, and therefore, a net decrease in dopamine availability (Willner, 1997). However, in the context of this model, it is important to emphasize that reward-*seeking* behaviour (something more closely linked to the concept of impulsivity) is conceptually distinct from the response to a reward when it is presented. The latter is often evaluated by preference ratings in studies with human subjects. Although it seems reasonable to think the two would go together – viz. wanting something and liking it – the distinction between them has a 'long and distinguished intellectual pedigree' and forms the basis for many theories of addiction, as we explain in Chapter 7 (Willner *et al.*, 1998).

A variety of studies have highlighted the importance of the dopamine reward pathway to behavioural activation. When compared to non-depressed subjects, both depressed and subclinically depressed subjects showed a decreased responsiveness to reward, but not punishment, in a verbal memory task that was carried out under three monetary reward conditions (neutral, reward, and punishment) (Henriques & Davidson, 2000). Another study monitored subjective responses to a mild dose of amphetamine and found that the degree of positive mood induced by the drug was strongly correlated with the severity of the subject's depression (Tremblay *et al.*, 2002). Depressed patients with severe symptoms experienced greater reward from the drug compared to control subjects, whereas the mood ratings of those with moderate depression were no different from control subjects. The investigators concluded that the hypersensitive brain reward-system response in the depressed patients is likely to reflect a downregulated or hypofunctional state in these patients.

While biological research has provided some insights into the causes of depression, cognitive explanations have also improved our understanding of depressive processes. Most cognitive models, including that of Beck and the later hopelessness/helplessness models, are based on a 'cognitive vulnerability hypothesis' and describe the way in which dysfunctional thinking patterns foster the development of depressive episodes (see Just *et al.*, 2001 for a review). In other words, negative thinking is not seen simply as a symptom of depression; it is also a causal antecedent stemming from the maladaptive way depressed individuals process information from their social world. For example, they may selectively attend to information that is unflattering to them, to interpret information negatively when there is some ambiguity, and endorse largely pessimistic beliefs – information that ultimately results in a

negative self-concept. As a result, they may pursue social goals that result in a lack of positive reinforcement or they may behave in a socially undesirable way because they lack the requisite social skills (Street *et al.*, 1999).

Many experimental studies conducted with pleasant and unpleasant word recall, or with autobiographical recollection, have shown that depressed people tend to recall more negatively toned past events than non-depressed individuals, and they do this more frequently than they recall positive events. In other words, they tend to remember and focus their attention on unhappy and unflattering information from the past. Some have suggested that this memory bias may be a *maintenance* mechanism in depression because it inhibits the individual from engaging in effective 'mood-repairing' activities (Watkins, 2002). For example, when depressed individuals are invited to a social event they are more likely to remember something unpleasant that occurred on a previous occasion they attended, which then leads to the view that parties do not improve their mood, and so the event would probably be avoided. In this way the depression is maintained, and even exacerbated, by reinforced negative memories, by increased social isolation, and by missed opportunities to develop more adaptive coping skills.

One hallmark of depressive thinking is *rumination* which, by definition, entails an attentional focus on past events. Although the intensity of one's thoughts during rumination suggests a high degree of cognitive control, in fact just the opposite is the case. There is a rather forceful *lack* of control in the ability to switch attention to other matters since negative thoughts seem to intrude automatically into the mind of the depressive, inviting more and more frequent gloomy thoughts. The work of Wegner and colleagues (1987), on the ironic effects of thought suppression, has had considerable impact on our understanding of ruminative thoughts in depression (see Purdon, 1999 for a review). In Wegner's original studies, subjects were asked either to suppress or express thoughts about a white bear whilst thinking aloud their stream of consciousness. Later in the study, the suppression/expression instructions were reversed, and it was found that subjects who had 'suppressed' first had more thought occurrences of the bear in the second phase. In other words, the very cognitive processes that are used to help us suppress thoughts paradoxically also seem to work to foster the elicitation of those same thoughts.

Thought suppression has been implicated in various psychological disorders, such as depression, that are characterized by the intrusive distress of unwanted thoughts. One explanation for why suppression of pessimistic thoughts tends to result in their more frequent occurrence is because, at least among the depressed, there is an absence of positive distracting thoughts and a hyperaccessibility of other negative thoughts. However, not all studies have found these effects when applied to the suppression of neutral thoughts, highlighting once again the important role of individual vulnerability in all psychological phenomena.

The above mention of *rumination* and *thought suppression* draws attention to another psychological disorder where those phenomena play a major role in the mechanisms of symptom formation and maintenance. We are referring to Obsessive–Compulsive Disorder, a condition which we consider in detail in the following chapter.

# C H A P T E R  6

## OBSESSIVE–COMPULSIVE DISORDER

### INTRODUCTION

As we have seen in the previous chapter, Obsessive–Compulsive Disorder (OCD) is listed in the DSM-IV as one of the Anxiety Disorders. While it is clear that patients with this disorder have some characteristics that overlap with the other disorders in this category, some have questioned the appropriateness of its inclusion, arguing instead the existence of an aetiology that is specific to OCD. Some have even suggested that anxiety is not causally implicated in the development of OCD, but rather that the disabling and distressing symptoms of the disorder give rise to the anxiousness that is typically observed in these patients.

Indeed, illustrative of the uncertainty of how to classify OCD is the fact that, different from the DSM, it is listed as a category separate from Anxiety Disorders in the ICD-10. One of the arguments for viewing OCD as a distinct disorder is the fact that it is consistently resistant to medications that are successful in treating most anxiety disorders. Other factors also distinguish the two forms of disorder. For example, OCD, unlike anxiety disorders, is characterized by deficits in the ability to inhibit irrelevant or distracting information. Its primary symptoms comprise intrusive and obsessional thoughts which are sometimes followed by repetitive, excessive, and intentional behaviours whose purpose is to neutralize the obsessions and reduce the distress they cause. Another interesting observation supporting the behavioural and biological separateness of these disorders is that nicotine dependence is highly prevalent in Generalized Anxiety Disorder and yet is very rare among OCD patients (Bejerot & Humble, 1999). Since nicotine is known to increase frontal lobe activity, it seems to exacerbate the symptoms of OCD, and is therefore an aversive behaviour for those suffering from this disorder.

Although OCD has been regarded as a unitary disorder since its introduction in the first version of DSM in 1952, its clinical features are, nevertheless, overtly heterogeneous so that any particular individual may have one – though more typically several – of a variety of symptoms which are present in varying degrees and combinations. Earlier attempts to deal with the symptom variability in OCD proposed a nosology of mutually exclusive subtypes, namely, Washers and Checkers. The more current view is that the clinical features of OCD are better described as 'moderately correlated symptom dimensions' – a framework which has been identified primarily through the use of factor-analytic procedures, and recognition of the great variability across patients in symptom severity (Mataix-Cols *et al.*, 1999; Summerfeldt *et al.*, 1999). Although studies have not completely agreed on the precise factor structure of OCD symptoms, either four or five primary dimensions seem to emerge, and are described in Table 6.1.

In a general sense, the inability to assess risk quickly and accurately is a core

**Table 6.1** Symptom dimensions in OCD.

> **Symmetry and ordering** are the most common symptoms of OCD typically involving obsessions about exactness, and repetitive counting and repeating activities that relate mostly to concerns about security and accuracy
>
> **Hoarding** relates to obsessions about saving, and to compulsions to collect, in excess, particular items such as old newspapers, cans of food or plastic bags of useless rubbish like old bits of paper
>
> **Contamination and cleaning** include obsessional concerns with bodily secretions, germs and dirt, environmental contaminants, and worries about illness. This factor also includes compulsions, such as excessive handwashing, grooming, and household cleaning
>
> **Aggressive obsessions and checking** comprise a range of fears, such as excessive worry about harming oneself or others, doing something embarrassing, acting on unwanted impulses, and obsessions of violent images. The compulsions typically involve checking door locks, stoves and other appliances; and carrying out acts which reassure that one hasn't harmed others. In severe cases, the checking rituals can be performed for hours each day, and to such a degree that the individual is scarcely able to leave the house
>
> **Sexual/religious obsessions** include the experience of forbidden or perverse thoughts and impulses which often concern things like incest and homosexuality, or concerns about sacrilege and blasphemy. When they occur in isolation of other symptoms, this is usually called 'pure obsessional disorder'

characteristic of all forms of OCD. However, the most subjectively distressing feature of OCD, and one experienced by patients of every symptom subtype, is the pervasive and overwhelming feeling of *doubt* – a sensation that cannot be eliminated by common sense or reasoning. For example, a woman may engage in some repetitive and ritualized behaviour like hand washing even though she knows logically that her hands are clean and that she has not touched anything dirty or harmful. But things just do not feel right so she remains compelled to repeat the washing over and over until the uncertainty disappears, and she senses that the behaviour has achieved its purpose. Some have described this moment as the 'just right' phenomenon, and explain that the individual can only achieve closure on the compulsive behaviour when this feeling occurs.

It has been largely implicit in the diagnosis of OCD that patients are able to recognize the excessive and unreasonable nature of their obsessions and compulsions. Predicated on the reliability of this assumption, OCD has always been firmly embedded among the 'neurotic' not the 'psychotic' disorders. However, this tenet does not always mesh with clinical reality since OCD patients exhibit varying degrees of *insight* into the validity of their thoughts and actions. Occasionally – studies suggest in less than 10 per cent of patients with OCD – insight is lost altogether, and their cognitive features begin to resemble delusions and take on the characteristics of a frank psychotic disorder. For this reason, some have suggested that obsessions and delusions, rather than being dichotomous categories, exist at either end of a continuum of insight, with what the DSM calls 'overvalued ideas' somewhere in the middle (Eisen *et al.*, 1999; Marazziti, 2001). How then do we classify OCD patients whose obsessions, at times, become delusional? Some have chosen to classify these patients as schizophrenic or simply psychotic, whereas others have introduced the term 'schizo-obsessive subtype' into psychiatric parlance to accommodate both aspects of the clinical profile. The DSM has also taken the middle ground by adding 'with poor insight' as a diagnostic qualifier for OCD patients who are partly convinced that their obsessions are reasonable. For more extreme cases of delusional OCD, the terms *delusional disorder* or *psychotic disorder not otherwise specified* were added. It seems that a key factor distinguishing OCD with delusions from psychotic psychopathology is a clear and logical link in the former between the delusional thoughts and the rituals they prompt (O'Dwyer & Marks, 2000). Much more about delusions, in the context of schizophrenia and other psychotic disorders, will be discussed in Chapter 9.

## NATURAL HISTORY OF THE DISORDER

Although OCD represents the fourth most common psychiatric disorder, it is still frequently underdiagnosed and undertreated in most populations. Indeed, 15 years ago OCD was thought to be a very rare condition, occurring in less than 0.5 per cent of the population. Now, however, estimates from more sophisticated epidemiological studies indicate that the lifetime prevalence of OCD is at least three per cent in females and two per cent in males, of whom the latter also have, on average, an earlier age of onset (Bebbington, 1998). Gender-related differences have also been observed in the symptom profile of the disorder. Generally speaking, women display more contamination and aggressive obsessions, and more cleaning rituals, whereas symmetry, exactness, sexual obsessions, and hoarding behaviours are more common in men (Bogetto et al., 1999; Pigott, 1998). Another interesting observation is that epidemiological samples provide a strikingly different symptom profile from those of patients who were identified and assessed in treatment facilities. For instance, the former are much more likely to have obsessive thoughts *without* compulsive behaviours, whereas most clinical patients report both. One plausible explanation for this difference is that compulsive acts are simply more obvious than obsessions, and therefore are probably viewed as more deviant by the individual and/or by friends and family – a factor which is likely to prompt a stronger motivation, in these individuals with noticeable compulsions, to seek treatment.

During the past decade or so, we have become aware that about a third to a half of adult OCD patients actually experienced the first symptoms of their disorder during childhood, although the disorder mostly went undiagnosed at this time (Robinson, 1998). There also seems to be a rather bimodal distribution in the age of onset with the first peak occurring between the ages of 12 and14 years, and the second peak between 20 and 22 years of age. This, coupled with the fact that an earlier onset is related to a poorer prognosis – especially in men – has prompted a particular interest in the study of paediatric OCD.

Although the diagnostic criteria for children are the same as for adults, the primary differences between the two are usually seen in how the children experience the illness. They are usually more frightened by their obsessions, and they frequently involve their parents or other close family members in their elaborate rituals. For example, mothers are sometimes required to perform time-consuming activities to cleanse themselves before washing the child's clothing. Or, others in the home are also required to carry out the checking compulsions of the child or to avoid the feared stimulus. In general, however, the degree of interference or distress caused by the symptoms may best be assessed in the context of schoolwork and peer friendships, which are often seriously compromised. Having said that, it is interesting that children with OCD do not typically exhibit the significant cognitive deficits that generally become apparent if the disorder persists and becomes chronic.

Another difference between adult and childhood cases may be seen in the presentation of the disorder. Children who show signs of OCD before the age of six years are much more likely to have compulsions than obsessions – pure obsessiveness is quite rare in these cases – and by far the most common are

washing rituals, followed by checking and counting. Another interesting observation is that if the child has an affected first-degree relative there is no consistent similarity in the nature of the symptoms, suggesting that mimicry or modelling of symptoms is not a feature of the disorder (Robinson, 1998).

Until recently, there have been few long-term follow-up studies of OCD, making it difficult to provide prognostic information to patients and their families. For that reason, a recently published prospective follow-up of 144 OCD patients over a 40-year period has been particularly helpful in framing a more complete picture of the natural course of the disorder; even more so because only a small proportion of the study patients had ever received pharmacological treatment for their disorder (Skoog & Skoog, 1999). By the end of the follow-up period, about 80 per cent of the patients showed improvement in their symptoms – many within 10 years of the onset of their illness. However, only 20 per cent of the patients ever achieved full remission, 10 per cent showed no improvement, and another 10 per cent had a deteriorating course of their illness. Also discouraging was the fact that approximately 20 per cent of the patients who showed early recovery, followed by at least 20 symptom-free years, were plagued by persistent relapses.

## CAUSAL EXPLANATIONS OF OCD
## BIOLOGICAL MODELS

Many have attempted to explain the cause of this debilitating illness whose symptoms have been described in psychiatric writings for over a century. Although it has not always been the prevailing viewpoint, there is currently a strong belief that OCD has its genesis in brain neuropathology. And, this viewpoint has spawned the development of several biological models of the disorder, all of which predict, in one way or another, the involvement of the prefrontal cortex, the basal ganglia, and the limbic system in the generation of OCD symptoms. Although a detailed description of neuroanatomy and neurophysiology is beyond the scope of this chapter, a brief consideration of some aspects of brain circuitry and functioning will help illustrate what we understand about the complex biology of this disorder.

117

The prefrontal cortex has direct neural circuitry to the basal ganglia via its connections with the limbic system. It also receives signals *from* these subcortical nuclei, and so, in response, can alter their activity. In other words, there are functionally reciprocal frontal-subcortical circuits which pass through the limbic system. Conceptually, each of these circuits is understood as having two loops – a 'direct' and an 'indirect' pathway – the former functioning as a positive feedback loop and the latter as a negative feedback loop.

Baxter and colleagues have outlined an elegant conceptual model of OCD pathophysiology by proposing that the function of the direct circuits is to execute 'pre-packaged' complex responses to what they call 'socioterritorial'

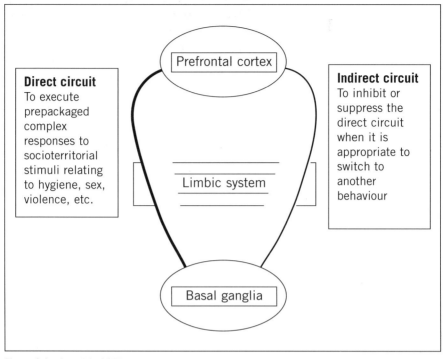

**Figure 6.1** A model of OCD.

stimuli – that is, things that are highly significant to the survival of the organism, such as hygiene, sex, safety, and keeping things in order (see Saxena *et al.*, 1998). These are responses that need to be carried out quickly in order to be adaptive, and which must operate to the exclusion of other interfering stimuli. The activation of these *direct* pathways tends to pin or rivet the execution of the behaviour until the attentional need to do so has passed. Part of the function of the *indirect* pathways is to inhibit or suppress the *direct* pathways when it is appropriate to switch to another behaviour – something we know that OCD patients have trouble doing. In healthy individuals, socioterritorial concerns pass through the direct pathway and are inhibited by the indirect pathway in a suitably timely manner. However, in OCD patients the excess activation of the direct pathway results in a fixation of these concerns. Because the appropriate inhibition has been too weak to turn off the signal, these concerns are experienced by the individual as repetitive and intrusive obsessions. In other words, as we can see in Figure 6.1, this model of OCD proposes a substantial imbalance in the tone or sensitivity of the direct–indirect pathway in OCD patients, which results in a response-bias towards socioterritorial stimuli; precisely the concerns which form the theme of most obsessions in OCD patients.

This popular conceptual model meshes well with neurobiological evidence

from a variety of sources. For example, neuroimaging studies have consistently shown *increased* prefrontal activity, most frequently involving the right orbitofrontal cortex, in unmedicated individuals with OCD. Indeed, it has been said that OCD patients display behaviours that are consistent with 'overheated' frontal lobes. Interestingly, these areas of hyperactivity seem to normalize when patients receive effective treatment, either pharmacologically or from behavioural therapy. Since the frontal cortex plays an important role in assessing the behavioural significance of biologically significant stimuli, it seems that heightened frontal activation may relate to obsessional thinking, but not necessarily to compulsions. On the other hand, the function of the basal ganglia and the cerebellum may modulate compulsive urges since the latter stores behavioural programs like conditioned reflexes. Also certain diseases with pathology localized to the basal ganglion, such as Parkinson's disease and Huntington's chorea, often show compulsive symptoms similar to those seen in OCD.

Other biological theories of OCD have focused more squarely on the role of neurotransmitter mechanisms. In particular, a dysfunction of brain serotonin (5-HT) has been proposed as a leading cause of OCD for several years. The so-called 'serotonin hypothesis' derived in large part from the clear and consistent efficacy of serotonin reuptake inhibitor (SRI) drugs in patients with OCD, and therefore the notion that OCD must be caused by a deficiency of 5-HT transmission (see Chapter 5 for a brief discussion of SRIs). More recent research using peripheral 5-HT markers, pharmacological challenge tests, and brain imaging techniques has also kept alive a strong belief in the involvement of 5-HT in this disorder (see Baumgarten & Grozdanovic, 1998; Delgado & Moreno, 1998 for reviews).

For example, there has been a number of case reports of symptom improvement when OCD patients use hallucinogenic drugs such as LSD, which are potent stimulators of brain 5-HT. Others have reported the exacerbation of symptoms after administration of 5-HT antagonist drugs. However, while 5-HT is clearly important to our understanding of the causal mechanisms in OCD, it would be greatly misleading to suggest that it tells the whole story, especially as accumulating evidence (which will be discussed later) indicates that dysregulation of other neurotransmitter systems – primarily dopamine – is implicated in OCD pathogenesis. Moreover, to give a balanced picture, we must also consider the limitations of the serotonin hypothesis. First of all, many patients are only partially responsive to SRI drugs, and nearly a third of patients do not respond at all. In addition, there is a range of other 5-HT agonists that have produced no symptom improvement at all – even a worsening of the condition in some patients. Also, studies that have used a 5-HT depletion paradigm were typically not able to show a reversal of the symptom improvement induced by SRI drugs – an effect that is seen consistently with depressive symptoms in patients with depression. Nor does 5-HT depletion have an ill effect on unmedicated, symptomatic people with OCD. One thing these particular results suggest is that whatever the role of 5-HT in the treatment of OCD, it is probably not the same as the role it plays in the treatment of depression.

On a more whimsical note, the observations of psychiatrists and poets have converged in the recent discovery of neurochemical similarities between OCD and romantic love! Perhaps this should not surprise. Certainly, writers have noted the commonalities between love and psychological disturbance for centuries, having written about falling 'insanely' in love or being 'lovesick'. Even in everyday parlance we say he is 'mad' about her when we describe the affection of a man for a woman. Indeed, it is not difficult to see that the obsessive preoccupation with, and the overvalued ideation about, one's love object during the early stages of romantic love are little different from the obsessions we see in OCD patients. Comparisons between OCD patients and a sample of healthy volunteers who reported having recently fallen in love, showed a statistically significant decrease in the number of 5-HT transporter proteins in the platelets of both groups compared to normal subjects (Marazziti *et al.*, 1999). Moreover, OCD patients who had recovered from their symptoms, and the volunteers who were no longer 'in love' when they were retested a year later, showed levels in this 5-HT marker that were indistinguishable from normal subjects. It is interesting to see how similar changes in the 5-HT transporter map onto the abatement of psychological symptoms in the two groups studied in this experiment.

A prime difficulty with the 'serotonin hypothesis' – and it reflects a mode of thinking that is common in other areas of psychiatric research – is that it may be based on faulty logic. Just because drugs such as SRIs increase 5-HT activity and are effective in alleviating the signature symptoms of the disorder, it does not necessarily follow that the *cause* of the condition is a dysfunction or deficiency in that neurotransmitter system; any more than taking an aspirin to cure a headache implies that headaches are caused by a deficiency of acetylsalicylic acid. In fact, with the development of more and more sophisticated neuroimaging techniques, it is becoming clear that a variety of lesions in the brain (either structural or functional) could lead to the development of symptoms without there being any impairment of 5-HT neurotransmission (Delgado & Moreno, 1998).

On the basis of the imperfect response to SRI drugs alone, it is clear that 5-HT is not the only neurotransmitter involved in the pathophysiology of OCD, or at least, not all forms of OCD. Accumulating evidence suggests that excessive dopamine availability may also play a role. One line of evidence comes from an interesting animal model known as the *quinpirole preparation* (Szechtman *et al.*, 1998). Rats treated chronically with this dopamine D2/D3 agonist drug, display ritual-like behaviours with a distinct similarity to the motor behaviours seen in OCD patients with checking compulsions. Since

compulsive checking is probably an exaggerated form of normal checking behaviour designed for the protection and security of the organism, this model suggests that checking (and perhaps other protective behaviours) may well be a dopamine-based behaviour.

Other evidence of dopamine involvement is that haloperidol – a dopamine D2 receptor antagonist – has been useful for improving the treatment response to SRI drugs. This makes sense theoretically because stimulation of D1 receptors is known to activate preferentially the direct orbitofrontal-subcortical pathways, and stimulation of D2 receptors has been shown to decrease activity in the indirect pathways whose function is to dampen down the hard-wired behaviours under the control of the direct pathway. In other words, by blocking D2 receptors, the indirect pathway is more efficiently able to counteract the action of the direct pathway.

## COGNITIVE MODELS OF OCD

Some clinicians and theorists have eschewed or discredited biological interpretations of OCD, instead favouring a more cognitive approach to the understanding of this illness. The early cognitive explanations relied mostly on a classical conditioning paradigm whereby traumatic learning caused certain stimuli to evoke anxious feelings and thoughts, which were then strengthened and maintained because particular behavioural rituals seemed to provide relief from this anxiety. There is a certain intuitive appeal to this idea since many cases of OCD have their onset after a stressful life event, and stress is a common trigger of relapse. Its limitation, however, is that it does not provide an explanation for cases that do not have an obvious or apparent traumatic precursor. Consequently, more recent cognitive accounts have moved beyond a strictly behavioural approach.

Currently, the most prominent cognitive theory is one proposed by Salkovskis (1985) and developed as an expansion of Clark's theory of depression and panic, which was discussed in some detail in Chapter 5. It starts from the premise that unwanted or intrusive thoughts are not only the precursor to, and the raw material of, obsessions, but more importantly they are part of universal and everyday cognitive experience. In other words, normal intrusive cognitions in healthy individuals are ideas, impulses, or images that interrupt one's stream of consciousness, and are indistinguishable in terms of their content from obsessional thoughts in OCD except that they are less intense, less long-lasting, and less distressing. Also, repetitive behaviours are especially apparent in childhood and are believed to reflect a strong need for predictability and order when a child is very young. It is also believed that maturation and the drive for mastery, control, and socialization are fundamentally dependent on repetition and elaborate rules of behaviour. In the average child, most of the normal childhood rituals – many of them fear-related and observable at night-time – have subsided by the advent of puberty.

However, it is important to emphasize that even though childhood compulsions are developmentally normal, the *extent* of these behaviours is highly correlated with anxiety. The more anxious children in all pre-adolescent age groups engage in a greater number and more intense ritualized behaviours than those who are less anxious.

In summary, the cognitive view is that obsessive-compulsive symptoms have their origins in, and are simply an extension of, normal behaviour. We might then ask what it is that turns a normal intrusive thought into an abnormal and tormenting obsession? Cognitive approaches identify two important factors in this transition: *misinterpretation* and psychological *vulnerability*; the latter increasing the likelihood that the former will occur. To be more specific, the transformation of a commonplace thought into something abnormal rests on the catastrophic way it is interpreted. For example, the individual believes that the intrusive thought is more important or threatening than it really is, or believes it has far greater personal significance than is logically warranted. A case example will help to illustrate this point.

---

**Case Study: Obsessive–Compulsive Disorder**

Walter, who is a 40-year-old devoutly religious man, with a highly developed sense of morality, had recurrent and obscene thoughts about the Virgin Mary. These were especially frequent when he was in church and was trying to pray. Instead of dismissing them as trivial and of no consequence, he immediately believed he was seriously sexually perverted and that his religious beliefs were flawed and insincere. Clearly, this catastrophic interpretation of his impure thoughts caused him great distress and fear. He soon stopped attending church services and began to eschew anything that contained Christian images. For instance, he used to enjoy visiting museums of art but could no longer do this because of the numerous pictorial references to Mary in the works of the old Masters.

---

However, theorists agree that the tendency to misinterpret or overinterpret is far more likely to occur in some individuals – like Walter – who are in possession of certain vulnerability traits. For example, there is a relationship between OCD and a particular cognitive style known as *thought–action fusion*. Typically, this can take two forms and describes tendencies with which we are all familiar, but which occur in an exaggerated form in some individuals. The first is the belief that having an unacceptable thought – such as imagining that the plane on which a loved one is flying is going to crash – increases the likelihood that the dreadful event will occur. The second is the belief that having a frightening or unacceptable thought is the moral equivalent of carrying out the action associated with that bad thought.

There has also been considerable interest in the use of cognitive experimental methods to examine whether information-processing

abnormalities in OCD could possibly give rise to the symptoms that characterize the disorder. McNally (2000) argued that the cognitive biases that describe these abnormalities are not 'mere epiphenomenal sequelae of the disorder, but rather constitute the pathogenic mechanisms themselves'. He also explains that although these biases may have their roots in the physiology of the brain, they cannot easily be reduced to concepts or explanations at the neurobiological level of analysis. Instead, we must rely on characterizing them functionally. Although information-processing abnormalities have been relatively understudied in OCD, when compared to their role in other disorders, there is already some evidence that certain cognitive deficiencies and derangements have been identified in this disorder.

One line of support is that individuals who develop OCD tend to have attentional biases that contribute to their recurrent obsessions. For example – and in ways similar to patients with anxiety disorders – those with OCD attend more persistently to threatening or potentially harmful stimuli. Data from various paradigms, including emotional Stroop experiments, have shown that OCD patients are more likely than healthy subjects to process obsession-relevant cues. Their attention also seems to be dysfunctional in its ability to ignore irrelevant or distracting information. This may give rise to the development of elaborate strategies to suppress the distracting thoughts. However, as Wegner's research has pointed out (see Chapter 5 for a discussion), active attempts to suppress certain thoughts – especially negative ones – usually result in an increase in their frequency. One can see how a vicious cycle of intrusive thoughts and suppressing rituals may develop and become habitual and persistent.

Other research has focused on the role of forgetting and the possibility that obsessional thoughts may result from a selective dysfunction in this ability, as well as from a hypersensitivity to the encoding of potentially threatening stimuli. Although studies have found that OCD patients were relatively unable to forget words construed as threatening, compared to neutral or positive words, it may well be because they have an enhanced memory for threat stimuli, rather than an impairment in their ability to forget (Wilhelm et al., 1996).

With respect to those who check compulsively, several cognitive explanations have been proposed and supported by research in the area of memory. For example, OCD patients may either fail to commit certain actions to memory, or they may have a diminished ability for retrieval from memory. Another possibility is that they may have a deficit in *reality monitoring* – that is, the ability to distinguish the *memory* of carrying out the action from the *intention* to do so. Although most studies have found no significant decrements in the ability of OCD patients to monitor reality accurately, these patients do often report a deficit in the confidence they place in their memory.

In summary, although we have good evidence that OCD symptoms might develop, in part, because of attentional biases favouring stimuli construed as potentially harmful, we are still not entirely clear about why certain stimuli become linked to threat and why others remain neutral. Nor are we entirely clear on how the emergence of obsessions gives rise to the particular compulsions that are used to neutralize their impact. Fear conditioning and an enhanced biological preparedness to target environmental stimuli related to safety and survival, may well contribute to the explanation.

## PERSONALITY FACTORS IN OCD

Before we begin this discussion, it is important to talk about some of the methodological difficulties inherent in trying to establish causal connections between personality factors, on the one hand, and vulnerability to OCD, on the other. The first problem concerns the longevity of the disorder. As we have seen earlier, a substantial proportion of patients experience the onset of OCD in childhood or adolescence, and only a small percentage ever recover fully. Therefore, the disorder is mostly a chronic condition, and although the symptoms may alter in severity over time, for most they have a lifelong presence. A second problem is that few, if any, studies of personality and OCD are prospective in design. Instead, most of the evidence is drawn from correlational data, obtained from patients in the full-blown throes of their disorder, allowing for little more than the assessment of relationships among variables. When considering both these problems together it is easy to see why some have disputed the meaningfulness of thinking of personality traits and OCD symptoms as discrete and separable entities or phenomena (Summerfeldt et al., 1998). Instead, it is argued that the severity of OCD symptoms confounds the valid assessment of personality traits. Existing research also makes it difficult to determine whether there is a specific profile of personality characteristics which increases the risk for OCD, or whether certain personality traits render the individual vulnerable to environmental stressors, which in turn interact with personality to cause the disorder. A third possibility – what some have called the 'scar hypothesis' – is that the chronicity and the distressing nature of the disorder irrevocably change a person's personality, as seen in their thoughts, their mood, and their behaviours. However, despite these methodological caveats, and irrespective of whether one focuses on the biological origins of OCD or one takes a more cognitive approach to its development, certain traits have emerged from the research with enough consistency for us to conclude that individual differences do play an important role in the development of OCD.

In the study of personality risk factors, some research information has come from case records and clinical observation, whereas other data have been obtained from self-report questionnaires and assessment interviews. Research has also approached the study of personality and OCD from two distinct perspectives. One has been to assess the comorbidity between OCD and the

124

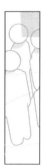

Axis II personality disorders, while the second has examined dimensionally constructed obsessive–compulsive personality traits in patients with OCD.

The logic guiding the former methodology is that comorbid personality disorders provide a key to uncovering underlying traits that increase risk for OCD. On the surface, this seems like a fruitful endeavour given the high comorbidity between personality disorders and OCD – estimates range between 33 per cent and 87 per cent (Bejerot et al., 1998a; 1998b). However, this approach has been criticized on a number of counts, and seems to have done little to inform us about the psychology that predisposes to OCD (see Summerfeldt et al., 1998 for a review). Nevertheless, a brief overview of the main findings from these studies is worth describing.

Although there is considerable variability in the findings from comorbidity research – indeed, all types of personality disorders have been found in these patients – the most consistently diagnosed personality disorders in OCD patients are avoidant, dependent, histrionic, schizotypal and, to a lesser degree, obsessive compulsive. In other words, the most prevalent personality disorders seem to come from Cluster C. However, as suggested earlier, we are limited in our ability to infer from these studies that specific personality traits are causally implicated in the development of OCD because of the distinct possibility that an illness as severe as OCD can foster abnormal personality traits rather than, or at least as often as, the reverse (Black & Noyes, 1997). The association of OCD with avoidant personality disorder serves as a good way to illustrate this point. As we have seen, OCD symptoms are generally severe, socially embarrassing, and time-consuming, causing sufferers to become isolated and withdrawn, and therefore to develop characteristics highly consistent with the diagnosis for avoidant personality disorder. In other words, this personality disorder may not be a primary cause of OCD, but rather a consequence of its symptomatology. Another problem of interpretation has been called 'criterion contamination' and applies aptly to the comorbidity between schizotypal personality disorder and OCD. For example, questionnaire items that were designed to assess schizotypal factors, such as cognitive distortion and magical thinking (for example 'No matter how hard I try, unrelated thoughts always creep into my mind'), may be endorsed by OCD patients for reasons quite distinct from the intended meaning of the item.

125

The great similarity in the diagnostic labels – Obsessive–Compulsive Disorder and Obsessive–Compulsive Personality Disorder – has led many to assume that the development of OCD requires a predisposing personality disorder of the same name. Or, argued another way, that OCPD is simply a milder form of OCD. Even intuitively this seems right since those with OCPD tend to be orderly, excessively organized, overly conscientious, and perfectionistic. They are also less prone than healthier individuals to let reward or pleasure guide their behaviour. These are all features that we see in a more exaggerated way in OCD. Therefore, it is rather surprising to find less overlap between the two disorders than one might imagine. For instance, in studies of patients with OCD, the reported prevalence of OCPD has ranged from as low as 4 per cent to approximately 50 per cent, suggesting that the two disorders are rather independent mental health problems that share some overlap but are not related in most cases (see Diaferia *et al.*, 1997).

However, before jumping to such a conclusion we should consider some factors that may artificially reduce the comorbidity of the two disorders. First, and as we have said before, OCD is such a debilitating condition that the reliable assessment of basic personality factors is extremely difficult and confounded by its clinical features. Second, if OCPD traits are not obviously present in a patient with OCD, we should not infer that these traits were unimportant in the development of OCD. We say this because at the extreme of some dimensions, a sort of 'chaos' ensues rather than an orderly progression of the underlying characteristic. This distinction may be made clearer by considering a physical analogy. Friction, such as that created by rubbing one stick against another, causes an increase in heat as the process continues. Eventually, a chemical reaction takes place and combustion occurs. The extreme heat becomes a spark of fire! However, the fire on its own gives no hint that it was the friction of two sticks rubbing together that gave rise to it. Similarly, there may be a qualitative difference rather than a quantitative difference in the clinical picture (such as we see in OCD) when the OCPD traits become very extreme (recall a discussion of this point in Chapter 2).

A final consideration is that the traits which describe OCPD may only be a precursor to certain types of OCD and not to others. For example, it may be that OCPD traits give rise to compulsions about symmetry and ordering, and/or to contamination and cleaning symptoms but not to the other forms of the disorder, such as compulsive hoarding. Since none of the comorbidity studies have examined OCD subtypes, instead treating the disorder as a uniform entity, this could obscure and underestimate the role of certain personality traits in the development of OCD. When we take all these possibilities into account, a more balanced view on the relationship between OCD and OCPD would be that although anancastic personality traits (or disorder) are not necessary or sufficient for the development of OCD, individuals with these traits are probably more prone to develop at least some forms of the disorder.

The dimensional approach to the study of personality and OCD does not really eliminate the methodological problems that we have already discussed. It may, however, make them easier to identify. Studies that have operated within this framework have identified a number of traits which seem to increase the likelihood of developing obsessional thinking. These include having an overdeveloped sense of responsibility, very high moral standards,

and striving for moral perfection (like Walter in the case study described earlier). Indeed, early, as well as contemporary, theories of OCD have assigned *perfectionism* a central role in the development of this disorder, even though there is no evidence of excessive perfectionism in OCD compared to many other psychiatric conditions, such as depression and anxiety disorders (Blatt, 1995). It seems, therefore, that perfectionism predisposes to many forms of psychopathology, but does not necessarily determine the precise form the disorder takes.

Other clinical studies have used broader dimensional constructs to assess personality, such as the self-report questionnaires developed by Cloninger (and described in detail in Chapter 3) to characterize the stereotypic patient with OCD. The data are consistent in describing a patient who tends to be high in harm avoidance and persistence, and low in reward dependence and novelty seeking – a profile that chimes well with the clinical features of this disorder.

The aetiological role of trait anxiety in OCD has fuelled much debate, and many have argued vociferously that anxiety does not have the primary predisposing role that it does in many forms of psychopathology (see Hoehn-Saric & Greenberg, 1997). There is no doubt that OCD patients have high scores on self-reported measures of anxiety, but it could be – and some physiological data support this idea – that the anxiety observed in OCD is a *state* characteristic consequent on the debilitating symptoms, rather than a *trait* which causes obsessional thoughts and compulsive behaviours. Others, however, believe that anxiety both contributes to, and exacerbates, the obsessional symptoms of OCD. For example, anxiety and the tendency to avoid harm is likely to foster a hypervigilance for threat and a bias toward the encoding of threatening stimuli which, in turn, will leave the individual in a state of persistent anxiety. Negative or depressed mood is also regarded as an important trigger to the onset of obsessive–compulsive problems because it seems to sensitize an individual's responsiveness to intrusive thoughts. Here it is worth noting that OCD patients are highly prone to comorbid depression.

Studies of healthy men and women have also examined relationships among personality, mood, and obsessive–compulsive symptoms (Wade *et al.*, 1998). In general, these have found that non-clinical obsessions and compulsions, such as antisocial urges, cleaning, and checking, are more likely to occur in those who are anxious, perfectionistic, morally principled, and depressive – evidence that converges with what we have learned from clinical research. These non-clinical findings have an important place in aetiological research since the study paradigm removes the symptom-severity that confounds clinical research.

Although biological and cognitive models of OCD each offer important insights into the pathogenesis of this debilitating disorder, on its own neither is sufficiently comprehensive to explain the heterogeneous aetiology, the varied clinical features, and the complex pathophysiology of OCD. Instead, what is needed are explanatory models in which neurochemical, anatomical, and cognitive factors are all fully integrated.

## OBSESSIVE–COMPULSIVE SPECTRUM DISORDERS

In recent years, there has been a growing trend to expand the boundaries of OCD classification – using the label Obsessive–Compulsive Spectrum Disorders (OCSD) – and to include a broad range of Axis I and Axis II disorders which are connected to OCD by virtue of loosely associated similarities in symptomatology, family history, neurobiology, comorbidity, clinical course, and treatment outcome. Among the plethora of syndromes included in the spectrum are those as diverse as somatoform disorders, tic disorders, epilepsy, autism, pathological gambling, borderline personality disorder, and the eating disorders (see Hollander & Wong, 1995 for a more comprehensive list). A common thread that seems to unite all these conditions is that each involves the difficulty, or the inability, to delay or inhibit repetitive behaviours. And, the principal reason investigators cohere these seemingly disparate syndromes is their collective responsiveness to the SRI drugs. However, owing to the obvious diversity among the spectrum disorders, a number of subgroups or clusters have been described within the broader category. These include the bodily appearance disorders, the impulse-control disorders, and the neurological disorders.

Whether this new classification represents a theoretical model with useful implications for improved treatment, or whether it simply obscures by overinclusion and simplification, has been disputed by those working in the field. Therefore, and in an effort to remain objective, we will try and give a balanced view of both positions in the remainder of this chapter. Eric Hollander, a leading proponent of the OCSD classification, has presented an interesting dimensional model of the spectrum disorders, proposing that they are appropriately conceptualized along a continuum of *orientation to risk*, with the compulsive disorders such as OCD, body dysmorphic disorder and anorexia nervosa, at the 'risk-avoidance' end of the continuum, and impulsive disorders such as borderline and antisocial personality disorders at the 'risk-taking' end. Psychologically, the two ends of the continuum are distinguished by differences in the motivation that drives the behaviours. In the case of *compulsivity*, the ritualized behaviours are carried out to reduce anxiety and discomfort, whereas the behaviours associated with *impulsivity* are seen to maximize pleasure and arousal. Hollander (1996) also described this spectrum within a conceptual biological framework, emphasizing the role of serotonergic dysfunction in all the disorders, though in different ways along the continuum – compulsivity being characterized by brain *hyper*frontality and increased 5-HT sensitivity, and impulsivity by *hypo*frontality and low pre-synaptic 5-HT levels. Of interest, and rather puzzling however, is that some people seem to have both impulsive and compulsive features simultaneously,

128

or at different times during the course of the same disorder.

Recent research suggests that a core feature of this risk-taking dimension is the varying ability to make good decisions, or to delay gratification, if doing so results in a better long-term outcome. The impulsive or high end of the dimension reflects a diminished capacity to do so, and the compulsive end of the spectrum displays a heightened tendency to inhibit reward. To illustrate, rats with a lesion in the core of the nucleus accumbens, a key brain area in the experience of pleasure and reward – and a topic that will be discussed in more detail in Chapter 7, on addiction – consistently chose small or poor rewards that were immediately available in preference to larger delayed rewards (Cardinal *et al.*, 2001). Similar findings have been observed in the human condition where those with bilateral ventromedial prefrontal lesions made choices on a gambling task that gave high immediate gains, but led to high future losses (Hollander & Evers, 2001).

While there is clearly some argument for viewing OCSD as a valid diagnostic entity – and there are many who do – other investigators have made the point that the commonalities among the disorders that comprise OCSD are more superficial than real, and that the differences between, say, OCD patients and patients with antisocial personality disorder, are substantially greater than their similarities (Rasmussen, 1994; Crino, 1999). Critics also point out that these disorders vary greatly in the cognitive component of their symptoms as well as the individual's motives for engaging in the behaviours. Questions too have been raised about the appropriateness of grouping disorders simply on the basis of similar drug treatment outcomes; in this case, good response to the SRI drugs. To illustrate this point, Rasmussen (1994) used the analogy of corticosteroids which are used to treat a variety of medical conditions that affect multiple organ systems. Yet no one, he argues, would think of linking, in a diagnostic way, all the diseases that are successfully treated with such drugs.

However, what we should really ask is whether there is anything to be gained from invoking the OCSD label, either in clinical practice or in terms of research. Moreover, and apart from the question of utility, the OCSD label itself is something of a misnomer and may serve to confuse and mislead. As Rasmussen (1994) reminds us, many of the so-called OCSDs have features that are quite unrelated, indeed almost opposite, to OCD. Furthermore, as we have seen throughout this chapter, OCD itself is a vastly heterogeneous illness or set of illnesses.

In this, and the previous two chapters, we have considered Axis I and Axis II disorders whose symptomatology has an intuitive and recognizable continuity with the personality and temperamental traits that – at least partly – give rise to them. In the next two chapters we will discuss two other disorders (addiction and the eating disorders) that display more complex, dynamic, and progressive patterns of behaviour. These are also disorders where volitional control is perhaps more salient than in other conditions, and where there seems to be a stronger aetiological role for social factors. It could also be argued that these disorders are primarily behavioural strategies – albeit maladaptive in their outcome – to cope with the psychological distress caused by the personality and other disorders described in chapters 4, 5 and 6. Therefore, one way to conceptualize the role of personality in addictive behaviours (Chapter 7) and the eating disorders (Chapter 8) is as a distal rather than proximal cause in their respective aetiologies.

# CHAPTER 7

## ADDICTIVE BEHAVIOURS

## INTRODUCTION

Even centuries ago people wrote about the enslaving properties of both opium and alcohol, so in a sense the *concept* of addiction has really existed for many years. Rather surprisingly, however, the use of these drugs did not seem to carry any moral condemnation, nor did an awareness of their non-medical effects have any real social or political significance until the 1800s, although the public generally recognized the potential of withdrawal symptoms and the risk of toxicity when these substances were taken in large doses. For example, before 1868, when the Pharmacy Act was passed in Great Britain, opium was readily available over the counter in any kind of shop (Berridge, 1997). However, these liberal ideas changed quite markedly during the Victorian era. By the end of the nineteenth century, both in Great Britain and the United States, heavy use of opium and alcohol was labelled *inebriation*, and this condition began to carry with it the stigma of moral corruption – even mental illness. We can probably say, therefore, that addiction, as a tangible construct, really emerged with the nineteenth century notion of inebriety since formal government legislation and drug policy followed soon afterwards. Nevertheless, for most of the twentieth century the issue of addiction and dependence was still largely restricted to alcohol and the opiates. Although certain other recreational substances became illegal during this period – for example, cocaine was banned in the United States in 1914 – this happened mainly because of evidence that cocaine could produce serious medical complications (Dackis & Gold, 1985). Marijuana was similarly criminalized in the United States in the 1930s. Again, this was not because of an association with addiction, but rather because of research linking it to violence and other socially deviant behaviours – a reaction that many believe was spawned by

131

public resentment of the influx of Mexican immigrants during the depression, and their recreational use of the marijuana leaf.

It was not until the post-World War II rise in psychiatry, and the 'rediscovery of addiction' (Berridge, 1997), that substances other than alcohol and the opiates were more formally added to the list of addictive drugs. Surprisingly, nicotine was remarkably slow to join and be fully integrated within the addiction model. In fact, public concern about smoking did not develop because of any real association with dependence, but rather because accumulating epidemiological evidence linked it to lung cancer. And, some have argued that it was not until the 1980s, and the advent of nicotine replacement therapy, that smoking-cessation difficulties really meant, unequivocally, nicotine addiction.

The field of addiction has been dominated for many years by the view that *psychomotor stimulant* drugs (see below) are at the heart of all addictive behaviours – indeed, so much so that the phrase 'drug dependence' has become almost synonymous with the term addiction.

---

### Psychomotor stimulant drugs

Psychomotor stimulant drugs are different from the general central nervous system (CNS) stimulants, such as caffeine, in that their action is more localized and evokes a particular set of psychological responses. In humans, and at moderate doses, these drugs tend to increase physical arousal and to improve cognitive performance on tasks related to reaction time, vigilance, and stamina. In animals, they increase locomotion at moderate doses, but at high doses animals display 'stereotypic' behaviour which is an exaggerated form of behaviours that are part of their natural repertoire. For example, laboratory rats will engage in excessive grooming behaviours or exaggerated exploratory rituals.

It is now commonly believed that it is the psychomotor stimulant property of a substance (or activity) that determines whether it is potentially addictive. The most commonly used psychomotor stimulants are crack/cocaine and amphetamines. However, even drugs which are mostly known for their CNS depressant effects, such as alcohol and the opiates (morphine and heroin), have psychomotor stimulant properties, and evidence suggests this is principally what makes them so addictive. At high doses, the sedating effects of the CNS depressants are the most pronounced. Interestingly, however, tolerance develops more quickly to their sedative effects than to their psychomotor stimulant effects. Alcohol is a good example. People who drink alcohol regularly often experience an enlivening effect from the first few drinks, rather than any feelings of sleepiness.

---

However, in recent years there has been an obvious paradigm shift, and many now believe that addiction extends beyond the use of conventional substances – those that can be injected, ingested or inhaled, such as heroin, amphetamine and marijuana – and includes certain compulsive *activities* such as gambling, internet use, and shopping (Griffiths, 2001; Orford, 2001).

Others have also argued that even natural rewards like eating and sex can be just as addictive as pharmacologic agents (Holden, 2001). Therefore, and in our discussions about addiction in the remainder of this chapter, we will adopt the perspective that addiction is not just about drug-taking, but rather that it comprises any behaviour that has the potential to become excessive, and that satisfies the set of commonly agreed criteria for addiction. Nevertheless, by adopting this broader viewpoint, we risk another difficulty – that of knowing where to draw the line between those behaviours that *often* cause addiction, and those that *seldom* do. For example, some have argued that it is possible to become addicted to work and to television – even to various forms of exercise, such as rock climbing (McIlwraith, 1998; Burke, 2000)! Although that may be true at one level, it is also clear that these activities do not share the same qualities as the core addictions, such as drug-taking, alcohol consumption, smoking, and gambling, both in terms of their reinforcing properties and in the strength of their addictive potential (see Orford, 2001).

## CLINICAL FEATURES

Although the experts have not reached complete consensus on the defining characteristics of addiction – nor on how they should be ordered by importance – at least most agree there are certain factors that should be included. Foremost is their progressively *compulsive* nature, even in the face of adverse consequences to health, safety, and social relations (Berridge & Robinson, 1995). In other words, to the serious detriment of conventional daily pursuits, such as looking after the needs of one's family, functioning well at one's job, and attending to normal social obligations, the addict spends more and more time carrying out the behaviour or seeking opportunities to do so. Nor is the addict deterred by the knowledge that the behaviour can cause serious medical problems, for example in the case of smoking.

*Tolerance* is also a defining characteristic of addiction and describes the experiential changes that occur as a result of chronic overindulgence. With continual and frequent exposure, the individual typically requires more of the behaviour to produce the same pleasurable or reinforcing effects. For instance, cocaine addicts repeatedly explain that they are never able to achieve the extremely euphoric feeling that came with the first few 'hits' of the drug. Tolerance effects have also been demonstrated in drug-administration experiments with animals. Initially, and at moderate doses, addictive drugs cause the animal to increase its locomotion. However, after repeated exposure to the drug, the animal no longer responds with the same degree of heightened activity.

In the early theories of addiction, and for many years to follow, *withdrawal* was seen as its core and quintessential feature; indeed, fundamentally necessary for its diagnosis. At that time, withdrawal had a very precise meaning and was inextricably linked to *physical* dependence and the symptoms of illness. Only

133

if cessation of the behaviour resulted in severe bodily discomfort was the substance thought to be 'addictive' and the person experiencing these symptoms, 'dependent'. However, among all the drugs that are now commonly abused, severe physical withdrawal symptoms only occur with the chronic and excessive use of alcohol and opium (and its derivatives, heroin and morphine). This fact probably accounts, at least in part, for the early belief that these were the only truly addictive substances.

Viewpoints about withdrawal changed quite dramatically in the 1980s when Western countries experienced the widespread and illicit use of cocaine and 'crack' – the latter being an affordable and arguably more addictive form of the powder. Currently, a vial of crack sufficient to produce an intense euphoria costs about $5 in most American cities, making it easily available to all members of our society, including adolescents. We now know that crack/cocaine are amongst the most potent and reinforcing of the euphoriant drugs, and yet abstinence, even after heavy and long-term use, is not associated with any very pronounced physical withdrawal symptoms. This fact has forced researchers and clinicians to rethink the central and prominent role that *physical* withdrawal has played historically in definitions of addiction. And when nicotine eventually joined the ranks of addictive substances, the evidence *against* the centrality of withdrawal was overwhelming since two of the most addictive substances in common use are virtually devoid of withdrawal symptoms, in the conventional physical sense. At this point, the World Health Organization declared that withdrawal was 'neither necessary nor sufficient' for a diagnosis of addiction.

However, in recent years, views on withdrawal have changed again, moving beyond a simple focus on physical effects, to include unpleasant feeling or emotional states. In other words, there has been a shift away from *physical dependence*, towards an emphasis on *motivational dependence* and the importance of withdrawal-induced dysphoria as powerful incentives for the continuation of addictive behaviours (Di Chiara, 1999). It is now abundantly clear that a pleasureless state and blunted affect – a condition similar to the *anhedonic* state that defines melancholy (see Chapter 5) – occurs when any addictive behaviour is discontinued, or its 'dose' is suddenly reduced. Anhedonic effects have also been seen in animals' behaviour after chronic drug exposure. Numerous studies have shown that if animals are allowed to self-administer large and intoxicating doses of any addictive drug over long periods of time, their threshold for natural reinforcers is elevated. For example, compared to baseline levels the animal will 'work' (for example, press a lever or run through a maze) for food, water, or access to a mate, at a significantly reduced rate after the drug administration. Clearly, the drugs have perturbed the animal's system in such a way that it is no longer as motivated to engage in previously rewarding activities. Later in this chapter we will explain more about the neurophysiological changes that cause this effect.

It seems, however, that the experience of withdrawal, either in its physical or psychological form, is probably not the greatest impediment to successful treatment for addiction, no matter how intense the symptoms may be. A more potent influence is the very strong *urges* that the addict experiences to continue or resume the behaviour. This 'craving' for the behaviour is often experienced as overpowering, and can persist even after a long period of abstinence. Indeed, according to the reports of addicts themselves, these cravings account, in large part, for their failure to stay 'clean' after treatment; and why some have suggested that addictions should be called 'chronic relapsing disorders' (Leshner, 1997) – despite the obvious pessimism that such a term conveys. What also makes relapse so difficult to overcome is that the cravings and feeling of 'loss of control' may be elicited by so many diverse factors. For example, external cues or triggers, such as a stressful situation, as well as internal factors, such as negative mood states, can give rise to cravings (el-Guebaly & Hodgins, 1998).

However, the most difficult to manage – because of their ubiquity and their relative uncontrollability – are the classically conditioned environmental cues. Objects or events which were repeatedly paired with the behaviour during the time the addiction was developing begin to function with the same strength, and in the same consistent way, as Pavlov's bell did to his salivating dogs (see Chapter 5). Their power is that they *signal* the approach of the rewarding event – food for Pavlov's dogs; drugs for the addict. For example, the environmental context in which the behaviour typically occurred – the neighbourhood bar for the alcoholic, the street where the drugs were obtained for the heroin addict, the tea break for the smoker – becomes the conditioned stimulus, and therefore has the ability to evoke the same intense cravings as those fostered by the addictive behaviour itself. In a series of elegant experiments, Childress and colleagues (1999) demonstrated the strong physiological effects of cue-induced craving. By use of positron emission tomography (PET) and measuring regional blood flow, these workers found that certain areas of the brain were activated to a very high level among cocaine abusers simply by showing them videotaped scenes of cocaine paraphernalia. More details about the specific brain regions that are activated will be discussed in detail in the next section of this chapter.

135

These and other similar studies have demonstrated the strong motivational properties that conditioned cues can have in pulling the addict towards the destructive use of their addictive behaviour. Cue-induced craving may also explain why relapse is less likely to occur during periods of detoxification, when addicts are usually in an institutional setting, than after they are rehabilitated and have returned to their familiar home environment. Even though the withdrawal symptoms may be the most severe during the detox period, the addicts are effectively removed from most of the conditioned environmental cues which tend to elicit potent cravings.

A glimpse at the current 'hot' topics in addiction research shows a clear bias favouring the view that addiction is a 'brain disease' (Leshner & Koob, 1999). There are probably many reasons for this emphasis, but one of the most important is the recent development of sophisticated brain-imaging techniques. Researchers now have an unprecedented opportunity to examine human brain-functioning in synchrony with subjective experiential reporting – a methodology that provides a clearer window than ever before into the brain–behaviour–motivation synthesis underlying addictions. Notwithstanding the apparent enthusiasm for a 'disease model' of addiction, most experts readily acknowledge that a multitude of other events influence the taking, and abusing, of addictive behaviours. These include factors such as availability, cost, peer pressure, and social tolerance. Therefore, any balanced and comprehensive view of addiction must take account of a combination of environmental factors, biological vulnerabilities, and a psychologically susceptible disposition. Leshner (1999) articulated this viewpoint by calling addiction 'a quintessentially biobehavioural disorder'. It occurs not only because of prolonged exposure effects on brain structure and function, but it also involves critical behavioural and social-context components.

But we also want to emphasize that addiction is not a condition that is passively conferred upon us; it does not suddenly overcome us like a major depressive episode or a panic attack might – without us taking any conscious or overt part in its development. Nor is it simply due to the concatenation of various risk factors that reflect our past history or our biological make-up. What makes addiction different from other psychological disturbances (except the eating disorders which we discuss in the next chapter) is that the individual is an *active* participant in the process. No one will ever become an alcoholic unless they take the first drink, nor a compulsive gambler if they never place a bet. And, addiction is a process that takes time to develop. With some substances, such as crack/cocaine, this can happen fairly rapidly. For others, such as cigarettes and alcohol, it generally happens over a period of years. In the following sections, we will briefly describe the brain mechanisms underlying addiction, including the acute and long-term effects of addictive behaviours on the structure and the function of brain biology.

## THE NEUROBIOLOGY OF ADDICTION

Some have used the term 'hijacked' to describe the effect of addictive substances on normal brain functioning. Although this may sound like a rather dramatic turn of phrase, its appropriateness stems from the fact that cocaine and other drugs – indeed, all potentially addictive behaviours – activate and can subvert areas of our brain which evolved to regulate and sustain the most basic aspects of our existence. In other words, the same brain circuitry which subserves feeding, sex, and other essential survival behaviours, also underlies the development and maintenance of substance abuse. And, because these non-natural behaviours 'trick' the brain into thinking that a survival need has been met, it is not surprising that addicts typically have a diminished sexual libido and appetite for food.

The *mesocorticolimbic dopamine pathway* is involved in the pleasure and reinforcement associated with natural reward states, such as eating, drinking, mating, and maternal behaviour, as well as with less basic needs, such as social interaction and novelty. As illustration, activation of the dopamine pathway was clearly seen in response to a palatable food in a recent brain-imaging study. When subjects ate a piece of chocolate and rated the experience as 'pleasurable', there was increased regional blood flow in the striatum (Small *et al.*, 2001). Moreover, when subjects felt highly motivated to eat more chocolate, the same brain regions (viz. the caudomedial orbitofrontal cortex) were active as those implicated in the experience of drug cravings. As an aside, it is interesting to note that chocolate has been identified as the single most craved food in studies of food preferences.

In another interesting study, investigators found that when men were exposed to pictures of female faces and asked to give preference ratings, only the 'attractive' female faces activated the brain's reward circuitry, not the faces which had been rated as 'neutral'. The men also took longer to rate the attractive faces, inferring that they looked at them longer because it was a more pleasurable experience. By contrast, when attractive male faces were shown to these men, they produced what could be considered an aversive reaction (Aharon *et al.*, 2001). How does one explain that? Evolutionary psychologists would probably say that the male aversion to other attractive males occurs because the latter represent a threat in the competition for accessible females.

Neuroimaging techniques have contributed greatly to our understanding of the biology of addiction. However, this is a relatively recent technology, and before we had regular access to these procedures, we relied mostly on what we could glean from animal research, making inferences about the rewarding properties of drugs from the way the animals behaved. Researchers have demonstrated repeatedly that cocaine, heroin, and a host of other addictive drugs are readily self-administered by several species of experimental animals (for example, laboratory rats or monkeys). There is also such a positive and strong relationship between the human abuse potential of a particular drug and the degree to which animals will self-administer the substance, that this experimental paradigm continues to serve as an excellent tool for our exploration of the neurobiology of drug reinforcement (Withers *et al.*, 1995). One disadvantage of this experimental approach, however, is that the animals cannot tell us anything about how they 'feel' when they take drugs!

Another sort of animal model – the 'knock-out' mouse (see Chapter 5) – has also proved useful in studying the role of dopamine in the reinforcing and addictive properties of drugs of abuse. For example, one strain of mice has been

137

genetically modified to lack the dopamine transporter (DAT), a membrane-bound protein found on the terminals of mesolimbic neurons, and whose role is to remove extracellular dopamine and carry it back into the cell body for reuse. Not surprisingly, these knock-out mice (DAT-KO) demonstrate the marked hyperactivity we would expect in the case of hyperdopaminergic tone, showing a 300-fold increase in the amount of time that dopamine spends in the extracellular space of their brains, compared to wild-type mice (Gainetdinov *et al.*, 1999). Also, when a dose of cocaine was given to DAT-KO mice it produced no further increase in their locomotion, as we would expect. It is interesting, however, that cocaine still maintains its rewarding properties in these mice – a fact that seems rather counterintuitive since we know conclusively that cocaine produces its euphoric effects by binding to the DAT and rapidly increasing synaptic mesolimbic dopamine availability. Part of the explanation relates to another neurotransmitter, *glutamate*, which activates brain cells devoted to dopamine, and is also involved in memory. Support for this notion comes from another strain of knock-out mice who lack a particular glutamate receptor, and who do not become dependent on cocaine, no matter how much they take. And the action of this glutamate receptor seems to be very specific to drugs like cocaine since the glutamate knock-out mice are just as motivated to approach natural rewards, such as food and water, as any other mice.

Although several anatomical structures and neuronal projections comprise the mesocorticolimbic dopamine system, and are implicated in the biology of natural and pharmacologic reward, the function of four of these regions is most clearly understood. The *ventral tegmentum* is an area in the midbrain, rich in dopamine neurons, which sends projections through the medial forebrain bundle to a set of limbic brain regions, including the nucleus accumbens and amygdala, and to the prefrontal cortex. Together these, and related structures, are known as the 'common reward pathway' because their activation or stimulation is experienced as pleasurable and reinforcing. In fact, if animals are given unimpeded access to self-stimulation of this circuit (via an electrode implanted in the brain which sends an electric current whenever the animal presses a lever), they will lever-press excessively and to the point of death from self-starvation.

Whereas several areas of the brain are associated with the subjective feelings of pleasure – or the euphoric 'rush' one gets from drugs like cocaine – increased dopamine transmission in the *nucleus accumbens* seems to play the most central role in mediating reinforcement. Indeed, the nucleus accumbens has been called the 'Universal Addiction Site' (Leshner & Koob, 1999) because most, if not all, drugs (or activities) of abuse stimulate extracellular dopamine in this area, albeit through interactions with different proteins and receptors (Gamberino & Gold, 1999). Some have also described the nucleus accumbens as a limbic–motor interface because increased dopamine release in this area

seems to have a pivotal role in providing certain stimuli with the incentive qualities needed to increase appetitive behaviour. The neurobiological mechanisms by which drugs increase extracellular dopamine in the reward pathway are considerably varied. Some, like amphetamine, stimulate the synthesis and release of dopamine from the cell body, others inhibit intra- and extracellular metabolism, and drugs like cocaine block the synaptic clearance of dopamine via the dopamine transporter (reuptake pump).

Interestingly, burst firing activity of the dopamine reward neurons has been observed with great consistency not only during the *consummatory* phase of rewarding activities but also well before the consumption begins. This strongly suggests that the common reward pathway is also involved in *associative learning*; that is, in establishing the conditioned reinforcement of environmental cues that signal the approach or the onset of the natural reward state. From an evolutionary perspective, this is clearly a very adaptive function since the organism will fare much better if it is able to discriminate between stimuli that predict when a rewarding event is likely to happen, and those that do not. A relatively large body of research supports the role of the *amygdala* in this process because it maintains a representation of the affective or emotional value of the conditioned stimulus (Jentsch & Taylor, 1999). One type of supporting evidence comes from studies of second-order schedules of reinforcement where it has been observed that experimental animals continue to respond to the presentation of a stimulus (the CS) that has been paired with a primary reward. We also know that the strength of conditioned reinforcement is greatly enhanced when the CS is paired with pharmacologic reward, such as cocaine, instead of a natural reward, such as food. However, when the amygdala is lesioned, animals show a clear and progressive impairment of responding under these second-order schedules of reinforcement (see Parkinson *et al.*, 2001). As we saw in Chapter 5, the amygdala operates as strongly for aversive and fear-provoking stimuli as for rewarding stimuli.

A final aspect of the functional neurobiology of addiction involves the *prefrontal cortex*. This area is thought to serve an 'executive' function in the brain by acting as a gating mechanism to moderate the suppression of limbic impulses. One method that scientists have used to study this area of the brain is to lesion or block its function pharmacologically with antagonist drugs. Another is to examine the behaviour of patients who have suffered frontal lobe damage. In studies where the function of the prefrontal cortex has been disrupted in one way or another, we see the person's inability to suppress inappropriate responses – in other words, a diminution in the ability to self-regulate one's behaviour and a frank loss of inhibitory control. In these cases, the individual's behaviour seems to be largely guided by previously conditioned responses which are not suited to the current situation (Jentsch & Taylor, 1999).

139

In recent years, the role of the prefrontal cortex has gained increasing prominence in our understanding of the addiction process; especially in our increasing awareness of its function in *decision-making* and in controlling behaviour that entails the risk of punishment (Bechara *et al.*, 2001). Currently, the evidence points to the fact that specific regions of the prefrontal cortex are responsible for regulating behaviour – specifically, for inhibiting the drive to respond to immediate reinforcement if the long-term consequences are likely to result in some negative outcome. Some have suggested that impairments in the capability of making good decisions stand at the core of addictive behaviours (for example, Grant *et al.*, 2000). In other words, addicts tend to choose immediate rewards even if they result in long-term negative consequences. However, what is not entirely clear is whether this impairment is a consequence of drug-taking and overactivation of the reward circuitry, or whether there is a premorbid tendency or handicap in the adaptive functioning of the frontal cortex that increases the risk for addiction. More on this will be discussed in a later section of this chapter.

## CHRONIC USE OF ADDICTIVE BEHAVIOURS

When the brain is activated excessively, and chronically moved beyond its natural or homeostatic state, neurochemical changes or alterations begin to occur. What is insidious about the overuse of addictive activities or substances, however, is that they change the brain in ways that contribute to further seeking and further use – a process that, over time, creates a vicious downwardly spiralling cycle of behaviours that are difficult to resist and highly prone to relapse if abstinence is attempted. Although the neuroadaptive responses that occur are complex, and vary from one substance (or activity) to another, there are some general adaptations that are common to all addictive behaviours. Paradoxically, the two most pronounced changes operate in virtually opposite directions – *desensitization*, on the one hand, and *sensitization* on the other.

Earlier in this chapter we discussed the phenomenon of *tolerance* and the fact that after prolonged and intense exposure to an addictive behaviour, more of it is required to produce the same subjective effect; that is, the same feelings of pleasure or reward. *Desensitization* is the neural mechanism underlying this aspect of addiction. When there are prolonged and repeated elevations of extracellular dopamine (hyperdopaminergia), the brain attempts to compensate for the excessive stimulation by changing its function in some way. We now have a pretty clear idea that long-lasting alterations take place at the *post-synaptic* level where a downregulation or reduced sensitivity of the dopamine receptors occurs. When trying to understand how this happens, it may be helpful to use a rather 'domestic' metaphor. Think of a house with a lot of open windows and suddenly the temperature outside drops and becomes very cold. The occupants cannot change the climate; all they can do to restore

140

a comfortable and normal temperature in the house is to close some of the windows. That seems to be the strategy our brain adopts when it becomes chronically overstimulated. Regrettably, one of the behavioural consequences of this neuroadaptation is that it seems to foster a desire for more extensive drug-taking since the individual needs to take larger and and/or more frequent doses to achieve the initial or desired effect of the behaviour. Recent evidence suggests that downregulation also functions at the level of the prefrontal cortex, and that reduced activity in this area (hypofrontality) underlies the difficulty that addicts have in resisting impulses to use their drug. In other words, the executive function of the prefrontal cortex is compromised.

Researchers have studied the neurobiology of desensitization in a variety of ways. Some have examined the cadaver brains of former drug addicts and found a reduced density of dopamine receptors compared to normal cadaver brains. However, a problem with this type of research is the question of causality. Did the drug addiction cause the reduced receptor densities (via downregulation), or were the addicts' brains like this before the addiction? And if so, did this factor contribute in some way to their addiction? Less confounded research has come from studies with animals. In one PET-imaging study with non-human primates, there was an observable downregulation of dopamine $D_2$ receptor density after animals had been chronically exposed to amphethamine stimulation (Ginovart et al., 1999).

*Sensitization* also plays a significant role in supporting addictive behaviours. Repeated but intermittent exposure to psychomotor stimulant drugs seems to produce heightened or increased behavioural and neurochemical responses to subsequent drug exposure. In animals, one way this can be seen is by increases in their activity levels – a behavioural marker of enhanced arousal or activation to the drug. Sensitization also appears to function at the level of stimulus-reward or associative learning. After an addictive substance has been used many times, we see an enhancement of its incentive value and that of its conditioned stimuli. The 'fatal flaw' of this neuroadaptation is that the addict's behaviour becomes more and more under the control of these conditioned reinforcers. Sensitization also controls behaviour because over time it increases the attention-getting properties of conditioned cues that reliably predict reward. In other words, addictive behaviours seem to enhance the attentional bias to stimuli that are associated with the addictive behaviour, thereby contributing to its increasingly compulsive use.

## VULNERABILITY TO ADDICTION

From an historical perspective, the emphasis on personality and personality pathology in the development of addictive behaviours has fluctuated considerably. In early theories, during the first half of the twentieth century, a disordered or maladjusted personality was believed to be the root cause of all addictions. However, by the 1970s, this perspective was mostly abandoned because a large body of research had failed to find one consistent *pre-addictive* personality (Verheul & van den Brink, 2000). In recent years, the tide has turned again, and personality pathology has now regained its prominence in the addiction risk profile. Presently, the most prominent aetiological viewpoint is that of a *stress-diathesis* model whereby addictions develop from a reciprocal interaction between the psychological and biological vulnerability of the individual, and their environmental circumstances. Even the most extreme environmentalists in psychology have been forced to acknowledge that genes contribute to individual differences in behaviour. However, behavioural traits are highly complex and therefore rarely affected by a single gene. Indeed, they have been characterized as polygenic, meaning that any given gene is likely to contribute only a small portion to the phenotypic (behavioural) variance (Crabbe, 2002).

It is now generally agreed that addictive behaviours can begin through two motivational routes: either the seeking of positive sensations, or the self-medicating of painful affective states. Recently, perhaps more researchers have favoured the latter perspective – that a disturbed affect and a difficulty with the regulation of unpleasant emotions are at the heart of most addictive behaviours (Khantzian, 1997; Leshner & Koob, 1999). In the remainder of this chapter we shall review the causal evidence linking certain personality factors to the development of addictions. However, when studying the personality aetiology of this disorder, we need to consider that the traits predicting who might *experiment* with substances (and other addictive behaviours) – even use them on a regular basis – may be quite different from those that influence who will *abuse* these behaviours.

Information about the role of personality in the aetiology of addiction, comes from three primary sources:

- Correlational studies in the general population, examining relationships between personality and use of addictive behaviours, such as drinking, smoking, and illicit drugs.

- The identification of traits that differentiate addicts from healthy individuals.

- Studies that assess the comorbidity between addiction and the personality disorders.

In this last regard, the evidence is somewhat compromised by the ongoing debate about whether, or to what extent, Axis II diagnoses in addicts are merely substance-related artifacts reflecting conditions created by the addiction rather than 'true' personality disorders with onset prior to, and independent of, the addiction (Verheul & van den Brink, 2000).

In current formulations about vulnerability to addiction, three primary causal or developmental pathways have emerged from the search for personality risk factors. The first body of research has focused on a construct we shall call *sensitivity to reward*, the second on *impulsive behaviour* and the third on *proneness to anxiety and negative mood*. Although these have mostly been studied as independent factors, we will see a certain amount of overlap among them, both theoretically and concerning underlying biological mechanisms. Interestingly, these domains of emotional experience are remarkably in step with the personality taxonomies of Eysenck, Gray, Zuckerman, and Cloninger, which were discussed in Chapter 3. By factor analysing the trait scores from all these measures of personality, Zelenski and Larsen (1999) identified three factors which they named 'reward sensitivity', 'impulsivity/thrill-seeking', and 'punishment sensitivity'. In a second phase of the study, these authors found that these three factors predicted different sensitivities to emotional states; reward sensitivity only predicted positive mood (or its absence at low ends of the dimension) and punishment sensitivity only predicted negative mood. Impulsivity/thrill-seeking, on the other hand, seemed to predict few emotions in either context.

In the following sections, we will summarize the findings that have emerged from the personality categories described above, and explain how each relates to the onset and progression of addictive behaviours.

## SENSITIVITY TO REWARD

Meehl (1975) was one of the first to suggest that within the general population the capacity for pleasure or reward exists as a normally distributed and biologically based dimension. Subsequent research has firmly rooted this personality construct in the neurobiology of the mesolimbic dopamine reward system. The sensitivity to reward dimension has also been associated with the *motivation to approach* rewarding stimuli, as well as with the ability to experience reward from engagement in these behaviours. In other words, the simple expectation of reward (usually triggered by some signal of forthcoming reward, such as the smell of cookies baking in the oven) tends to produce a feeling of pleasure and increases motivation to engage in the rewarding behaviour (see Germans & Kring, 2000). In the context of addiction research, we shall see that traits located at both ends of the sensitivity to reward continuum have been implicated in the development of addictions – albeit for different reasons.

143

The term *anhedonia* was coined to describe the low end of the sensitivity to reward dimension. As we learned in Chapter 5, this term refers to the *diminished* ability to experience pleasure and reward from natural reinforcers, and is thought to reflect compromised, hyposensitive, or sluggish dopamine availability. Indeed, neuroscientific research has strongly supported the hypodopaminergic tone underlying anhedonia. For example, Breier *et al.* (1998) found that personal detachment and indifference to other people was associated with reduced density of striatal dopamine $D_2$ receptors and dopamine availability in the brain reward areas. Also, a distinctive personality type characterized by introversion, apathy, and low preference for novelty has been associated with Parkinson's disease – a degenerative condition caused by a diminution of dopamine neurons in the substantia nigra and ventral tegmentum areas of the brain (Slaughter *et al.*, 2001). There is also some animal support for the notion that anhedonic characteristics may be more about an hedonic deficit in approach motivation than an actual deficit in the ability to experience pleasure, although compelling human evidence is tentative at this point (Heinz, 1999).

The high end of the sensitivity to reward continuum describes an enhanced motivation to engage in natural rewards, such as eating, mating, and maternal behaviour. *Novelty* is also a state that both human and non-human animals tend to find rewarding. For example, in place-conditioning experiments, rats chose to spend more time in the environment that had previously been paired with a novel stimulus than in the non-conditioned area. However, recent physiological evidence suggests that the mechanisms of novelty *reward* are rather different from those underlying novelty *seeking* – the former, but not the latter, involving the dopamine system (Bevins *et al.*, 2002). Another finding, highly relevant to the subject of addiction, is that novelty seems to potentiate the reward of other pleasurable stimuli. In one study, it was observed that the striatum was activated more in rats who received a combination of amphetamine and novelty than in control rats who received either a novel stimulus, or a dose of amphetamine on its own (Badiani *et al.*, 1998). But perhaps that should not really surprise, as most of us would agree that food tastes much better in an interesting restaurant when dining with friends than it does when we eat roughly the same thing at home by ourselves.

While there are clearly inherent aspects to the variability in sensitivity to reward, anhedonia may also be induced by environmental and behavioural factors. In this context, Wise (1982) was the first to introduce the term 'anhedonia' to the field of addiction research after it had become clear that activation of mesocorticolimbic dopamine played a central role in animals' responses to a variety of reinforcing stimuli, such as food and water, intracranial self-stimulation, the opiates, and a variety of other psychomotor stimulant drugs; and when it was found that neuroleptic drugs (that is, dopamine receptor antagonists) blocked the positive reinforcement associated with these stimuli. Since then, many other studies have demonstrated that a relatively long-lasting anhedonic state may also be induced by prolonged exposure to psychomotor stimulant drugs (see Gamberino & Gold, 1999) and to chronic mild stress (Zacharko, 1994). We now have a fairly clear idea that state-induced anhedonia is primarily mediated by downregulation of postsynaptic dopamine receptors. Although repeated administration of addictive substances results in synaptic deficits in two brain neurotransmitter systems – dopamine and serotonin – the former seems to underlie the

anhedonia associated withdrawal, whereas the latter is associated with negativity and poor impulse control (Rothman *et al.*, 2000).

As we said earlier, there is accumulating evidence that individual differences in sensitivity to reward are related to susceptibility to addiction, with risk being conferred from both ends of the continuum. We shall begin first by citing some evidence related to the low end of the continuum. We know, for instance, that a strain of alcohol-preferring rats has lower levels of dopamine concentration in the nucleus accumbens compared to non-preferring rats (see Cloninger, 1987 for a review). Also, genes of the dopamine system have been studied as candidates for risk. For example, certain forms of the dopamine transporter (DAT1) gene (viz. the 9-repeat allele and rare shorter alleles) are considered 'low risk alleles' for addiction because functionally they are associated with a less efficient DAT and therefore greater availability of extracellular dopamine. On the other hand, the 10-repeat (and rarer longer alleles) are considered 'high risk alleles' for the opposite reason – a more efficient DAT and therefore less dopamine availability (Rowe *et al.*, 1998; Waldman *et al.*, 1998). In addition, a form of the dopamine $D_2$ receptor gene (the A1 allele) has been associated with reduced density of dopamine receptors, and those with this genotype (compared to the A2 allele which has been associated with increased receptor density) are more likely to exhibit compulsive and addictive behaviours, such as alcoholism (Noble *et al.*, 1991). In an interesting and relevant study of gene–gene interactions, a 50 per cent reduction in smoking risk was found for those with the 9-repeat DAT1 gene and the dopamine $D_2$–A2 gene (Lerman *et al.*, 1999). This pronounced effect was attributed to the combination of greater availability of synaptic dopamine, and higher functioning of the dopamine receptors.

Lastly, in an elegant study highlighting the risk potential conferred by specific genes, Volkow and colleagues reported that subjects who experienced the effects of a cocaine-equivalent drug as 'pleasurable' had significantly lower dopamine $D_2$ receptor levels than those who found the effects 'unpleasant', suggesting that potent stimulating drugs may exert their positive subjective effects because they boost a sluggish dopamine system in those less sensitive to reward (Volkow *et al.*, 1999). To explain these findings, Volkow and her colleagues have proposed a particularly intriguing hypothesis related to risk for addiction. They suggest an optimal level, inverted-U, relationship between hedonic tone and dopamine activation where too little or too much of the latter is subjectively aversive (Figure 7.1) For those with high $D_2$ receptor levels (more hedonic individuals), a normal increase in dopamine stimulation – like that found from natural rewards (for example, food and social interaction) – is likely to be perceived as pleasant, whilst a larger increase, such as that created by potent drugs like cocaine, would be experienced as unpleasant (as the study by Volkow *et al.*, 1999, demonstrated). Alternatively, low $D_2$ receptor levels (associated with anhedonia) could predispose to addiction by favouring initial pleasant responses to drugs, and other potent dopamine agonists, as this activation does not take them beyond their optimal level of dopamine activation.

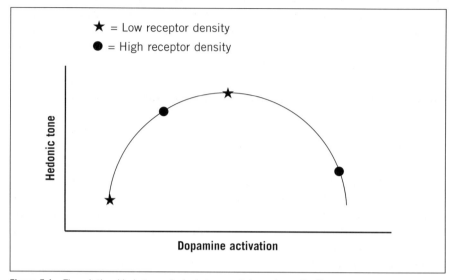

**Figure 7.1**  The relationship between hedonic tone and dopamine activation.

There is good support for the notion that some anhedonic individuals engage in arousing behaviours as a form of compensation for their blunted affect and their inability to experience activation from weak levels of stimulation. For instance, one study found that skydivers were more anhedonic (independent of any depressive episode) than control subjects, suggesting that this highly arousing behaviour may partly serve a mood-enhancing role (Pierson *et al.*, 1999). Anhedonia has also been associated with nicotine dependence, especially among depressed and schizophrenic patients.

It is easy to see that certain people make better decisions than others in their choice of self-regulating behaviours. The factors that move some in the direction of adaptive options, such as exhilarating sports, whereas others turn to drugs are not entirely obvious, but must clearly involve a host of environmental influences like peer pressure, cost, and the opportunity for experimentation. Other personality factors are also likely to be influential. Indeed, epigenetic models propose that temperament traits like sensitivity to reward do not exert direct and invariant effects but, rather, depend on a relationship with other traits, such as self-control. Some have also suggested that temperamental traits may become amplified over time through a 'chain of failures' in the development of self-regulation (Wills *et al.*, 1998).

In the preceding account, we have seen how anhedonic traits may foster addictive behaviours because they serve a compensatory function for blunted

affect and motivation. However, an argument may be made – and the evidence is supportive – that individuals whose personality locates them at the *high* end of the sensitivity to reward continuum are also more likely to engage in addictive behaviours, but for very different reasons. Those high in sensitivity to reward tend to be more motivated to approach, and more easily pleased by, natural rewards, the primer of which is eating. Indeed, research has supported the relationship between eating and sensitivity to reward, as we shall see in the following chapter on eating disorders. From an evolutionary perspective, there is good reason why our genetic legacy has favoured high hedonic reward from eating. In times of famine and seasonal food shortages, an inherent love of eating was clearly adaptive. However, this same capacity has a very obvious disadvantage in environments such as ours where highly palatable and calorically dense food is too readily available. One result of this clash between our environmental and our biology is the staggering percentage of overweight and obese individuals in most Western countries. Current estimates from the UK and North America indicate that more than 50 per cent of the adult population is overweight. Not surprisingly, the emerging viewpoint, as we saw earlier, is that eating can be just as addictive as snorting cocaine or drinking alcohol (Holden, 2001).

There are other characteristics of those high on sensitivity to reward that may contribute to their involvement in addictive behaviours. By definition, hedonic individuals tend to be more extraverted, more sociable, and more attracted by novelty. This is especially relevant because many addictive behaviours occur in social settings, or are likely to be initiated in the presence of other people. Think for a minute about social drinking, the influence of peers on smoking, or the club scene, and illicit drugs like Ecstasy. Even the use of caffeine is an activity we mostly do with others, as seen in such social idioms as the 'coffee break', and the current popularity of the coffee shop as a daytime venue for meeting friends. It is also the case that many addictive behaviours occur in the presence of some novelty, and this is especially true for adolescent experimentation with illicit drugs and sex. For the more sociable and extraverted individuals, the addictive behaviours themselves – the cigarettes, the alcohol, or the casino – may not be the primary appeal. What they may find more rewarding is the social contact and the novel experiences that are so often a part of engaging in these behaviours, especially in the early stages. In other words, for some individuals, addictions may be a secondary effect, developing as a consequence of their location within social events. However, over time, and after repeated exposure, the behaviours themselves take on primary appeal.

## IMPULSIVE BEHAVIOUR

Impulsivity is one of the most elusive personality constructs in the field of addiction research, probably because it has attracted so many definitions and such subtlety of meaning. Some see restlessness and the tendency to be easily distracted as essential elements of impulsivity. Others have described impulsivity as poor tolerance of frustration which drives the individual to act spontaneously, whereas others still have focused on the disinhibition of responding at times when inhibition is the appropriate response in a particular situation. In other words, impulsivity is about poor self-regulation whereby behaviour is predominantly and inappropriately controlled by appetitive stimuli. According to Gray's and Cloninger's theories, impulsivity is a component of both novelty seeking and reward sensitivity. From a more cognitive perspective, some believe that impulsive behaviour is primarily about poor decision-making, exemplified by the tendency to choose small or poor rewards that are immediately available in preference for larger but delayed rewards. And lastly, among those who focus on the seriously disordered end of this trait, impulsivity is often used to describe strong drives or temptations to perform acts that are risky or even harmful to ones self or others. In this context, acts of self-mutilation and aggressive behaviour are subsumed in the DSM category of Impulse-Control Behaviours.

One theory brings together many of these rather loosely connected ideas by proposing that impulsivity is at the low end of a dimension of 'behavioural self-regulation'. Other components of poor behavioural regulation include inattention, hyperactivity, and aggression. It is also interesting to speculate whether intelligence is an independent factor, or whether it plays a role in determining where any given individual falls along this continuum since we know from studies with children that those who show good self-control are more competent socially and intellectually (see Blair, 2002).

Considerable research has also investigated the biological basis of impulsivity. However, the general ambiguity of its meaning has also contributed to measurement confusion, and a certain inconsistency in the findings. Most agree that aggressive impulsivity is related to lower serotonergic activity, perhaps at the level of the amygdala (Oquendo & Mann, 2000). On the other hand, those studying the more cognitive elements of impulsivity tend to implicate the prefrontal cortex in this process. For example, an interesting series of studies over the past 30 years has shown that

frontal lobe brain lesions in animals enhance the degree to which the animal's behaviour is controlled by conditioned reinforcing stimuli – or what has been called 'Pavlovian approach behaviour'. In other words, after the lesion, the animal is less able to shift its behaviour from conditioned reinforcing stimuli to a new task. As we have seen in an earlier section of this chapter, the strength of conditioned responses is correlated with the degree of dopamine activation in the nucleus accumbens – a process that occurs when natural or pharmacological rewards, such as food or addictive drugs, respectively, are present. We will also recall that prefrontal input to the midbrain is the mechanism by which cortical structures can modulate or gate conditioned response tendencies. Therefore, inherent individual differences in the functioning of this dopamine-based regulator system – either a *hyper*sensitive tendency to respond to appetitive stimuli, or *hypo*active cortical modulation of these impulses (or both) – appear to form, at least in part, the biological explanation of some aspects of impulsivity (Jentsch *et al.*, 2000).

The insidious nature of potent rewarding behaviours (like taking addictive drugs) is that they tend to create a snowball effect by fostering the drive to do more of the same. One way this seems to happen is that repeated exposure to drugs of abuse can produce reductions in cortical dopamine, which in turn diminishes the efficiency of the executive function of the prefrontal cortex, resulting in the exaggerated responding to pleasurable stimuli and the thrill or sensation seeking that is typically associated with impulsivity (Taylor & Jentsch, 2001). In summary, drugs of abuse can affect behavioural processes that contribute to addiction, including enhanced stimulus-reward learning and Pavlovian approach behaviour, and decreased behavioural inhibition.

For many years, addiction research focused on the compulsive aspects of this disorder, and the prominent role that cravings seem to play in its astonishing resistence to treatment and its high rate of relapse. However, in recent years there has been increased interest in the part that impulsivity plays in this process. This change in focus was prompted partly because clinical evidence failed to show that all drug use occurs in response to overwhelming cravings. It seems that some happens in a rather spontaneous, impetuous, and unplanned manner (Moeller *et al.*, 2001). Many studies have also shown a strong relationship between impulsivity and addictive behaviours (see Brady *et al.*, 1998 for a review). For example, impulsivity has been associated with greater experimentation with drugs, greater frequency and severity of use, and poorer treatment outcome. Aggression is also strongly associated with drug-taking, both preceding and following drug use, and one characteristic linking the two behaviours is impulsivity (Allen *et al.*, 1998). In addition, a number of studies have shown a higher than expected prevalence of personality disorders, especially antisocial and borderline, among groups of addicts (Clark *et al.*, 1997; Grilo *et al.*, 1997). However, in much of this research, the causal association between impulsivity and addiction is open to question since many studies are either correlational and/or have tested groups of drug-dependent subjects. The major problem, as we have seen earlier, is that chronic drug-taking can directly cause the behavioural characteristics that are tapped by most measures of impulsivity.

More compelling evidence of the link between impulsivity and addiction comes from longitudinal studies, and studies that track the chronology of comorbid disorders. For instance, Verheul and colleagues studied a large group of mixed substance abusers and found that remission of the addiction was not significantly associated with remission of their personality disorder – an outcome which suggests that personality pathology and addiction tend to follow an independent course. Another study compared adolescent sons of

149

substance-abusing fathers, over a two-year period, with an age-equivalent group of boys whose fathers had no history of addiction or other psychiatric disorders, and found a higher presence of poor behavioural self-regulation among the former (Dawes *et al.*, 1997). This characteristic also predicted more deviant peer affiliations and poorer school performance – characteristics which frequently precede substance abuse. What was also interesting was that the factors that comprise poor behavioural regulation in the boys (such as impulsivity and inattention) were largely present in their respective fathers.

## PRONENESS TO ANXIETY AND NEGATIVE MOOD

A number of irrefutable facts, such as the high comorbidity between substance abuse disorders and a variety of anxiety disorders, has spawned the search for causal links between anxiety and addiction. Studies have found, for example, that the lifetime prevalence of substance abuse is 300 per cent greater in those with generalized anxiety disorder and 200 per cent greater for panic disorder compared to rates in the general population (DeHaas *et al.*, 2001). There is also good evidence that a personality profile – the main component being neuroticism, and which the Eysencks have called the 'addictive personality' – is significantly higher in all addict groups, including substance abusers, compulsive gamblers, and those with eating disorders.

However, because many of the studies supporting the association between anxiety and addiction have used addicts recruited from treatment and rehabilitation centres, some have disputed the aetiological role of anxiety, arguing that it is simply the distress of withdrawal that we are assessing in these studies rather than a premorbid, causally prior, risk factor. While this may be true in some cases, longitudinal studies of personality, and retrospective accounts of the order of onset of comorbid anxiety disorders in addiction, offer fairly strong support for a causal model. For example, teacher's ratings of high harm avoidance in school children predicted their subsequent substance abuse in adolescence and early adulthood (Wills *et al.*, 1998). Several studies have also shown that anxiety disorders precede the substance use disorders in a large percentage of comorbid individuals (Merikangas *et al.*, 1998).

One factor motivating the use of addictive behaviours is simply their powerful ability to reduce the painful emotional consequences of stress. The *stress-reduction* or *self-medication pathway* to addiction has received a great deal of research attention in recent years and predicts that individuals who are high on traits, such as anxiety and neuroticism, are more reactive to stressful life events than more stable individuals and, in turn, that this reactivity provides the motivation to seek quick and effective psychological relief from distress, in the form of drugs. Consistent with this hypothesis is the argument proposed by Khantizian (1997) that the drugs that addicts select are not chosen randomly but instead are the result of an interaction between the psychopharmacological action of the drug and the form of the individual's distress. For example, he argues that heroin addicts prefer opiates because their powerful muting action subdues the rage and aggression they experience, and cocaine has its appeal because it can relieve the distress of depression. It follows then that the stress-reduction pathway is perhaps more relevant for addiction to alcohol, tranquillizers, and the opiates than for the popular stimulant drugs, such as crack/cocaine.

In recent years, cognitive theorists, investigating the links between anxiety and addictive behaviours, have proposed the notion that *anxiety sensitivity* is an important variable in the development and maintenance of addiction, and various models have been proposed to explain how this might occur. Although convincing empirical support for any of these is inconsistent or lacking, some do have a certain intuitive appeal. One 'moderator' model, proposes that the association between anxiety and substance use will be greater in those who are also high in anxiety sensitivity. Because the symptoms of stress will be more extreme in these individuals, they may be more likely than others to self-medicate with anxiolytic substances. Indeed, the evidence linking anxiety sensitivity and addiction is most convincing in the area of alcohol abuse, and to a lesser degree, nicotine addiction (Norton *et al.*, 1997; Norton, 2001). A second moderator model, coming from the opposite direction, specifies that the anxiety-dampening effects of taking substances such as alcohol will be greater in those with high anxiety sensitivity, thereby reinforcing its use. Mediational models could also explain the links between anxiety and substance abuse. For example, it could be that those high in anxiety sensitivity intensify drug withdrawal symptoms, especially those related to alcohol and smoking, because of their similarities with anxiety symptoms – putting them at greater risk for continuing the behaviours (Stewart & Kushner, 2001).

The role of stress in the vulnerability to addiction has been approached from at least three angles:

- How proneness to anxiety can potentiate the individual's reaction to challenging or distressing environmental events.

- How early prolonged stress can modify neuroanatomical development, which in turn, can foster behaviours which increase risk for addiction.

- How stress can trigger the relapse of addictive behaviours.

Although stress affects practically all physiological systems, one of the most important includes its activation of the limbic-hypothalamic-pituitary-adrenal (LHPA) axis. Briefly, the hypothalamus secretes corticotropin releasing factor (CRF), which leads to the subsequent release of adrenocorticotropic hormone (ACTH) from the pituitary gland, culminating in the sercretion of cortisol and other hormones from the adrenal glands. While the acute action of these stress hormones are life-saving because they mobilize the resources we need to respond quickly and efficiently when the situation is threatening (as we saw in Chapter 5), their protracted effects can be seriously detrimental to one's health (Majewska, 2002). It is relevant that drugs of abuse also activate the LHPA axis. However, the causal mechanisms linking stress and addiction are not fully understood, except for the consistent acknowledgement that it is a multidimensional relationship that depends on the neurobiological, genetic, and developmental make-up of each individual.

Although we could cite many examples, some taken from animal research will highlight our limited understanding of the complex relationship between LHPA axis function and drug effects. Many studies have shown that laboratory rats who respond with increased locomotion when placed in an inescapable novel environment like the 'open-field' box (high reactives) are more likely to self-administer a wide range of addictive drugs than their less active counterparts (low reactives) (Piazza *et al.*, 1989). The best explanation for these findings is that the high physical activity reflects a higher sensitivity to stress because these animals also have a stronger and longer-lasting corticosterone (a stress hormone in rats) response to this environment. Furthermore, other research has shown that the high reactives do not differ from the low reactives in their sensitivity to a novel environment that is freely chosen (Robinet *et al.*, 1998). Puzzling, however, is another animal paradigm producing exactly the opposite results. Two inbred strains of rats (Lewis and F344) were compared on their susceptibility to drug self-administration. The Lewis rats acquired drug self-administration significantly more rapidly than the F344 rats, and although the former also displayed a high locomotor response to novelty, they had a more *hyporesponsive* HPA axis function to stress than the F344 rats. Kosten and Ambrosio (2002) proposed a rather elegant fusion of the two seemingly contradictory findings by suggesting a non-linear, inverted-U relationship between HPA activation and behavioural sensitivity.

Extrapolating from their theory, some individuals (like the Lewis rats) may have low responsiveness to stress and to drugs, and may therefore seek out drugs to increase their arousal. Here we can see parallels to the ideas we presented in the earlier section on Sensitivity to Reward. Other individuals who are highly responsive to stress (like the high reactive rats) may also seek out drugs to ameliorate their hyperresponsiveness to stress. In other words, both those who are not easily stressed and those who are very easily stressed may find drugs rewarding, but for different reasons.

Other interesting research linking anxiety-induced stress to addiction was carried out by Volkow and colleagues (1996a; 1996b). Healthy male subjects were given either an intravenous dose of methylphenidate (a cocaine equivalent drug) or a placebo injection in a double-blind study. At the same time brain PET images were taken and subjects were asked to rate how they

felt on an adjective checklist (for example, *anxious*, *restless*, *happy*, etc.). It was found that subjects' 'anxious' ratings during placebo were positively correlated with the degree of dopamine concentration in the mesolimbic area during the drug condition. From these results, the authors concluded that a proneness to anxiety may be associated with a more reactive dopaminergic system. In other words, addictive behaviours may have a greater reward potential for these individuals than for those who are less anxious, increasing the likelihood of their use.

Finally in this section, we shall examine the role that early environmental stress may have on increasing vulnerability to addiction. A substantial body of research has documented the relationship between addiction and trauma. For example, victims of childhood physical and sexual abuse consistently report greater use of alcohol and other illicit drugs. Other studies have also shown high rates of victimization among female substance abusers, and rates as high as 50 per cent of post-traumatic stress disorder in clinical samples of substances abusers (Gordon, 2002). Although causation is always difficult to establish – and, indeed, may be bidirectional – one obvious explanation is that drugs and other addictive activities are used to provide relief or escape from the stress of ongoing abuse, or its painful memories. On the other hand, there is also clear evidence that early aversive life events can modify neurophysiological development of the LHPA axis. Animal research also indicates that early developmental stress causes the enhanced self-administration of drugs when these animals are adults (Kosten *et al.*, 2000). There is some indication that downregulation of certain serotonin receptors may be one of the biological mechanism linking early life stress to increased risk for addiction. Other evidence has implicated reduced cortisol levels (see Chapter 5 for a more detailed discussion of developmental influences on fear and anxiety). Although the neurochemical correlates of early developmental stress are still only vaguely understood, the behavioural correlates are quite consistent. Animals raised under stressful conditions tend to be shyer, less explorative, and fall into lower levels of the social hierarchy. In the human condition, it is more difficult to untangle environmental stress, innate temperament, and the interaction between the two, especially because this appears to be an evolving relationship. However, observations of orphan children show behaviours comparable to those seen in animals, such as a greater occurrence of emotional disturbances relating to sleep and feeding, and a substantially higher incidence of anxiety and depression at later ages.

In summary, there is substantial evidence that personality and personality pathology are involved both in the aetiology of addiction and in the course the disorder takes. There is even some tentative suggestion that personality factors may play a role in the *type* of addiction one develops – whether to alcohol, nicotine, or food. A clearer understanding of the personality pathways has considerable practical importance and is crucial to the development of improved treatment methods. If we can understand the psychology of those at high risk for addiction we can also improve our ability to target prevention efforts. A recognition of the heterogeneity of personality risk factors is also fundamental to the development of strategies to predict relapse since certain treatments may be more effective with some patients than with others.

# C H A P T E R 8

## EATING DISORDERS

## INTRODUCTION

Descriptions and explanations of eating disorders have changed considerably over time, and according to the authorities who have written about them; and it is fairly safe to say they will do so again. However, within the current DSM (version IV) system of classification, eating-related disorders subsume three separate diagnoses. Each has distinct clinical features; at the same time they have many characteristics in common. Although diagnostic *categories* have certain merits for research and treatment, they are nevertheless rather arbitrary, and sometimes obscure the heterogeneity of the disease in terms of predisposing or causal factors. An alternative approach has taken a dimensional perspective on the eating disorders; the premise being that differences between a preoccupation with weight and diet, and the clinical form of the disorder, are essentially quantitative, and that the behavioural and psychological characteristics vary more in degree than in kind. In other words, the full-blown syndrome is viewed as the end-point along a continuum that begins with normal dieting, advances to excessive concern about weight, the emergence of some clinical symptoms, and finally a severe and pathological illness (Fairburn & Beglin, 1990; Kendler *et al.*, 1991). In recent years, this viewpoint has become more prevalent – even in mainstream psychiatry – so that most would now agree that the eating disorders are more appropriately regarded as a 'spectrum of pathology' than as discrete disease entities. And so, although we continue to employ the DSM-IV diagnostic criteria and terminology for convenience, in practice our assessment of symptomatology typically reflects the dimensional view, and patients with milder forms of the disorders are treated alongside those with a more severe illness.

# CLINICAL FEATURES

*Anorexia nervosa* is currently defined as a self-imposed state of [semi]starvation, motivated by an excessive pursuit of thinness and characterized by the failure to maintain a body weight above 85 per cent of what is expected for one of the same age and height. Patients with this disorder also report an extreme fear of gaining weight even when they are severely emaciated and in a medically unstable state. For those who are female and post-pubertal, ammenorrhea, or the absence of menstruation for three consecutive months, is also a diagnostic requirement.[1] Another common symptom of this disorder is a distorted image of one's own body. Many patients seem unable to perceive their body size in an accurate way, and claim to feel fat even when they are severely emaciated. Also, the majority of patients with anorexia nervosa engage in excessive amounts of physical exercise; for example they will walk miles each day or spend several hours at the gym. Some display a more generalized hyperactivity that takes the form of relentless pacing, and a feeling of restlessness that makes sitting still difficult. What is most surprising, and rather counterintuitive, is that physical activity levels are generally at their highest when patients are at a very low weight and eating next to nothing (Davis *et al.*, 1994; Davis, 1997). Their apparently boundless energy is difficult to reconcile with the stark emaciation of their bodies. Weight loss and exercising seem to operate synergistically in these patients. In the most typical cases, an exponential decrease in body weight is matched by an exponential increase in physical activity. We shall discuss the biological underpinnings of this relationship in more detail later when we discuss the pathophysiology of eating disorders.

Because of the varied clinical picture of those with anorexia nervosa, the DSM identifies two subtypes of the disorder according to the way in which weight loss is achieved. Those of the *Restrictor* type have the set of symptoms we most commonly associate with anorexia nervosa. Typically, and over time, both the quantity of the food eaten, and the nutritional quality of the diet, is systematically reduced so that an escalating state of energy depletion and malnutrition occurs. For example, a common sequence of behaviours begins with a young woman's decision to adopt a strict vegetarian diet which soon evolves into a vegan regime and the elimination of dairy products such as milk and cheese. In time, the complex carbohydrates, such as bread and potatoes, are also removed from the diet, leaving only a limited selection of vegetables and fruits. Eventually, even these can take on a 'forbidden' quality. In some extreme forms of the disorder, patients will refuse all food and even restrict their intake of water.

---

[1]Although there are cases of men with eating disorders (estimates suggest about one in ten sufferers are male), the focus of this chapter is on females with the disorder. Research indicates substantial differences in the risk profile between the genders. For thorough reviews on the topic of males with eating disorders see Andersen (1990) and Andersen *et al.* (2000).

For others – those of the *binge-eating/purging* (B/P) type – self-starvation takes a different form. Periods of food restriction are punctuated with episodes of binge eating, followed by efforts to rid themselves of calories by self-induced vomiting or the abuse of laxatives and diuretics. Here, the DSM classification system seems particularly arbitrary because in many ways this form of anorexia nervosa is more similar to bulimia nervosa than to its 'restrictor' counterpart. For reasons that are not entirely clear, the DSM has chosen to use *body weight* as the unifying characteristic for the anorexia subtypes – both have in common a weight well below normal – instead of classifying the eating disorders according to their psychobehavioural similarities.

*Bulimia nervosa* is the diagnosis given to those who binge-eat (at least twice a week for a duration of three consecutive months) and then engage in some inappropriate behaviour (like vomiting) to compensate for the calories they have ingested. In addition, their body weight is either within the normal range or they are overweight. Clearly, it is a matter of clinical judgement whether to issue a diagnosis of anorexia nervosa of the B/P type, or one of bulimia nervosa, since the diagnostic demarcation is really a matter of the patient's weight. We suggest that menstrual status is probably the most useful marker of the distinction between the two, whenever this is an appropriate consideration.

At this point, we should emphasize that a 'binge' is a very subjective event and is not simply a matter of the quantity of food that is eaten. In the most typical cases, it refers to eating considerably more than most people would eat in a similar period of time. However, for some who have lived on very little food for a long time – most particularly those with anorexia nervosa of the B/P type – a 'binge' may be similar to what most of us eat at a normal meal. The most salient characteristic of a binge is that there is a feeling of loss of control over the eating; the sense that one is unable to stop once eating has begun.

As with anorexia nervosa, the DSM has also specified different types of bulimia nervosa depending on what compensatory behaviours are used. The *purging* type regularly engages in self-induced vomiting, or uses laxatives, diuretics, or enemas to expend unwanted calories. The *non-purging* type is more likely to follow a binge with periods of fasting or excessive amounts of physical activity. Concerning the latter, it is probably fair to say that this form of the disorder represents the most secretive, and the most difficult to recognize. Because exercising is so highly valued in our culture, and because we associate a myriad of benefits with regular physical activity, the exercising bulimic is likely to be seen by undiscerning friends and family as the picture of health – unlike her anorexic counterpart whose emaciation usually draws attention to her obsessive exercising. In addition to a relative absence of external scrutiny of the exercising bulimic, there is also the likelihood of *self-delusion*. In other words, she may even convince herself that nothing is wrong with her behaviour since physical activity is so 'healthy' and so strongly promoted in our society.

157

A third diagnosis, listed in the DSM under the vague descriptive category 'Eating Disorder Not Otherwise Specified', is *binge eating disorder*. The primary distinction between this disorder and bulimia nervosa is that individuals do not regularly engage in any compensatory behaviour following a binge episode. They also frequently initiate binges when they are not feeling physically hungry, and will continue eating until they are uncomfortably full. Not surprisingly, these patients are almost always obese, and they feel great guilt and remorse for the large amounts of food they consume, even though they recognize that the binge is usually motivated by feelings of depression and/or anxiety. Although not a criterion of the disorder, individuals with binge-eating disorder are generally older than those with bulimia nervosa.

## HISTORICAL PERSPECTIVES

Until relatively recently, explanations of the eating disorders tended to avoid, or disregard, biological theories and models in favour of those that focused on psychosocial and family influences. For example, historically – at least from the time that anorexia nervosa was formally identified as a disorder, distinct from other forms of self-starvation, in the mid-nineteenth century – the family was believed to be the root cause of the patient's denial of food. From this perspective, treatment was relatively straightforward and simple. It consisted of the gradual introduction of food, but, most importantly, the removal of the patient from her home lest the family interfere or disrupt her recovery. In more modern times, the causal role of the family has diminished in importance and our efforts to understand the eating disorders have focused, not exclusively, but more emphatically, on environmental factors; the most prominent derive from feminist and cultural theories.

There has been, for instance, a strong belief that the increase in eating related disorders after the 1960s was a direct consequence of the emergence of ultraslenderness as the ideal of female sexual attractiveness in Western society. This standard has been most explicit in the visual media. And the fashion industry, in particular, has been vilified for its overt sexualization and objectification of very young and very emaciated women. Indeed, at the present time, the thinness of the female body image ideal has reached such extremes that a substantial proportion – estimates reach as high as 80 per cent – of TV actresses, supermodels, and *Playboy* magazine centrefolds have a body weight that would meet the diagnostic criterion for anorexia nervosa (Katzmarzyk & Davis, 2001; Szabo, 1996; Wiseman *et al.*, 1992). However, the most insidious aspect of the media images of women is that anorexia nervosa is often associated with images of glamour and success. Although this disorder has the highest mortality rate of any psychiatric disorder, including depression and alcoholism, all too often highly paid fashion models or accomplished female athletes are described, almost reverently, in the media as 'anorexic' in appearance!

While it is intuitively appealing to blame the prevalence of eating-related disorders on our cultural standards of female beauty, it behoves us to take a more balanced view of the evidence. Although most women experience the pervasive media messages about attractiveness and thinness, the population incidence and prevalence of eating disorders are actually relatively low. Estimates suggest that between 0.5 per cent and one per cent of adolescent and young adult women suffer from anorexia nervosa, and a slightly higher rate – perhaps two to three per cent – from bulimia nervosa (see Drewnowski *et al.*, 1988; Van't Hof & Nicolson, 1996 for reviews). If our glorification of the slender female body was the *principal* cause of eating disorders, we should find a far higher prevalence of these disorders in our population than we do.

On the other hand, we must also be careful not to discredit the psychological impact of these cultural factors. Clearly, they set the stage; they provide the backdrop; they heighten awareness; and they create, for many, the initial motive for dieting. Moreover, we know that eating disorders are almost non-existent in societies that are untouched by Western ideals and also that these disorders emerge quite suddenly when countries became Westernized. A good example of the increasing prevalence of eating disorders was seen in eastern Europe in the 1980s after the collapse of Communism and the transition to Western capitalism. What we can then say, with confidence, about media images of women is that the power and pervasiveness of advertising are primarily responsible for the normative discontent that many young women – and more recently men – feel about their physical appearance, and for the extraordinary methods they will use to improve their body image. The diet and fitness industries are dual conspirators in this process, and continue to make a fortune from the insecurities and dissatisfaction they have fostered in our society.

It is also important to emphasize that these cultural influences are especially strong among the young teenage girls in our society. It is not a coincidence that early adolescence is currently the most common age during which eating disorders, in particular anorexia nervosa, develop. Moreover, the age of eating disorder onset has been decreasing in recent years so that it is now not atypical to see patients as young as eight years old. Adolescence is a time when young women are particularly vulnerable to prevailing attitudes about thinness and sexual attractiveness. During the early teenage years, a secure self-concept and sense of personal identity are in the formative stages of development and are therefore more fragile than at most other times in the lifespan. For a variety of reasons, this is also a time when much of the female adolescent's self-esteem is focused on her physical appearance, and this focus is more emphatic in our current image-driven and media-based culture than ever before. We know that the desire to be thinner, an emphasis on dieting, and an awareness of what one is wearing and how one is viewed by others, is occurring at earlier and earlier ages. Studies have shown that young pre-pubescent girls regularly complain

159

about being fat (Childress *et al.*, 1993). We need only consider the pop-star clothing styles that are being successfully marketed for children in the five- to nine-year-old range – short skirts, tight-fitting leggings, and belly-baring shirts – to see the overt sexualizing of children in our culture. These days, lessons in the importance of appearance come long before adolescence!

Adolescents are also characterized by a particularly inflexible way of thinking about the world. They tend to employ a cognitive style that psychologists have called *dichotomous thinking*, which simply means that they tend to view the world as 'black and white'. In other words, there is a reluctance or inability for them to see things in half measures. Let us consider a nutrition example. If the adolescent has come to believe, for whatever reason, that dietary fat is 'bad', this stance becomes completely incompatible with the notion that we all need some fat in our diet for optimal health and well-being. For the reasons described above, it is easy to see why the young are especially gullible consumers of information. They have developed neither sufficient skill nor the cynicism to evaluate the quality of the media's messages, and they have not had enough experience to know that not everything in print is accurate.

Relatively recently, there has been a shift in our thinking about the eating disorders, with a movement away from explanations that rely solely on sociocultural factors, to ones that include a consideration of neurophysiological and genetic influences (Kaye, 1999). Consequently, the prevailing view is that the eating disorders are not only highly complex with respect to their clinical features, but also that multiple factors determine their risk and their severity. Although there is little doubt that environment plays a role in the initiation of dieting, we now believe that it is primarily the psychological vulnerability of the individual that takes normal dieting from something relatively benign, to a life-threatening illness. Before we discuss these individual risk factors in more detail, it is appropriate to review the ways in which clinicians and scientists study the aetiology of eating disorders, and the specific difficulties that these disorders bring to the business of research design and methodology.

## RESEARCH METHODOLOGY

When trying to determine what premorbid personality factors increase the risk for eating disorders, it is more difficult to untangle cause and effect than it is with most other psychiatric disturbances, simply because the biological abnormalities that define these disorders, viz. starvation, malnutrition, and dehydration, are known to alter the chemistry and structure of the brain in ways that dramatically influence psychological functioning. Probably the clearest evidence we have of these effects comes from the semi-starvation study conducted by Dr Ancel Keys at the University of Minnesota soon after the Second World War (Keys, 1950). In this landmark study, a group of 36 young men agreed to participate in a six-month period of severe food deprivation during which they consumed only 50 per cent of their daily caloric

requirements. This followed an initial three-month period of extensive medical testing. On average, the men lost 75 per cent of their baseline body weight and experienced a host of bodily changes. Although the physical symptoms were pronounced, and included lethargy, dizziness, and feelings of coldness, the men uniformly reported that the most prominent changes, by far, were the psychological ones. They became very irritable, depressed, lacking in libido, and preoccupied with thoughts and images of food. What is important for us to consider when we undertake clinical research is that all these characteristics are regularly seen in patients with eating disorders, in particular anorexia nervosa. Therefore, and in a powerful way, the Keys study illustrates the inherent difficulties in trying to identify psychological *causes* by comparing patients who are medically unstable with healthy control subjects. Their starved state rather than their true psychological make-up may be responsible for any differences we observe. On the other hand, we must be careful not to err in the opposite direction and assume that the psychological characteristics commonly seen in eating-disordered patients have been induced *solely* by their malnourished physical state.

It is also wise to recognize that there are some significant limits on our ability to generalize from participants in the Keys study to patients with eating disorders. First of all, the former were all men, and the majority of eating-disordered patients are women. This is relevant because we now have good reasons to believe that gender may influence the response of the individual to a dieting regime, both psychologically and biologically (e.g. Walsh *et al.*, 1995). Second, the men in the Keys study were vigorously screened for selection in the study in order to ensure they were in excellent physical health. Perhaps most importantly, participation in the study required those who were sociable, psychologically stable, and completely free from emotional distress. Regrettably, this is not the premorbid psychological profile of most women who develop eating disorders!

Given the physically unstable state of most eating-disordered patients, and the unreliability of data collected from those who are medically compromised, how then can we study the aetiology of eating disorders? In other words, how are we able to gather causal information that is scientifically valid and not confounded by physiological factors? In the field of epidemiology, it is well-established that longitudinal or prospective studies provide the best data for establishing causal links. In general, this type of study requires the initial assessment of variables that are believed to be aetiologically significant, from a large number of individuals representing the population at risk. Following a reasonable lapse of time – usually years rather than weeks or months – the individuals are reassessed to establish how many developed the criterion disorder or illness. From the identification of cases, researchers can establish which baseline factors significantly differentiate those with the disorder from those who remained healthy.

Although this is considered the most sophisticated and most valid method to use, it does have certain practical drawbacks. For example, this type of research is a very costly way to establish risk for a disease that occurs relatively rarely – recall that the eating disorders have a combined prevalence of about three per cent in the population – because of the necessity of testing a very, very large sample of participants in order to identify a sufficiently large number of cases to allow for suitable statistical analyses. An added problem is attrition and the feasibility of tracking a large number of people over an extended period of time, especially when, in the case of eating disorder research, recruitment is aimed at adolescents. For all these reasons, large-scale prospective studies are relatively rare in eating disorder research and, by necessity, other paradigms have found greater favour among researchers.

One popular approach has been to study recovered patients who are, at the time of assessment, weight-restored and symptom-free. The assumption in this kind of study is that any characteristic that differentiates the recovered patients from an age- and sex-matched group of subjects without a history of an eating disorder, must be significant in the aetiology of the disorder. At first glance, this seems a reasonable assumption. However, we must also consider the possibility that the experience of 'having the disorder' has fundamentally altered individuals so that even long-term recovery does not return them to their pre-disordered state. Presently, we are still fairly uncertain about the long-lasting psychobiological effects of starvation, and so we must be suitably cautious about drawing strong causal inferences from the data of recovered patients.

Another problem inherent in the research of recovered patients is that these studies are often long-term follow-up studies conducted a considerable period of time – usually years – after the initial diagnosis (Herzog *et al.*, 1999). A striking example of this was a study that compared a sample of women ten years after their hospital treatment for anorexia nervosa. Among those who had recovered from the disorder, there were virtually no persisting clinically significant signs of psychopathology (Schork *et al.*, 1994). Since the former patients were not distinguishable from the general population, we may be tempted to use this as evidence that no identifiable personality risk factors exist for anorexia nervosa. However, that would be a hasty and unwarranted conclusion since recovery in this study is confounded by the passage of time. In other words, more has happened to the patient in the intervening ten years than simply the end of her illness. She has also matured and, in many cases, has experienced the psychological changes that accompany the passage from adolescence to adulthood.

Another type of research design – and one that is based squarely on the assumption that psychological disturbance is a continuation of normal personality variation – is to investigate the relationships among aetiological

factors and subclinical symptoms of the eating disorders (such as weight preoccupation, for example) in a cohort of the population that is believed to be at greatest risk. With respect to the eating disorders this would typically be a sample of adolescent or young adult women. On the positive side, findings from this type of research are not confounded by the physical symptoms of the disorder, and the data can be obtained relatively easily. The most serious limitation, however, is that these data are usually collected at a single point in time, and the statistical analyses are mostly correlational. Therefore, it is difficult to know, with any certainty, which factors influence which other factors. For instance, several studies have found that self-esteem is lower in young women who report dissatisfaction with their body shape. However, we cannot say for sure whether the feelings of poor self-worth contributed to the individual's disparagement about her body, or whether other, perhaps social or family, factors fostered a negative evaluation of the individual's body, which then eroded the way she felt about herself in a more general way.

A further approach to the study of cause and effect relies on animal models. However, here the limitations are also clear, and focus primarily on the degree to which we can extrapolate our findings from laboratory animals, usually rodents, to the human condition. Obviously, there are boundaries – and some would say these are reached very early on – beyond which our knowledge of animal behaviour cannot enlighten our knowledge of human behaviour. Without venturing into a discussion of the ethics and morality of the use of animals for experimentation, the fact remains that they are used (as we have seen in some of the previous chapters), that we can do invasive procedures that would be prohibited with human subjects, and that our understanding of the brain–behaviour relationship has been much enhanced by this research. In the area of eating disorders, two interesting animal models have contributed to our understanding of the biobehavioural disease process.

The first has been variously named the *exercise-induced weight-loss syndrome*, the *activity–stress paradigm*, or *activity anorexia*, and describes a phenomenon whereby rodents (and certain other animals) will systematically, and to a fatal outcome, increase their wheel running and decrease their calorie intake after an initial period of food restriction (see Epling & Pierce, 1996). Since the pattern of these behaviours shows a remarkable similarity to the progression of exercising and dieting in patients with anorexia nervosa, we have been able to investigate the neurochemical alterations that take place during the development of this syndrome in a way that would be difficult, if not impossible, to study in human subjects. The second animal model is one of *spontaneous self-starvation* (Treasure & Owen, 1997). This syndrome also bears a striking resemblance to the behavioural characteristics of anorexia nervosa and is found in a genetically lean strain of pigs. Farmers who raise these animals have consistently observed that during periods of stress, such as early separation from the sow, a proportion of young, mostly female, pigs spontaneously restrict their intake of food and become hyperactive.

As we have discussed above, all the methods commonly used to study the aetiology of eating disorders are in some way flawed. On its own, each, albeit for different reasons, limits or compromises our ability to draw firm conclusions from our data. However, study outcomes are much more scientifically compelling if we look at the broader picture. When a particular question has been studied using a variety of different paradigms, and the combined results provide a consistent outcome, we can be fairly confident in drawing valid conclusions from the collective evidence.

## TEMPERAMENT AND PERSONALITY

The psychopathology of anorexia and bulimia nervosa comprises a number of clinical symptoms and traits, some that are common to both disorders, and others that occur more frequently in one or the other. We also have evidence that the dimensionality of personality disturbance correlates with the severity of behavioural symptoms; the lowest levels of pathology occur in the general population, the highest levels in the most severe and intractable cases of eating disorder, and mild cases somewhere in the middle. Since many of the personality traits associated with eating disorders have at least moderate heritability, we can infer the existence of a genotypic vulnerability, expressed by a cluster of phenotypic psychobiological markers. However, what is not entirely clear is whether these markers reflect a specific diathesis for eating disorders or, instead, a predisposition to a broad range of psychological disturbances. Having said that, much of the evidence suggests that, compared to many other forms of psychopathology, restricting anorexia nervosa represents one of the strongest cases for a direct relationship between personality traits and a specific behavioural disorder (Kaye, 1997; Klump *et al.*, 2000; Davis & Woodside, 2002).

One of the difficulties in studying risk or vulnerability in the eating disorders is the degree of patient movement across diagnostic categories. On the one hand, anorexia and bulimia nervosa seem distinctly different in their 'pure' forms – the rigidity and restraint of the restrictor anorexic is antithetical to the bingeing, purging, and impulsive behaviours associated with the bulimic. However, the clinical picture is rarely this clear-cut. Across time, approximately half the patients with anorexia nervosa become bulimic, and many bulimic women have a prior history of anorexia nervosa. Regrettably, in many studies, patients are assigned to diagnostic categories simply on the basis of their current symptomatology. Although this is less frequently done in studies of anorexia nervosa – most recent studies do draw a distinction between the restrictor and binge/purge subtypes – rarely is a differentiation made between bulimic patients with and without a history of anorexia nervosa. This oversight is particularly problematic when we are examining aetiological factors.

A second consideration in studying the role of personality is the fundamental importance of body size in any formations about risk for eating disorders. In a culture such as ours, it is not abnormal for those who are overweight – women in particular – to be more preoccupied with their weight, more dissatisfied with their bodies, and more likely to diet. These tendencies only become aberrant or pathological when they arise in the context of one who is of low weight or even underweight. Therefore, it is important to remove or control, in a statistical way, the influence of body size before we can accurately assess the associations between eating disorder symptomatology and personality factors.

For the reminder of this chapter, we will discuss the most prominent psychological risk factors, their biological underpinnings, where relevant, and how they seem to influence the onset and the progression of the eating disorders.

## OBSESSIONALITY AND THE EATING DISORDERS

Perhaps the most consistently reported association is between eating disorders – in particular, anorexia nervosa – and obsessive–compulsive disorder (OCD), with valid estimates of lifetime comorbidity rates between 35 per cent and 40 per cent (Halmi et al., 1991; Thiel et al., 1995). There is also a much higher than expected lifetime prevalence of eating disorders among patients diagnosed with OCD, with rates as high as 12 per cent (Rubenstein et al., 1992). Clearly, there are many clinical similarities between the eating disorders and OCD, such as involuntary ruminations, uncontrollable urges, and a preoccupation with trying to control unwanted thoughts and images. Therefore, let us consider how the two disorders might be connected phenomenologically, and the manner in which OCD tendencies could give rise to the symptoms of an eating disorder.

One possibility is that the sociocultural context of the past 30–40 years has simply altered the form of certain OCD symptoms in a particular and susceptible cohort of the population. Indeed, some have claimed that anorexia nervosa is simply a 'modern variant' of OCD (Holden, 1990; Rothenberg, 1986). This is certainly a plausible explanation since we have good clinical evidence that a change in one's environmental circumstances can alter the symptomatology of OCD. Take, for example, the case of a young woman who was obsessed with fears of personal contamination, and who had engaged in the common washing and cleaning rituals for a number of years. However, after the birth of her first child these personal fears subsided and moved quite suddenly from herself to her child. She became obsessively fearful that the bottles of milk she prepared for the baby were tainted. Each day she emptied and refilled the bottles, repeatedly sterilizing them each time.

Many patients with anorexia nervosa are excessively fearful of eating. For them, food, particularly fatty food, is the dietary equivalent of the more

165

conventional obsessions we see in OCD, such as fear of dirt and germs. And, expending calories through some form of physical exercise is analogous to the conventional washing and cleaning rituals. Both are used to reduce the anxiety associated with their respective obsessions. Currently, there is a strong emphasis in Western societies on the health risks associated with high-calorie diets and physical inactivity, so it is not difficult to understand that for certain vulnerable individuals – especially those with obsessive–compulsive tendencies – such messages can have a great impact. In our super-hygienic, antibiotic world, for some young women, fat has replaced germs and dirt as 'the enemy'.

Indeed, in our own clinical work we have been alarmed to discover the number of young patients who tell us that their dieting and exercise routine first began after warnings they were given in health education classes at school. In past generations young school children were taught about the need for cleanliness and the role that bacteria play in the spread of disease. However, in our society where obesity is a major health risk – current estimates of overweight populations in the UK and in the USA have exceeded 50 per cent among adult men and women – educational prevention has turned to harsh warnings about the evils of overeating and lack of exercise. It seems that the fear of infection experienced in previous generations has become the fear of fatness in current times! One anorexic patient even confessed that during the most severe form of her illness she believed that rubbing suntan oil on her skin was unhealthy and would make her fat.

An obsessive need for exactness, orderliness and attention to detail is another common trait found in patients with OCD, and one that takes a food-related focus in patients with anorexia nervosa, irrespective of their nutritional status. Many patients spend a considerable amount of time counting the calories in the food they eat and obsessively balancing these against the number of calories they waste in daily exercise. The ritual of calorie counting is attended to with excruciating detail, and great distress occurs if the calories taken in are not negated, or exceeded, by the calories expended. In the most severe cases, much of the day is consumed with reading food labels, and ruminating about the nutritional content of the little food they eat. Again we can see how the conventional OCD symptoms – checking and ordering to reduce the possibility of physical harm – take on a culturally specific meaning manifest in the checking and ordering of food to remove the risk of getting fat. In a world that is relatively free from the life-threatening dangers we once encountered, fat has become more fearful to many women than the possibility of physical injury.

Much has also been written, albeit sometimes in a non-specific way, about the central role of 'control' in the phenomenology of the eating disorders (e.g. Fairburn *et al.*, 1999). The impression that is often given – and we think erroneously – is that eating-disordered patients have had so little 'control' of

other aspects of their life that they try and compensate by exerting control over what they eat. But where is the logic to this? How does self-starvation give one more direct control of one's life? Moreover, it is difficult to reconcile this concept of 'control' with the clinical features of the disorder since severely ill and malnourished patients are hardly in personal 'control' of very much, especially what they eat! One is more likely to describe them as 'out of control'. Therefore, when we think about the issue of control, we must be mindful that the term subsumes a number of meanings, and is more likely to operate *indirectly* in the lives of most eating-disordered patients. For some, diet and exercise may be a way to 'control' their shape and appearance. For others, their illness is a way to 'control' other people and foster attention, caring, and sympathy. And for still others, the behaviours of the disorder, such as dieting and bingeing, may help to 'control' their unpleasant moods and emotions. Each of these motives can be a significant causal factor in the initiation and maintenance of self-starvation. It is also important to be reminded that concern with control is also a core feature of OCD. Obsessions and compulsions are about gaining control over frightening impulses, anxious thoughts, and disturbing fantasies.

## PERFECTIONISM AND THE EATING DISORDERS

By continuing to frame the links between obsessionality and the eating disorders, we must also consider the role of obsessive–compulsive personality characteristics in their development. Perhaps the most salient of this constellation of traits is *perfectionism*. In recent years, considerable interest has focused on its aetiological significance in the eating disorders, and on the genetic basis of this trait. However, before we consider the biological underpinnings of perfectionism, we should first explain what is commonly meant by this term, and how it might relate to the initiation and progression of eating disorders.

Although early theorists tended to view perfectionism as a unitary construct, today most would agree that several distinguishable facets comprise this trait. Perhaps the most parsimonious way to structure the components of perfectionism is to distinguish between its *adaptive* or positive, and its *maladaptive* or negative, manifestations. On the one hand, perfectionism can describe a set of characteristics that is highly socially desirable, and appears to contribute to healthy psychological functioning. High striving and painstaking efforts are mostly associated with personal satisfaction, feelings of achievement, and an ensuing sense of self-esteem. On the other hand, perfectionism may also describe the tendency to set impossibly high personal standards whilst experiencing an intense need to avoid failure. Here, we see the darker side of the construct in attitudes and behaviours that are clearly maladaptive.

A number of studies have found a significantly higher degree of perfectionism in patients with anorexia nervosa – irrespective of subtype –

compared to healthy age-matched women (Bastiani *et al.*, 1995;Terry-Short *et al.*, 1995). The most distinguishing aspect of perfectionism in these patients is their strong drive to avoid mistakes and parental criticism, their desire to adhere to standards of excellence, and their doubt about whether they have done the right thing. In addition, greater perfectionism in anorexic patients has been associated with more severe symptomatology and the tendency to engage in excessive amounts of exercise (Davis *et al.*, 1999). Also, the fact that perfectionism is typically not diminished by weight restoration – unlike other core symptoms of starvation – strongly suggests that this trait is a common premorbid characteristic of anorexic patients, and therefore is likely to play a predisposing role in the development of the disorder (Deep *et al.*, 1995). Other support for a causal link is the evidence of strong family transmission, and the association between perfectionism and weight preoccupation in non-clinical women (Hewitt *et al.*, 1995). Lastly, there is also a high occurrence of OCPD in patients with an eating disorder, and perfectionism is clearly a discriminating characteristic of this personality disorder.

One can see that cultural messages about attractiveness – of the sort we have described earlier in this chapter – are much more likely to provoke extreme behavioural measures when they collide with the personality of a young woman with obsessional traits. First, her perfectionism will foster higher expectations, tougher standards of acceptable body image, and a greater need to seek approval from others, than in one less so predisposed. Her rigidity and methodical nature also lend themselves well to the rigours of a strict dieting and exercise regime, and her perseverance guarantees that once she sets herself a task, she is more likely than most to succeed. As one young anorexic patient confided to us: 'All my friends decided to go on a diet last summer. I just happened to do it better than everyone else'!

The association between perfectionism and bulimia nervosa is much less consistent and strong than that with anorexia nervosa. Although some studies have found a significant relationship between perfectionism and bulimic symptoms, others have not (see Goldner *et al.*, 2002; Polivy & Herman, 2002). One of the difficulties is that many of these studies have failed to consider the heterogeneity of patients with bulimia nervosa. In other words, they have failed to distinguish bulimic subjects with a history of anorexia nervosa from bulimic subjects who have never had a significant weight loss. Furthermore, if we consider the relationship theoretically, bingeing is a rather paradoxical and counterintuitive behaviour in the context of a highly perfectionistic and obsessional woman who aspires to the nearly impossible task of achieving the cultural standards of ultrathinness, since it sabotages the very goals she wishes to reach. Nevertheless, the fact that some research has found elevations on measures of perfectionism in currently ill and recovered bulimic patients suggests a certain amount of shared vulnerability on this trait for both disorders.

# IMPULSIVITY AND THE EATING DISORDERS

A role for perfectionism in bulimia nervosa is also empirically incompatible with the much stronger evidence that impulsivity, low tolerance for frustration, and emotional instability are the most consistent personality traits found in bulimic patients during the active stage of their illness (Steiger *et al.*, 2001b; Penas-Lledo *et al.*, 2002). However, it is worth noting that although the DSM makes no specific distinction, many believe there are two clinically divergent groups of bulimic patients based on significant differences in their psychopathology (Vitousek & Manke, 1994). One type of patient is relatively passive, extremely compliant, and shows a great dependence on external rewards. The second, the so-called *multi-impulsive type*, is not only characterized by impulsive and disinhibited behaviour in relation to eating, but manifestations of impulsivity can be seen in other aspects of these patients' lives. For example, there is a high incidence of self-harm behaviours, such as skin cutting and burning (Favaro & Santonastaso, 1998; Schroeter *et al.*, 2002). Alcohol and other substance abuse disorders occur more frequently in these patients than in other diagnostic groups, and there is evidence of more overt family conflict and hostility (Polivy & Herman, 2002; Tiller *et al.*, 1995). There is also high co-morbidity with the 'erratic-dramatic' Cluster B personality disorders, such as Borderline (Steiger *et al.*, 1996; Steiger *et al.*, 2001a).

If we turn to the biological underpinnings of the identifiable traits of both anorexia and bulimia nervosa, one compelling theory combines the anancastic and the impulsive traits within the same biological framework. It is proposed that the symptom and trait differences in anorexia and bulimia nervosa reflect bipolar opposites on a dimension of responsiveness of brain hypothalamic serotonin (5-HT) pathways. Elevated function contributes to certain symptoms and characteristics seen in restricting anorexia nervosa, and decreased function gives rise to those seen in bulimic patients. In other words, dysregulated 5-HT function seems to characterize both forms of the disorder, albeit in opposite directions. In addition to the biological evidence supporting this theory – that is, low peripheral markers of 5-HT in bulimia nervosa and higher levels in anorexia nervosa – the eating behaviours that distinguish the two disorders map onto the role of 5-HT in the regulation of food intake. High activity is associated with increased satiety and food avoidance, whereas low levels foster overeating (see Chapter 5 for details and references).

A similar continuum model has been proposed to explain the relationship between impulsivity and obsessive–compulsiveness, as we have seen in Chapter 6. Like the eating disorders, this model has been defined within a biological framework with obsessive–compulsive traits reflecting heightened frontal lobe activity and increased 5-HT reactivity, and impulsivity reflecting hypofrontality and low 5-HT levels (Hollander & Wong, 1995). Considered together, both the symptomatology of bulimia and the personality traits of those who suffer from this disorder may be described as lacking in inhibition,

169

being emotionally reactive, and having a strong approach to activities which maximize pleasure or reduce distress, irrespective of the associated risk. On the other hand, anorexia nervosa is a disorder of extreme constraint, persistence, and avoidant behaviour.

## ANXIOUSNESS AND THE EATING DISORDERS

A number of conceptually similar, and highly correlated, personality traits have been studied in the context of eating disorders. As we have seen in Chapter 3, several different labels have been used to describe a predisposition characterized by negative affect, proneness to stress, and a tendency to worry – viz. neuroticism, anxiety, and harm avoidance. In general, individuals high on these dimensions are also hypersensitive to rejection and social disapproval. Compared to the general population, eating-disordered patients of *all* diagnostic categories have significantly elevated levels of these traits (Casper *et al.*, 1992; Davis & Claridge, 1998; Davis *et al.*, 1999). Moreover, these traits do not seem to diminish with weight-restoration or the interruption of other symptoms such as bingeing and over-exercising, suggesting they play a causal role in the development of eating disorders. A large body of research with non-clinical subjects also demonstrates that these same anxiousness traits are strong and consistent correlates of body dissatisfaction and weight preoccupation (for example, Davis *et al.*, 1996; 1997).

Another approach to the study of anxious personality traits has been to examine the comorbidity rates between the eating disorders and other Axis I and Axis II disorders that relate most closely to these traits. In both anorexia and bulimia nervosa, the most frequently reported anxiety disorder is *social phobia*. As we have seen in Chapter 5, prominent features of this syndrome are the extreme anxiety reactions that occur in anticipation of, or exposure to, social situations – in particular those where the individual is expected to perform, or where some sort of personal evaluation is required, such as an audition, a job interview, or an academic test. We also recall that social phobia typically begins in childhood or early adolescence and is often comorbid with other conditions, such as depression and substance/alcohol abuse. However, these conditions are usually secondary to social phobia; depression tending to result from the social withdrawal and isolation; and drugs often used to self-medicate (Brunello *et al.*, 2000). The fact that eating disorders are also secondary in at least 50 per cent of cases suggests a strong causal role for social phobia, and for the personality characteristics that predispose to it.

How then do anxious traits give rise to the behaviours that define the eating disorders? To answer this question we need to consider both environmental and biological factors. A key characteristic of the socially anxious is their hypersensitivity to criticism or disapproval – a factor that is typically exacerbated during adolescence when self-assurance is shaky at the best of times. Heightened levels of social anxiety can affect an adolescent's behaviour in a number of deleterious ways.

In our culture, with its focus on fashion, fitness, and 'looking good', it is easy to understand the strong associations that can form in the minds of young women between achieving a thin body shape and gaining social approval. Adolescence is a time when the need for peer acceptance is at its greatest. Ironically, it is also a time when unkindnesses and jealousies among friends and classmates are at their worst – sentiments which often take the form of teasing and bullying. Many socially sensitive young women begin to diet in the hope of enhancing their physical appearance and gaining greater popularity. Others may begin to restrict their food in response to spiteful or jealous remarks about being overweight. Still others may begin to diet at a time when their mother is actively trying to lose weight. If the child's weight-loss success is rewarded by parental praise, this too can reinforce the continuation of dieting if the child is strongly sensitive to, and dependent on, her parent's approval.

We can also think of anxiousness in a more 'dynamic' sense. Instead of simply examining its *direct* effects on body-image disparagement, weight preoccupation, and other signs of disordered eating, we can examine anxiousness through its contribution as a *moderator* variable. In other words, we can look at how it modulates the role of other personality influences on eating-related attitudes and behaviours. A few examples from our own recent work will illustrate this point. The first comes from a study on physical attractiveness (Davis *et al.*, 2001). There is some evidence that families of patients with anorexia nervosa tend to be more than normally concerned with social appearances, and place considerable importance on looks and physical attractiveness, both for the parents and for their children (Marcus & Wiener,

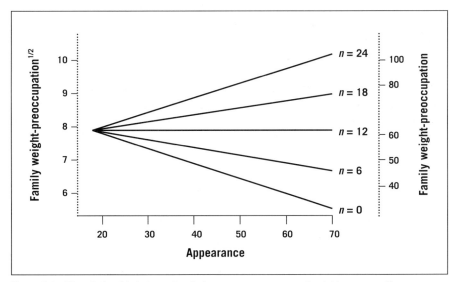

**Figure 8.1**  The relationship between family focus on appearance and weight preoccupation.

1995). Although we know that attitudes to dieting and body image may be learned through a daughter's modelling of her mother's behaviour, it has also been argued that parental behaviours are not sufficient, on their own, to produce disordered eating in their offspring *unless* combined with certain 'third factor' vulnerabilities of the child. The results of a recent study illustrate how neuroticism (N) fulfils this modulating role. Among those who had low to moderate levels of N, there was no relationship between a family focus on appearance and weight preoccupation. However, among those with increasingly higher levels of N the relationship between these two variables became increasingly more positive. In other words, and as we can see in Figure 8.1, family focus on appearance only predicted weight preoccupation among women who were psychologically vulnerable as indicated by their relatively high scores on N.

Our second example concerns a trait discussed in some detail earlier. Perfectionism has frequently been associated with eating disorder symptomatology, including the poor body image that forms part of the syndrome. However, again, research suggests this relationship is very much influenced by neuroticism, as we can see in Figure 8.2. At high levels of N, the commonly identified relationship does exist; namely, that highly perfectionistic woman do report low levels of body esteem. However, among individuals with more moderate levels of N this relationship disappears. And, among very stable individuals – those with low scores on N – the relationship

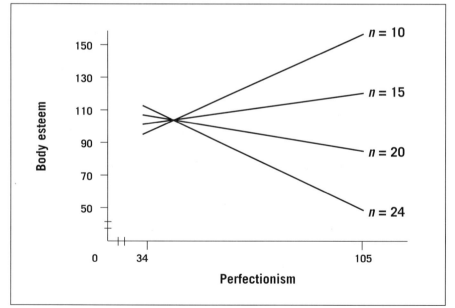

**Figure 8.2** The combined effects of perfectionism and anxiousness in association with eating disorder symptomatology.

between perfectionism and body esteem actually reverses into a positive one (Davis, 1999).

This example illustrates the combined effects of perfectionism and anxiousness – probably the two most prominent characteristics associated with risk for an eating disorder. Sensitivity to criticism and to the social pressures to pursue a thin body image – when coupled with a tendency to set unrealistically high standards and to persist in trying to achieve these goals – can clearly be a lethal combination! Indeed, we have consistently found that a personality characteristic which has been called *neurotic perfectionism*, and which combines the most pathological features of both the traits that form its name, is the strongest psychological correlate of disturbed eating and poor body image in both clinical and non-clinical subjects (see Mitzman *et al.*, 1994; Davis, 1999).

An important consideration in the links between anxiousness and eating behaviour is the role that stress can play in the progression from psychological disposition to disorder (see also Chapter 5). However, in most cases, stress is a matter of subjective interpretation. That is, cognitive appraisal will determine whether an event is perceived as stressful, neutral, or positive, and experience tells us that there is great variation across individuals in the evaluation of many daily events. For example, most can identify with the experience of writing an examination. However, some find the experience challenging, arousing, and stimulating, whereas for others it is a highly nervous-making event which causes great distress.

The findings from several studies suggest that a deficit in appropriate coping skills renders those who develop an eating disorder less able to deal effectively with stress (Henderson & Huon, 2002; Koff & Sangani, 1997). Moreover, they are likely to experience more events as stressful because of their anxious traits. There is also agreement that stress can have a marked effect on eating behaviours; the difficulty is that the reactions do not seem to be uniform. Both animal and human experimentation indicates that stress can lead to increased or decreased consumption depending on many factors including the type, the duration, and the intensity of the stressor (Dess, 1997; Steptoe *et al.*, 1998; Rutledge & Linden, 1998). These factors may also be mediated biologically. When an individual is stressed, a number of biochemical changes occur, including the release of corticotropin-releasing factor (CRF), a hypothalamic neuropeptide which has been associated with decreased or restricted eating behaviour. However, other hormones secreted during stress can affect the body's glucose tolerance levels and foster an increase in appetite. Heightened sensitivity in either of these hormone systems could be a contributing factor to individual differences in eating behaviours during stress. Alternatively, the hormonal influence might be biphasic. For example, we know that at low or moderate levels, agonists of certain opioid receptors increase food intake, whereas at high levels they decrease it (Glass *et*

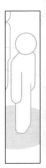

173

*al.*, 1999; Johnson, 1995; Martin-Bevins & Olster, 1999). Other factors that influence emotional eating can clearly be learned. Food is paired with so many pleasant social events – in fact, it is difficult to think of a celebration that does not include food – that it can take on the properties of a conditioned stimulus. Food is also used to distract from, or compensate for, distress. We see this every time a child is offered a biscuit to stop it crying.

We have seen how anxious traits can increase the impact of social pressures to lose weight. It has also been suggested that for some highly anxious individuals self-starving can be a powerful device to ameliorate negative affect (Kaye, 1999). This might occur because of diet-induced alterations to the brain serotonin (5-HT) system. More specifically, restricted food intake reduces the availability of the amino acid, tryptophan, the precursor to 5-HT, which in turn decreases 5-HT output. As we have seen in Chapter 5, high levels of this brain neurotransmitter are associated with harm avoidance, behavioural inhibition, fear and anxiety – in sum, an excessive overconcern with the anticipation of negative consequences. Conversely, relatively low levels of 5-HT are associated with impulsivity and aggression. There has been considerable interest in the role that 5-HT may play in the development of eating disorders, and 5-HT activity has been studied both in the ill state and among patients after recovery. Cerebrospinal fluid concentrations of the 5-HT metabolite, 5-HIAA (5-hydroxy-indolacetic acid) are commonly used to provide information about central nervous system serotonergic activity. Using this metabolite, studies have found that concentrations are elevated in woman who are weight-restored and long-term recovered from their illness (Kaye *et al.*, 1993). Moreover, there was a persistence of their anxiety and harm avoidance. As we said earlier, Kaye and colleagues suggested that severe dieting may actually have a mood-enhancing effect on patients who had relatively high levels of 5-HT before their illness began. Indeed, this maps onto the reports of many anorexic patients who claim that their greatest fear in facing recovery is the return of their anxious mood and obsessional thinking.

The story is somewhat more complicated, and perhaps less intuitive, for the role of 5-HT in the symptomatology of bulimia nervosa. What is particularly difficult to reconcile are two apparently conflicting pieces of evidence. On the one hand, there is a very different approach to food in the restrictor anorexic who increasingly resists food, compared to the bulimic patient who typically alternates between compulsive overeating and periods of fasting. On the other hand, recovered bulimic patients (like recovered anorexic patients) also have elevated 5-HIAA concentration in the cerebrospinal fluid. Some have proposed that bulimic patients suffer from a modulatory 5-HT defect, and may learn to crudely regulate their mood by 'starving and stuffing', because of their respective effects on brain tryptophan and 5-HT function (Kaye *et al.*, 2001; 2002). However, this explanation does not mesh well with the fact that the compulsive overeating of most bulimic patients resembles the impulsive

behaviours associated with low 5-HT activity (Steiger *et al.*, 2001c). Moreover, an enhancement of food consumption has consistently been observed with receptor antagonists and other drugs that decrease 5-HT activity. Again, one of the difficulties in this field is that many of the studies have failed to use 'pure' groups – that is, anorexic subjects of the restrictor type and bulimic subjects with no history of anorexia nervosa – when examining biochemical markers.

## SENSITIVITY TO REWARD, ADDICTION, AND THE EATING DISORDERS

Over the past few years, there has been an increasing interest in the parallels between eating disorders and addictive behaviours such as drug and alcohol abuse. Therefore, important research advances in the study of *vulnerability* to addiction may also inform our understanding of risk for the eating disorders.

The links between addiction and eating disorders can be mapped out at two levels. First, there is substantial lifetime comorbidity between the eating disorders, especially bulimia nervosa, and other addictions – a fact for which several, albeit not entirely incompatible, explanations have been proposed (Holderness *et al.*, 1994; Wiederman & Pryor, 1996). For example, some have suggested that a common set of personality traits predisposes to a range of behaviours that can alleviate the individual's painful affective states (Koob & Le Moal, 1997; Leshner, 1997). The particular behaviour that is chosen – for example, whether one becomes a gambler, a smoker, or an overeater – depends, of course, on a plethora of personal, environmental, and social factors. In support of this position is the evidence that anxiety and depression often pre-date substance abuse and other addictions (Grant & Harford, 1995; Kessler *et al.*, 1997). As we saw earlier in this chapter, these same affective disturbances are frequent pre-morbid characteristics of patients with eating disorders (Deep *et al.*, 1995; Vitousek & Manke, 1994). We have also found that among eating-disordered patients, irrespective of subtype, scores on a measure of *addictive personality characteristics* were comparable to those found in groups of drug addicts and alcoholics (Davis & Claridge, 1998). Complementary to this viewpoint, is also the idea that an addiction to one behaviour reinforces a certain style of 'coping' pattern that leaves the individual vulnerable to developing another type of addiction (see Holderness *et al.*, 1994).

A second, and somewhat different, position is that the behaviours which define the eating disorders are themselves addictions because they satisfy all the established clinical criteria for substance abuse disorders (Heyman, 1996; Robinson & Berridge, 1993; Tiffany, 1990; Wise & Bozarth, 1987). In Chapter 7, we described in detail the most salient characteristics of addictive behaviours. These find direct parallels in the core eating-disordered behaviours, such as dieting, exercising, and binge-eating, all of which tend to become excessive over time. Like other addictive behaviours, there is also a strong compulsion to continue these behaviours despite serious medical complications – a fact that is reflected in their prolonged morbidity, their high rate of relapse, and the substantial risk of sudden death. To illustrate, a recent study reported that the median time for full recovery from anorexia nervosa ranged between 41 and 73 months depending on the symptom profile of the patients; and, only 75 per cent ever achieved that status (Strober *et al.*, 1999). Other data also confirm that anorexia nervosa (to a greater degree than bulimia nervosa) is characterized by high rates of partial recovery and low rates of full recovery (Herzog *et al.*, 1999).

At the biological level, there are also parallels between eating disorders and addiction. We know, for instance, that *strenuous exercise* and *starvation* stimulate the release of endogenous opiates in the brain (Bergh & Sondersten, 1996). In the manner of all psychological and physical stressors, these behaviours stimulate the hypothalamic–pituitary–adrenal (HPA) axis and the release of beta-endorphins which, in turn, activate dopamine neurons in the nucleus accumbens and the ventral tegmentum – brain structures which we have learned are strongly associated with reward and dependence (Gianoulakis, 1998). These biological events have led to the formulation of what has been termed the *auto-addiction opioid* theory of the eating disorders – a theory which proposes that a chronic eating disorder is an addiction to the body's production of brain opioids, and therefore is identical to other forms of substance abuse. In other words, both starving and exercise serve as 'drug delivery devices' since they increase circulating levels of these opiates – specifically, the beta-endorphins – which are as potentially addictive as the exogenous opiates like heroin and morphine because of their ability to stimulate dopamine in the brain's mesolimbic reward centres (Heubner, 1993; Marrazzi & Luby, 1986).

As we have seen in Chapter 7, a key concept in current formulations about risk for addiction concerns individual differences in *sensitivity to reward*. This describes individuals' ability to experience pleasure and their motivation to engage in pleasurable or rewarding activities. We are reminded that the 'common reward pathway' in the brain evolved or developed to subserve survival behaviours such as eating. Recent studies have shown that sensitivity to reward is also useful for understanding certain behavioural differences between anorexic and bulimic patients such as the fact that the former display a facility for self-starving and report a decreasing interest in food, whereas the latter have difficulty resisting food and become compulsive overeaters. As was predicted, anorexic patients have a significantly *lower* sensitivity to reward than the general population, and those with bulimia nervosa tend to be somewhat *higher* than normal (Davis & Woodside, 2002). These findings support the premise that individual differences in reward sensitivity contribute to the avoidance and approach relationships to food found, respectively, in the two patient groups.

And yet, the inevitable question arises. Do these differences reflect premorbid – and therefore potentially causal – characteristics, or do they

result, in the case of anorexia nervosa, from the stress of starvation? In other words, in the case of anorexia nervosa there is the possibility that differences in the ability to experience the positive-incentive value of food may be diminished in response to an extended period of food deprivation making it easier, over time, for severely anorexic subjects to starve themselves (Pinel *et al.*, 2000). Interestingly, a similar explanatory conundrum exists when we consider the findings from a recent obesity study. Using PET scans, Wang and colleagues (2001) found that a group of grossly obese adults had significantly lower dopamine receptor densities – a biological characteristic that has been associated with low sensitivity to reward – than normal weight adults. What is not clear is the underlying mechanism. Did the obese subjects overeat as a *compensatory* behaviour for inherently low baselines dopamine levels, or did their overeating cause a downregulation of the dopamine system as occurs after chronic use of psychomotor stimulant drugs? One way to answer this question is to examine the relationship between eating and sensitivity to reward in healthy individuals. Studies carried out in this context have found that high sensitivity to reward is associated with overeating and with eating in response to stress and negative emotional states (Davis *et al.*, 2002).

In summary, when we take all factors into account, there is good evidence for the position that the eating disorders are a form of addiction. Clinically, the behaviours that define these disorders are very similar. Moreover, very similar biological mechanisms can explain the progression from 'use' to 'abuse' that we see in both disorders – in the case of drugs, from a recreational habit to a state of pathological dependence; in anorexia nervosa, from casual dieting to a life-threatening refusal to eat; and in bulimia nervosa to the increasing inability to resist large quantities of food. Finally, there is support for a common psychobiological vulnerability. We know, for instance, that individuals tend to 'self-medicate' their affective disturbances with a variety of rewarding behaviours based, to some extent, on the specific effects of each (Chutuape & Dewit, 1995; Khantzian, 1997; Markau *et al.*, 1998). Here, it is interesting to consider why some individuals choose nicotine, others alcohol, and others food to regulate mood. Clearly, personality, environment, and sociocultural factors have considerable influence in the choices that are made. The obsessional, perfectionistic, anxious, and conforming nature that characterizes many anorexic patients makes it easier to understand the compelling attraction of appearance-enhancing behaviours, such as dieting and exercise, since there are many social and psychological rewards that accrue to those who can achieve the cultural standards of thinness.

## THE PATHOPHYSIOLOGY OF EATING DISORDERS

However, in order to understand the motivation to continue these behaviours beyond the point of body-image improvements – and in the face of life-threatening medical complications – we must move beyond psychosocial explanations. When a person begins to diet, what often starts as a casual attempt to lose a few pounds can become, in certain vulnerable individuals, a time-consuming preoccupation with weight and body shape. Indeed, for some, the initial loss of weight is even involuntary, stemming from a mood or illness-induced absence of appetite. In some case, these behaviours and attitudes become even more extreme and ultimately they tip into a downwardly spiralling cycle of pathology. For many eating-disordered patients, food restriction is also accompanied by sport or exercise activities which, too, become extreme and compulsive over time. Studies have estimated that lifetime prevalence rates of hyperactivity or excessive exercising are about 80 per cent in patients with anorexia nervosa, and about 50 per cent in those with bulimia nervosa (Davis, 1997a).

Although most would agree that psychosocial factors are proximally causal in the initiation of the core eating-disordered behaviours, such as dieting and exercise, it is also becoming clear that the *pathophysiology* is perhaps a more important influence in the persistent and extreme continuation of these behaviours, even to the point of death. There is good evidence that the vicious psychobehavioural cycle that develops in the eating disorders is perpetuated, to a large extent, by the very behaviours that define the syndrome; that is, the physical malnutrition and the hyperactivity (Davis *et al.*, 1994, 1999). Both excessive exercising and self-starvation are activities which share a strong relationship with obsessionality. For example, several studies report that high-level exercisers typically display a compulsive behaviour pattern, as well as an obsessional and rigid personality profile (Davis & Claridge, 1998). As we have seen earlier, eating-disordered patients also tend to have personality traits, such as rigidity, restraint in emotional expression, and greater impulse control, which increase the likelihood that the goals they set, and the behaviours they engage in, will be tackled with enduring persistence.

Therefore, although we can see that the psychobehavioural links between exercise and self-starvation are well-established, it is only relatively recently that we have understood some of the biological connections. Interestingly, we have known for over 30 years that physical activity can be fatal for laboratory animals who are placed on restricted feeding schedules. Numerous studies have demonstrated that this phenomenon – sometimes known as *starvation-induced hyperactivity*, or as *exercise-induced weight loss* – is easily inducible and highly reliable (see Epling & Pierce, 1996). In the generic experimental protocol, food-restricted rats, with free access to a running wheel, reduce their food intake and their body weight in almost direct proportion to an increase in physical activity. In fact, in a relatively short period of time the animals can literally run themselves to death! There seems little doubt that strict calorie restriction and strenuous exercise are reciprocal behaviours which eventually become self-perpetuating and resistant to change.

In many ways, the exercise-induced weight-loss syndrome is a valid analogue of eating disorders in the human condition. Among other things, about 75 per cent of patients with anorexia nervosa report an inverse relationship between food intake and physical activity level during the acute weight-loss phase of their eating disorder (Davis *et al.*, 1994). Moreover, in describing this behaviour pattern subjectively, patients uniformly state that their involvement in physical activity progressed from a voluntary and mostly enjoyable endeavour to a state where the behaviour became 'obsessive' and 'out of control' – something they often wanted to stop doing, but simply could not! And this occurred most typically during a time when their food restriction was at its most severe.

Over the past decade, there has also been substantial biological support for the utility of the *exercise-induced weight-loss syndrome* as a psychobiological model for anorexia nervosa (Broocks *et al.*, 1990; Lett & Grant, 1996). One of its most significant experimental features is the ability to control for the general effects of weight loss by including, in the testing protocol, a non-exercising weight-matched group. This affords the opportunity to tease out biological changes that cannot be attributed to the secondary consequences of weight loss. On the other hand, a weakness of the model is its inability to control for the general effects of excessive exercise since there is no suitable way to stimulate normal weight animals to run freely to the same extent.

In recent years, several neurochemical mechanisms have been proposed to explain this syndrome, the most prominent of which have implicated both the monoamines and the endogenous opiates in the reinforcing properties of running. Because physical activity increases dramatically during periods of food restriction, one is obliged to infer either that exercising is accompanied by some pleasurable and rewarding effect or, alternatively, that it compensates for some unpleasant condition created by the state of hunger. One line of supporting evidence is the reduction of norepinephrine turnover in semi-starved sedentary animals while the opposite occurs in semi-starved animals who are able to run (Broocks *et al.*, 1990). It is possible that reduced norepinephrine turnover might be one internal stimulus for the induction of hyperactivity. Similarly, starvation-induced decreases in dopamine turnover were significantly increased in semi-starved animals who were allowed to run. These bits of evidence have led to the conclusion that exercising may be reinforcing because it compensates for the effects of semi-starvation which reduces turnover rates of dopamine in the brain. Strenuous physical activity also produces a release of endogenous opiates which are known to elevate mood (see Belke, 1994 for a review). This meshes well with our clinical observation. Many hyperactive patients report that once the disorder has become established, their extensive exercising is used more to regulate a disturbed mood than for body-image reasons.

## CONCLUSIONS

In this and the previous chapter, we have described behavioural disorders where personality is clearly influential in their origins, but is not so obviously continuous with their symptoms as in those described in chapters 5 and 6. The former are conditions whose link with normal personality relates mostly to a general *vulnerability to disorder* rather than to the specific form it takes. More than other psychological disturbances, the behavioural disorders are influenced by environmental factors, and by the interface between a psychobiological diathesis and a host of external events. Different from the mood and anxiety disorders, and OCD, both addictions and the eating disorders may be viewed as 'maladaptive strategies' that individuals use to function in their environment, rather than as extreme forms of their personality. In other words, the behaviour – whether it is trying to lose a few pounds to look better or taking a drink to relieve the stress of a social event – is primarily a way of coping with the exigencies of everyday life. Regrettably, behaviours that profoundly alter our neurobiology, such as self-starving, overeating, and substance use, have consequences beyond their ability to improve our immediate circumstances.

# CHAPTER 9
## PSYCHOTIC DISORDERS

## DEFINITIONS AND DESCRIPTIONS

Of the types of abnormality discussed in this book, psychosis and the psychotic disorders challenge our understanding most. They have generated a bewildering array of biological, psychological, social, sociological, and even political, research, with proportionately the least return in the way of comprehension of their nature and causes. Opinions about them are invariably wildly polarized, backed by evidence that is often unreplicated, flatly contradicted by other findings, or deliberately chosen to suit the argument. Because the topic is so unusually vast and untidy we, too, will need to be selective in the material we include here. It is therefore highly likely that we will also present a one-sided view – and the reader should be aware of that. But, given space limitations, some angle on the topic had to be chosen if we were to give a coherent account of a highly complex field. We were helped in this by the fact that one of the major issues about the psychotic disorders is precisely the one that is the central theme of the book.

In the case of psychosis, dimensionality, the possibility of an association between normal and abnormal, between personality and pathology, is much more controversial than for anything we have discussed so far. In the non-psychotic domain, debate certainly exists and opinions differ about the extent of dimensionality in clinical disorder and about other matters, such as the importance of genetic dispositions, the influence of biological – as against, say, cognitive – explanations, and so on. But the discussion there is of a different order from that surrounding psychosis. This has something to do with 'believability', or intuitive feel, or a sense of 'there but for the grace of...'. Most people, however rabidly against the view that biology plays a part in mental illness (or disagreeing with other things we have said), will have some insight into the disorders we have discussed so far – a realization of some connection to their own personal experience, or possibility for experience. That is usually not so true for the psychotic disorders, which for many of us seem alien, something which only the truly mentally diseased could suffer.

Nevertheless, dimensionality in the psychotic disorders is an issue that is currently the subject of live debate in psychiatry and abnormal and clinical psychology. This gives us a ready-made framework for organizing the material here and we shall make dimensionality the central theme of the chapter. For this reason, a fairly large part of the discussion will be taken up with theoretical and clinical questions relevant to the topic, alongside examining empirical evidence that bears on it. But, first, some terminology.

Actually, much of the vocabulary we need has been mentioned at various points throughout the book. And, in any case, the kinds of clinical state we shall be discussing will, in general terms, already be fairly familiar to the reader; corresponding, that is, to what in everyday discourse we refer to as the mad, the crazy, the lunatic, or the insane. Nevertheless, it is worth briefly recapping the more technical language used in connection with these disorders, now that they are the topic of a single chapter.

'Psychotic' (and 'psychosis') we introduced right at the beginning when outlining a broad framework for the layout of the book. We noted that, although there is no single criterion for defining psychotic, there would be a general consensus that, once recognized as in need of help, a person would be said to fit that description if he or she showed certain features: loss of touch with reality and lack of insight into weird behaviours, and strange thoughts, perceptions and feelings which, on the face of it, seem outside the range of normal experience. In current usage the other major distinction that would then need to be made is between, on the one hand, the schizophrenic form of psychosis and, on the other, manic-depressive psychosis. (In the DSM and the ICD the latter has now been renamed 'bipolar affective disorder', but here we shall use both terms interchangeably.)

On the personality side we have also already encountered the notion of 'psychoticism', in at least two guises. One is in a generic sense, to articulate the idea of some kind of dimensionality connecting the normal to the abnormal in the domain of psychosis. The other is more specific, as a third dimension in Eysenck's theory, intended to account, in combination with his other two personality dimensions, for underlying dispositions to schizophrenic and manic-depressive psychosis. Then, while discussing the personality disorders, we came across the DSM Axis II 'Mad' cluster, the clinical features of which have a reference point in the symptoms of Axis I psychotic illness. Lastly, also in Axis II we noted that Borderline Personality Disorder, although in a different cluster, has some connections to psychosis.

We also need to note a potential point of contact, yet also distinction, between the content of this chapter and our coverage of depression in Chapter

5. As discussed there, depression was taken to mean low moods of varying severity, symptom content, and perhaps different biologies. Some of those features might be shared with the form of depression found in bipolar affective disorder. However, the latter was left out of Chapter 5, for two reasons. First, the presence of the manic element in bipolar disorder helps to identify some potentially different aberration of mood from depression occurring on its own. Second, research on manic depression has conventionally formed part of the psychosis literature, rather than that on depression *per se*.

We shall discuss manic depression in more detail towards the end of the chapter, but it is convenient to summarize its distinguishing characteristics now. These are shown in Table 9.1, where we emphasize the more extreme features of the disorder.

**Table 9.1**  Bipolar Affective Disorder (Manic depression): main features.

| Mania | Depression |
|---|---|
| Elated mood | Suicidal mood |
| Overactive behaviour | Sluggish behaviour |
| Racing thoughts and speech | Slow thinking and reduced speech |
| ('Flight of ideas') | Delusions of sin, poverty, etc. |
| Delusions of grandeur | Hallucinations |
| Hallucinations | |

Most of the depressive symptoms will be familiar from Chapter 5; the manic ones perhaps less so, but they do fairly obviously contrast, cognitively and emotionally, with those of depression, However, we should clear up one misconception about the 'bipolarity' of manic depression. Contrary to some belief, mania and depression do not correspond exactly to the 'happiness' and 'sadness' of normal mood. Thus, mania – or what is often referred to as 'hypomania' – is not the same as happiness. Manic individuals may become very irritable if thwarted in attempting to carry out unrealistically grandiose schemes or, if asked to do so, judge their prevailing mood as depressed (Lester & Kaplan, 1994).

Turning to schizophrenia, its diagnostic features, according to the DSM-IV, are listed in Table 9.2. The schizophrenia construct raises several issues, some to be discussed in following sections, but one general observation should be made at this point. It is evident from Table 9.2 that, under the DSM-IV, an individual could be diagnosed as 'schizophrenic' by meeting only two, and any two, of a range of quite different criteria. Indeed (see under 'NOTE' in the table) only *one* criterion needs to be met if the symptom happens to be of a certain, peculiar quality: what is described as of the 'first rank'.

183

**Table 9.2** Schizophrenia: diagnostic criteria (DSM-IV).

| **Two (or more) of:** |
| --- |
| Delusions |
| Hallucinations |
| Disorganized speech (for example, frequent derailment or incoherence) |
| Grossly disorganized or catatonic behaviour |
| Negative symptoms, that is, affective flattening, alogia or avolition |

*Note*: Only one criterion if symptom of 'first rank' type.

The notion of first rank symptoms, first proposed by the German psychiatrist Kurt Schneider (1959), is an important one in helping to articulate some questions that have always puzzled, and continue to bemuse, researchers on schizophrenia. What *are* the 'fundamental' features of schizophrenia? Is there some unique feature that is sufficient to define the condition? What is it about the disorder that ultimately needs to be explained? The dilemma is illustrated in Table 9.3, which contrasts two different views on this. One is the first rank symptom position just mentioned: that certain experiences of people clinically labelled 'schizophrenic' are so bizarre, incomprehensible, and distant from the normal that we are surely convinced that these must be central to the disorder.

**Table 9.3** Primary symptoms of schizophrenia: two perspectives.

| **According to Bleuler** |
| --- |
| *Disorder of thought process:* |
|     Loosening of associative thought |
|     'Splitting' of cognition and emotion |
| **According to Schneider** |
| *First rank symptoms:* |
|     Audible thoughts and 'third person' hallucinations |
|     Delusions of external control over emotions, thoughts, willed action |

In contrast is the view traceable to Eugen Bleuler who, some 100 years ago, coined the term 'schizophrenia' (Bleuler, 1911). He believed that hallucinations and delusions were what he called accessory symptoms, viz. *secondary*, psychological consequences of a more primary, physiological process that constituted the core of schizophrenia. A particularly important defining feature of this primary process was the loosening of associative thought which, in the subsequent terminology popularized by Schneider, could be elaborated into first rank (but, according to Bleuler, aetiologically secondary) symptoms. It is evident from Table 9.2 that current professional practice for diagnosing schizophrenia is a confused mix of these two positions; for example Criterion 3 – thought and speech derailment – represents the Bleulerian tradition. The bias, however, is clearly towards the view that first rank symptom diagnosis is pre-eminent. This is understandable. Reporting that aliens in outer space are responsible for the thoughts in your head certainly seems more crazy than bemusing your neighbour with your stream of consciousness style of conversation!

## THE ISSUE OF HETEROGENEITY

It is already obvious that psychosis shows considerable clinical variability. But how do we interpret this? Are the disorders literally independent of one another and of quite different origins? Or do they represent different expressions of a single underlying cause or combination of causes? There are really two debates here. One concerns the separateness, or otherwise, of schizophrenia and manic depression; the other relates to heterogeneity within schizophrenia itself. We shall look at each of these in turn.

## ONE PSYCHOSIS OR TWO?

It has become the received wisdom in psychiatry that manic depression and schizophrenia are distinct disorders, with quite different aetiologies. This view is even prevalent outside professional circles, where the two ways of going crazy are viewed very differently, even to the extent of social evaluation. Schizophrenia – indeed anything with 'schizo' in the label – is usually judged malign, dangerous, deteriorating, and irreversibly damaging to the person. The moods of manic depression, on the other hand, although recognized in their extreme form as signs of illness, are viewed as less permanently dysfunctional – in some quarters even as vaguely romantic, through supposed connections to things such as artistic talent and the creative process.

Yet it is important to realize that, historically, the bipolar/schizophrenia dichotomy currently in vogue in psychiatry actually represents only one of the possible perspectives on psychosis. Indeed, separating out two 'types', as in the current psychiatric nosology, is relatively recent, owing much to Emil Kraepelin, the great nineteenth-century classifier of mental disease (Kraepelin, 1919). It was the two forms of insanity he recognized – manic depression and *dementia praecox* (later renamed 'schizophrenia' by Bleuler) – that have became enshrined in modern diagnostic manuals. Yet, long antedating Kraepelin, there was a school of thought favouring a 'unitary psychosis' (or *Einheitpsychose*) theory. This proposed a single mental aberration which, shaped by different influences, resulted in varied expressions of madness (see Berrios, 1995).

Despite the monopoly of Kraepelinian thinking about insanity, the unitary viewpoint never died entirely. In fact, outside psychiatry, in the personality domain, it continued to have a strong influence on the way some psychologists thought about psychosis. Most obviously, it survived in Eysenck's notion of 'psychoticism' as a personality dimension common to all forms of psychosis. The idea formed part of his theory from its inception; but Eysenck's opinion on the matter was either ignored or ridiculed by psychiatrists. However, in recent years the unitary view of psychosis has enjoyed some revival among clinicians and medical researchers, and is now beginning to re-emerge as a strong contender on how we should construe schizophrenia and manic depression: as entirely separate disorders or as variations on a common theme. We shall look at the arguments and evidence for this later in the chapter, when we come to discuss bipolar disorder.

## ONE SCHIZOPHRENIA OR SEVERAL?

Distinguishing schizophrenia from bipolar disorder does not solve the problem of heterogeneity in psychosis; it merely narrows the domain that we need to puzzle over. As noted when discussing the diagnostic criteria for schizophrenia, there is potential for considerable variability in its clinical presentation. This should not surprise us. Bleuler never intended to refer to a single syndrome. From the very beginning he talked, instead, of 'the schizophrenias' as a group of disorders, with different clinical features. It was mostly the awkwardness of linguistic usage that subsequently caused the term to be used in the singular, a convention which – having made the point – we shall continue to follow here.

There have been many attempts to deal descriptively with the clinical variability of schizophrenia. The traditional diagnostic approach – perpetuated in both the DSM and the ICD – has been to name subtypes, defined according to the cluster of symptoms that predominates in the patient. Types include 'catatonic', 'paranoid', and 'hebephrenic' (a quaint label from the very early history of psychiatry). We shall not dwell in detail on this subtyping, except to make two points. First, in both the DSM and the ICD the main subdivisions of schizophrenia are supplemented by reference to other varieties of psychosis, such as 'delusional disorder' and 'brief psychotic disorder'. Even without manic depression, the heterogeneity of psychosis is well catered for in the diagnostic manuals. The second point to make about this subtyping concerns its relative lack of utility for (and use in) scientific research on schizophrenia. Where researchers have paid attention to clinical variability in their samples (which mostly they have not) they have tended to look elsewhere for subclassifications. These have taken many forms, ranging from simple, empirical dichotomies – for example paranoid versus non-paranoid – to more elaborate, statistically derived, clusters or dimensions.

Currently, the most widely quoted research classification is based on a distinction between positive and negative symptoms (Andreasen & Olsen, 1982;

Crow, 1985). Positive symptom – or what is sometimes called Type I – schizophrenia is defined by the presence of active symptomatology, such as hallucinations, delusions, and florid thought disorder. Negative symptom (Type II) schizophrenia is characterized by a lack or poverty of behaviour: thought, feeling and motor activity, perhaps driven by a low motivational state. Although still very popular, this dichotomy may be faulted on a number of grounds:

- Subjective accounts of the psychotic experience suggest that it is doubtful whether 'negative' symptoms define a *type* of schizophrenia. It is more likely that positive and negative symptoms represent alternating *states* occurring at different times within the same individual (Bouricius, 1989).

- If it does define a 'type' of schizophrenia, the 'negative' form probably refers to the chronic end-state, without florid symptoms, into which some individuals progress after years of adaptation to the illness.

- Diagnosing schizophrenia at the first episode solely on the basis of negative symptomatology, in the absence of positive symptoms – classically the core feature of psychosis – is unconvincing. How is it distinguishable from depression?

- The meaning of 'negative symptomatology' is ambiguous. It could be: a way of coping with the positive symptoms of schizophrenia (for example, as social withdrawal); an effect of antipsychotic medication; or part of a manifestation of depression.

- Research suggests that a simple two-syndrome dichotomy is oversimplified. Statistical analyses now suggest that there are at least three (and possibly as many as five) dimensions in schizophrenic symptomatology (Arndt *et al.*, 1991; Lindenmayer *et al.*, 1994). This does include negative and positive symptom features. But, in addition, an important subdivision of the positive aspect is now recognized: one part corresponds to first rank symptoms of the kind described earlier, whereas the other has to do with disorganized, derailed thinking, more in line with Bleuler's conception of the primary disorder in schizophrenia.

187

Despite these criticisms, the negative/positive distinction – or some elaboration of it – probably is along the right lines, as a rough template, easily recognizable to clinicians, of how schizophrenic symptoms can vary.

## DIMENSIONAL ASPECTS OF SCHIZOPHRENIA

Appreciating that, in whatever form, there is *some* kind of dimensionality in schizophrenia is important because it is no longer possible fully to understand the disorder, or research being conducted on it, without paying attention to that aspect. This is true in several respects: the genetics of schizophrenia; the various models currently being formulated to explain the illness and the predisposition to it; and methodological issues that arise in trying to investigate these topics. But, compared with the other disorders, how dimensionality applies to schizophrenia has become more controversial and the special questions it raises need considering further.

## QUASI- VERSUS FULLY DIMENSIONAL MODELS

As noted elsewhere in the book, 'dimensionality' enters into disorder in two quite different ways. One is as continua of personality dispositions, for example strength of anxiety traits. The other is as variations in illness severity; for example number or severity of anxiety symptoms. The existence of the latter kind of dimensionality in schizophrenia is not particularly contentious, since the symptoms of the illness can sometimes appear in a rather muted form. It is this observation that has given rise to the idea of the *schizophrenia spectrum* and to connections between schizophrenia and the personality disorders. Of the latter, Schizotypal Personality Disorder (SPD) has received most attention, as a possible mild variant of schizophrenia. The reasons for this are obvious as can be judged from the clinical criteria for SPD, shown in Table 9.4; it can be seen that this personality disorder is defined very much in terms of dilute versions of schizophrenic symptoms.

**Table 9.4**  Schizotypal Personality Disorder: diagnostic criteria.

| |
| --- |
| Ideas of reference |
| Odd beliefs or magical thinking |
| Unusual perceptual experiences |
| Odd thinking and speech (vague, circumstantial) |
| Suspiciousness |
| Inappropriate or constricted affect |
| Odd eccentric behaviour or appearance |
| Lack of close friends |
| Excessive social anxiety |

As we know, SPD is not the only representative of the 'Mad' cluster in the DSM Axis II; viewed more broadly, the 'schizophrenia spectrum' could be said to take in the other Cluster A disorders, viz. Paranoid Personality Disorder and Schizoid Personality Disorder (Maier *et al.*, 1999). This would acknowledge both the severity implications of the spectrum, as well as its heterogeneity; reflecting schizophrenia itself. However, the main point is that the

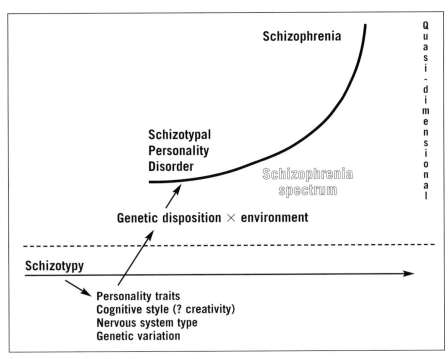

**Figure 9.1**   Comparison of two dimensional models of schizophrenia.

dimensionality we are looking at here refers to a continuum within the *illness domain*, consistent with the well-recognized medical principle that diseases frequently do present with different intensity.

An alternative, more radical, view of the dimensionality of schizophrenia would go further than that. It would argue that schizophrenia is, in principle, no different from the other illnesses discussed in this book; just as anxiety traits predispose to anxiety symptoms, so 'schizophrenic' personality traits predispose to schizophrenic symptoms.

Figure 9.1 illustrates the essentials of these two models – denoted, respectively, 'quasi-dimensional' and 'fully dimensional'. Two points should be noted. First, according to the fully dimensional view, in moderate amount the underlying traits predisposing to schizophrenia are perfectly adaptive features of personality; in the same way that mild trait anxiety can be beneficial. It is this proposal that has created most controversy in debates about dimensionality and schizophrenia: to many critics the suggestion that there could be anything healthy in a seriously disabling condition like schizophrenia seems absurd. The second point to note about Figure 9.1 is not specific to schizophrenia. It is simply a reminder about how the two forms of dimensionality relate to each other and how the fully dimensional model is more inclusive than the quasi-dimensional model. This is naturally the case since traits at the personality level are more universal than symptoms; the latter only occur once the person has passed the threshold into illness (as depicted in Figure 9.1 moved from the bottom to the upper half of the diagram).

Irrespective of the model of dimensionality adopted, the central concept that has guided research on the topic is 'schizotypy'. The term is owed to Rado (1953), a psychoanalyst, but the construct was later developed by Meehl and his followers (Meehl, 1962, 1990; see also Raine *et al.*, 1995) within a genetic theory of schizophrenia. The Meehl school is very firmly grounded in a quasi-dimensional theory: schizotypy is regarded as the phenotypic expression of a genetically determined biological malfunction which, unless compensated for, will result, to varying degree, in schizophrenic illness. The fully dimensional view is more relaxed about the 'normality' of schizotypal traits; as noted above, these are perceived as part of natural variations in personality, an idea that obviously owes much to theories in the Eysenckian tradition.

These two contrasting formulations of dimensionality have often led to different conclusions about schizophrenia and schizotypy, and ways of studying them. To illustrate, fully dimensional theorists have made considerable use of the notion of 'healthy schizotypy', to denote (perhaps the majority of) individuals who are high on the dimension but who show no evidence of illness (McCreery & Claridge, 2002; see also Claridge, 1997). For quasi theorists this is an impossible idea! According to them, genuine schizotypy is *always* a sign (or potential sign) of schizophrenia, however mild and/or concealed. True, there are cases, it is argued, where the person's behaviour mimics schizotypy but, in genetics jargon, these are what are called 'phenocopies', individuals in whom the superficially similar behaviour arises for different reasons.

These different conceptions of schizotypy have a knock-on effect on research methodology. In looking in the general population for signs of schizotypy – neurocognitive, biological, or whatever – quasi theorists always search for indicators of *defect* in very targeted subsets of individuals; these will be subjects who have already been strictly screened, for example by questionnaire, as falling into the schizotype category, or 'taxon' as it is called (Lenzenweger, 1993). Fully dimensional theorists, on the other hand, assume that schizotypal characteristics are widespread as signs of naturally occurring variation. Hence, they will use the same methods as those employed elsewhere in individual differences research, such as correlational analyses in unselected samples of subjects. As discussed later, fully dimensional theory has also tended to assume that evidence of schizotypy in healthy individuals need not necessarily show up as performance deficits. Instead, it might be found in perfectly functional behaviours.

## MEASUREMENT OF SCHIZOTYPY

Despite the above differences in research aim and interpretation, the descriptive measurement of schizotypy itself has been a shared endeavour, common to both schools of thought on the topic. This has resulted in the

construction of a large number of self-report questionnaires for use in non-clinical populations. Scales have been devised from a number of different points of view and for different purposes: as specially developed research instruments, as scales modelled on the DSM criteria (for example, for SPD), or as derivatives of existing questionnaires (Edell, 1995; Mason et al., 1997). Of most interest to us here are the many factor analyses of these questionnaires that have been carried out, by several research groups (see Mason et al. (1997) for a summary of studies up to that date and Schizophrenia Bulletin (2000) for several later reports).

Unsurprisingly, all investigators conclude that 'schizotypy' is not a single construct, but consists of more than one component. Almost without exception, every study has demonstrated a minimum of two dimensions that correspond to, respectively, the positive and the negative symptoms seen in schizophrenia itself. Beyond that, however, there is some difference of opinion. Looking across all studies, the consensus is that schizotypy consists of three dimensions. However, this may reflect the number of scales included in the various analyses. One study, the most comprehensive to date – in terms of number of scales included, as well as sample size – has suggested that there may actually be *four* schizotypy components (Claridge et al., 1996). These are shown in Table 9.5, together with typical self-report items that help to define them: these are taken from a questionnaire – the O-LIFE – developed from the factor analysis (Mason et al., 1995).

**Table 9.5** O-LIFE – typical items.

---

**Unusual experiences**
Are your thoughts sometimes so strong you can almost hear them?
Have you ever felt you have special, almost magical powers?

**Cognitive disorganization**
Do you ever feel that your speech is difficult to understand because the words are all mixed up and don't make any sense?
No matter how hard you try to concentrate do unrelated thoughts always creep into your mind?

**Introvertive anhedonia**
Do you feel very close to your friends? (–)
Are people usually better off if they stay aloof from emotional involvements with other people?

**Impulsive Nonconformity**
Do you ever have the urge to break or smash things?
Are you usually in an average kind of mood, not too high and no too low? (–)

---

The first three of the components listed in the table are virtually identical to those reported by other workers; they correspond, at the trait level, to what in the clinical sphere is now agreed to be a fair summary of schizophrenic symptomatology. The fourth factor – *Impulsive Non-conformity* – possibly represents some set of personality traits relating more to the affective form of psychosis. We will return to that point again when discussing manic depression.

# EXPLAINING SCHIZOPHRENIA

## RESEARCH PROBLEMS AND STRATEGIES

Compounding the difficulty of grasping conceptually what is meant by 'madness' is the problem of studying it scientifically. The two are, of course, connected and there are many practical ways in which the bizarre quality of the psychotic state affects its empirical investigation. We have already mentioned the heterogeneity of schizophrenia; taken together with the similar picture found for schizotypy, this means that attempts to give a single explanation of a single disorder are almost bound to fail. And variability almost certainly extends beyond *between*-subject differences to *within*-subject variation. It can be shown that, even for simple physiological responses, such as the galvanic skin response, individual schizophrenic subjects show enormous day-to-day fluctuation (Claridge & Clark, 1982). Few, if any, studies of schizophrenic subjects bother to take more than a one-off reading of whatever it is they are interested in measuring. That, of course, is also true of research in other fields of abnormal psychology. But it might be particularly serious in the case of schizophrenia, because what causes this individual instability of function could itself be an important clue to the nature of the disorder. Certainly it was once said that the only consistent observation about measures taken from schizophrenic subjects is their variability.

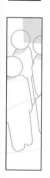

192

Other research hazards stem from the effect of the clinical state on the measurement process itself This is particularly serious for psychological studies, for example of performance on laboratory tasks that are widely used in research on schizophrenia. What does it really tell us about schizophrenia if, throughout testing, the subject is listening to hallucinatory voices or distracted by delusional thoughts about the experimenter – or merely not looking at the computer screen on which the test stimuli are being displayed! A partial way round the problem is to study subjects whose more acute symptomatology is controlled by antipsychotic drugs, a procedure generally forced on researchers anyway since most schizophrenic subjects are on some form of medication. But this creates its own difficulties because it is never clear what is being measured: a genuine feature of the illness or the effect of the drugs being used to treat it. Which of course is a critical consideration; not just for psychological studies, but also (perhaps more so) for those of a biological nature.

To a much greater extent than for other disorders, research on schizophrenia is therefore very largely a matter of playing swings and roundabouts with methodology, balancing the ideal against what is practical. Or, alternatively, trying to step around the difficulties altogether and seeking other research strategies. It is here that studies of schizotypy come in. The reasoning behind this is quite straightforward. If, as is argued, high schizotype subjects share important features with schizophrenic subjects, then studying them, instead of people with the full-blown clinical illness, should help because it then becomes possible to study 'schizophrenia' without the confounding effects of acute mental disturbance or medication. Selection of highly schizotypal individuals for this purpose is either by means of the questionnaires referred to in the previous section, by equivalent interview procedures, or – in the case of clinical samples – by virtue of subjects meeting the criteria for Schizotypal Personality Disorder.

All of the above refers to the use of the 'schizotypy strategy' to examine possible *mechanisms* of psychotic disorder. But studying schizotypy has another purpose, established in its own right. This concerns the identification of features that help to put people at risk for schizophrenia. Here, the genetics of the disorder are becoming an increasing focus. It is now generally accepted that, in so far as genetic factors have a rôle to play in schizophrenia, these are likely to be complex, with many genes involved and graded effects being the order of the day. Conceptualizing the genetic architecture of schizophrenia in this way sits well with the dimensional perspective intrinsic to schizotypy which is now beginning to emerge as a 'strong' construct that could capture at least some of the underlying genetic disposition to schizophrenia. Thus, any objective measurements of schizotypy that are unearthed are potentially useful indicators of risk for the illness; just as – to recall our earlier analogy – blood pressure acts as a measure of risk for hypertension and, beyond that, more serious vascular disease.

## GENETICS AND RISK FOR SCHIZOPHRENIA

Although much of the detail is still missing, the contribution of genetic influences is one of the few factual certainties about schizophrenia. Even in the absence of the discovery of specific genes, this is clear from kinship data, as shown in Table 9.6. Notably – and a sure sign of the heritability of a trait – monozygotic twins are much more concordant for schizophrenia than dizygotic twins *and* the degree of risk for the illness changes in an orderly manner according to the closeness of the kinship, from first- to second-degree relatives, and so on (Gottesman, 1991).

**Table 9.6**   Risk for schizophrenia according to kinship (per cent).

| | |
|---|---|
| Monozygotic twins | 43 |
| Monozygotic twins (reared apart) | 58 |
| Dizygotic twins | 12 |
| Two Schizophrenic parents | 46 |
| One Schizophrenic parent | 6 |
| Sibling | 10 |
| Aunt | 2 |
| First cousin | 2 |
| Unrelated | 1 |

There is, however, a caveat about the observation that the concordance rate in monozygotic twins is approximately 50 per cent. It could be argued that the figure looks vaguely suspicious, given the great heterogeneity of 'schizophrenia'. Individual studies of monozygotic concordance for schizophrenia have ranged from zero to more than 90 per cent. Is it possible that the value of 50 per cent now generally quoted is merely some average of a range of heritabilities for entirely different psychotic disorders, different variants of schizophrenia, or just illnesses of different severity? Certainly, on the last point it is known that calculated heritabilities for schizophrenia vary proportionally with judged severity among the cases sampled (Gottesman & Shields, 1982). More intriguing – and rather puzzling – is an observation about heritabilities calculated on the *same* sets of twins, diagnosed, on one occasion, according to first rank symptoms and, on the other, by broader criteria for schizophrenia, taking in more Bleulerian features (Farmer *et al.*, 1987; McGuffin *et al.*, 1987). For broad criteria the results were very much those we have quoted above – approximately 50 per cent concordance for monozygotic twins. In contrast, the heritability of first rank symptom schizophrenia turned out to be zero! This tends to suggest that, despite their convincingly 'psychotic' appearance, first rank symptoms do not tap directly into whatever is inherited in schizophrenia; instead, they may indeed be secondary elaborations of some more fundamental (inherited) cognitive processes, along the lines visualized by Bleuler.

One thing that *is* certain from the genetics data is that environmental influences must also be important in the aetiology of schizophrenia. This has been interpreted in sharply different ways. A biological school in schizophrenia research has emphasized the importance of ante- or perinatal trauma as a possible factor, interacting with genetic disposition, to trigger the illness. A body of evidence supporting this claim has come from observations that schizophrenic subjects more frequently have a history of birth

complications (Verdoux *et al.*, 1997). A recent elaboration of this idea is the 'two-hit hypothesis' to which we referred in Chapter 2; the notion that genetically predisposed individuals may be made even more vulnerable by exposure to physiological stressors at critical points in development and then, through later trauma, be precipitated into illness (Bayer *et al.*, 1999).

In contrast, a social interpretation of the genetic/environmental interaction is typically to be found in the classic study by Tienari (1991). He examined the rate of schizophrenic breakdown in subjects adopted away from their biologically schizophrenic mothers. As expected, having a biological mother who was schizophrenic increased the rate of schizophrenia in the offspring, even though reared in a non-schizophrenic family. But – and this was the important finding – the schizophrenia genetics revealed itself *only* if the adaptive family was psychologically disturbed. Put another way, it looked as though even individuals who were strongly loaded genetically towards schizophrenia could be protected from breakdown if their rearing family was healthy.

By itself neither of these formulations of the environmental influence in schizophrenia tells the whole story. For just as there are different clinical presentations, so there is almost certainly more than one route to psychotic illness. The only common factor seems to be some genetic disposition. But we could even ask about that: What does it mean? We have already seen that there are genetic influences in almost every kind of human variation, including the more familiar features of temperament and personality. Is it possible – as the fully dimensional model mentioned earlier would assume – that the network of traits contained within schizotypy/psychosis proneness is merely another example of that: personality dispositions waiting to be transformed into a variety of disorders? Certainly some thinking about the genetics of schizophrenia is moving in that direction, as Figure 9.2 illustrates.

The author of the model, Weinberger (2002), explains it as follows:

> An argument can be made that schizophrenia is not a genetic illness *per se*, but a varying combination of component heritable traits (and genes) that comprise susceptibility and that interact with each other, with modifying alleles, and with the environment to produce the complex clinical phenotype. (Weinberger, 2002)

195

Of course, this is a terribly catch-all position: it can scarcely be wrong! But it is probably the best we have and better than claims – so far largely unsubstantiated and, with the odd exception, mostly abandoned – that there is a gene for schizophrenia. Returning to Figure 9.2, it would obviously help if we knew more about possible genes involved and the functional processes for which they code. But progress there has so far been fairly limited. Admittedly, claims have been made for several gene loci, some of which do have interesting connections to other aspects of schizophrenia. An example is a proposal that

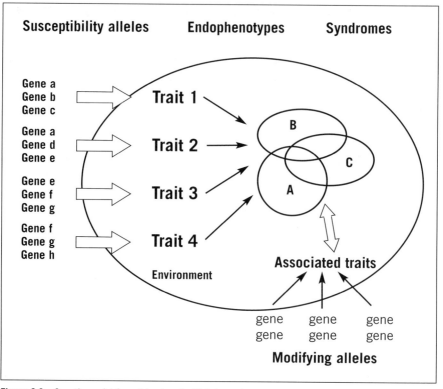

**Figure 9.2** Genetic model for schizophrenia (Weinberger).

the alpha-7 nicotinic receptor gene may contribute to the risk for developing schizophrenia. It has not escaped notice that this might relate to the long known fact that schizophrenic subjects smoke a lot (Hughes *et al.*, 1986). But in other respects such observations sit rather in isolation, describing small effects that do not in themselves account for much of the variance in schizophrenia risk.

One notable development in genetics research on schizophrenia – implicit in Figure 9.2 – has been the realization that the clinical diagnosis is a very blunt, inaccurate phenotype for exploring the heritability of psychosis. In its place, it is argued, we should substitute, and look for the genetics of, intermediate phenotypes, or *endophenotypes* (Gottesman, 1991). These are measures that do not, at first glance, seem to have much to do with psychotic symptomatology; they are assumed instead to tap more basic – albeit quite narrow – behaviours that look as though they might underlie the clinical state. A widely quoted example is an index of *smooth pursuit eye movement* (SPEM). This has been extensively investigated following observations that a proportion of schizophrenic subjects showed an abnormality in their ability to follow, effectively, a swinging pendulum. Similar irregularities have been reported in other relevant target groups, including first-degree relatives of schizophrenic subjects and schizotypal and schizoid individuals (Levy *et al.*, 1993).

Reiterating an earlier comment – and as will be illustrated further in the following sections – studies of schizotypy are a potentially rich source for discovering endophenotypes for schizophrenia. Notably – and this is a crucial point – much of the research to date has concentrated on the *positive symptom* aspects of schizophrenia (and schizotypy). Yet, the *negative* component – corresponding to anhedonia in schizotypy – might prove to be just as important, if not more so, in contributing to schizophrenia breakdown in vulnerable individuals (Tsuang, 2002). One piece of evidence to support this comes from a follow-up study of individuals administered schizotypy scales covering both positive and negative aspects, viz. magical ideation/perceptual aberration and anhedonia. Although the base rate of subsequent psychopathology was low, the positive symptoms scales did predict a somewhat greater frequency of general psychotic experiences (Kwapil *et al.*, 1997). However, it was the *negative* symptom measure (social anhedonia) that was more able to predict specifically schizophrenia spectrum disorders in the subjects (Kwapil, 1998).

These findings should not surprise us too much. As we know, positive symptoms show almost no heritability. And, as experiences, they are quite common in the healthy population: this is true both for hallucinations (Johns & van Os, 2001) and delusions (Peters, 2001). Indeed, occurring as religious or other spiritual experiences they can be quite constructive, even problem-solving for the individual (Jackson, 1997). Unless they lead to outrageous or noticeably 'sick' behaviour, positive symptoms are likely to pass, at worst, as eccentricity. By comparison, anhedonia – both physical and social – looks more malignant and it is easy to see how, occurring in conjunction with aberrant cognitive experiences, some of the more disabling social and emotional signs of schizophrenic illness could develop.

## EXPERIMENTAL PSYCHOPATHOLOGY OF SCHIZOPHRENIA

Over the more than 100 years since it was first described almost everything imaginable has been measured in schizophrenic subjects. This ranges from head size and facial appearance (still going on) to the constituents of sweat; the latter motivated by the observation that schizophrenic subjects smell differently (only abandoned as a clue to a possible chemical explanation when the cause was understood to be a combination of living in an institution, personal neglect, and treatment with paraldehyde, an old-fashioned sedative that exudes in the perspiration!). As always, current approaches still divide roughly along medical/non-medical lines: the search for the neurology and biochemistry of disease, as against more systematic enquiries, often by psychologists or psychophysiologists, into the mechanisms and correlates of schizophrenia This distinction is becoming increasingly blurred as biology more and more influences psychology, cognitive becomes neurocognitive, and perspectives on schizophrenia that originated outside medicine, such as the dimensional view, begin to have an influence on psychiatric thinking about the illness.

In trying to pick a way through what is still nevertheless an untidy literature, we shall take as our starting point what is often referred to as the *experimental psychopathology* of schizophrenia. This is particularly suited to our purposes here for three reasons. First, it draws very much upon research by experimental psychologists trying to get a handle on schizophrenia. Second, from its inception the area has been a natural breeding ground for research on dimensional models. Third, because there is an encouraging degree of continuity in the development of ideas about schizophrenia, over what amounts to nearly 50 years of research on its experimental psychopathology.

To enlarge briefly on the last, historical, point the aim from the beginning was to try to find ways of studying in the laboratory what were seen to be the core psychological processes that lie behind the manifest symptoms of schizophrenia. Given the clinical features of the latter, these processes were considered to be predominantly (though not exclusively) broadly cognitive in nature; in the terminology of the time to involve some or all of the stages in information processing. Clinical observation and experimental study converged to suggest that the cognitive functioning of schizophrenic subjects could be deviant at all points – from the simplest sensory analysis of a stimulus through to its highest level of representation in language and thought (Table 9.7).

**Table 9.7** Psychological processes disturbed in schizophrenia.

| **Sensation and Perception** | |
| --- | --- |
| Auditory – sounds louder, distorted, for example music backwards | |
| Visual – objects brighter, duller, larger, smaller; no perspective/constancy | |
| Other – tactile, olfactory, synaesthesia | |
| **Attention** | 'flooded', *or* over-narrowed |
| **Thinking & language** | incoherent, blocked *or* coherent, logical, but bizarre |
| **Emotion** | fluctuant: blunted *or* hypersensitive ('skinlessness') |

The common problem was what Venables (1964), one of the foremost workers in the field at the time and a psychophysiologist, designated 'input dysfunction' – an inability to handle information in an orderly and stable way. Venables was also one of the few researchers, then or since, to have taken

account of the great heterogeneity of schizophrenia. Table 9.7 demonstrates why he felt he needed to do this. The schizophrenic's functioning could operate at two extreme and quite opposite ways: thinking and attention could be highly focused or all over the place, emotion be lacking or personally overwhelming, and so on. Venables's idea therefore was that the schizophrenic nervous system has problems in input dysfunction in two directions: the 'gating in' of stimuli and their 'gating out'. This causes it to be either abnormally open to, or closed off from, information, a fact reflected in the individual schizophrenic subject's clinical symptomatology.

Venables's theory of input dysfunction continues to be the inspiration for much contemporary research on schizophrenia by experimental psychopathologists. Significantly, it has also influenced parallel work on schizotypy, in particular the search for endophenotypes that might index the risk for schizophrenia. Illustrative here are studies by Braff and colleagues (Cadenhead & Braff, 2002). They identify three measures of sensorimotor gating that seem to be especially robust indicators of the input dysfunction; robust because all show deviations not only in diagnosed schizophrenic subjects but also in biological relatives of schizophrenics, individuals with the SPD diagnosis and healthy schizotypes selected by questionnaire. We have already mentioned a version of one of these measures – eye movement deviation. The other two are as follows:

- *Pre-pulse inhibition of the startle response.* This is a measure of the extent to which weak prestimuli, presented at brief intervals, reduce the magnitude of the blink reflex component of the startle response. Schizophrenic subjects and related risk groups show *less* of this normal inhibition, so that startle is relatively greater than usual.

- *P50 event-related* (ERP) *suppression.* In this EEG measure two auditory clicks are presented sequentially to the subject, a comparison being made of the corresponding evoked amplitudes in the wave occurring at a latency of 50 msec (P50). Typically, the secondly P50 is reduced in size: again this suppression occurs to a lesser degree in schizophrenic subjects and related groups.

199

The emphasis on *inhibition* as a critical mediating process in these measures is significant. In a number of different experimental and clinical contexts it has been argued that the relative failure of some kind of inhibitory process in the nervous system might account for many of the core features of schizophrenia; not least the tendency to irregular, unstable functioning that so characterizes the disorder. Gating abnormalities, such as those just described, are one application of this inhibition theory in schizophrenia research; another, at a higher level of psychological functioning, is the use of the construct to explain performance differences on cognitive tasks.

An example is *negative priming*, based on the Stroop colour–word paradigm (Moritz & Mass, 1997; Williams & Beech, 1997). Here, subjects are put through the usual procedure where they are asked to ignore the word meaning and name the hue of colour words written in incongruous colours; for example *blue* written in *red*. In the negative priming format the sequential pairs in the word list are related in meaning; in such a way that the hue to be named in any given stimulus is the same as the word ignored in the previous stimulus; for example *blue* (ignored) written in *red* (named) may be followed by *yellow* (ignored) written in *blue* (named). Negative priming refers to the extent to which colour naming speed is impaired, compared with a control condition in which the stimuli in the sequence are unrelated. The method has been widely used in schizophrenia research, with performance differences observed on the task being ascribed to variations in 'cognitive inhibition'. The argument is that response speed will depend upon the extent to which the temporarily ignored word stimulus has been actively screened out of immediate attention and, therefore, the ease with which it can be recalled for colour naming on the following trial. Having less cognitive inhibition, schizophrenic subjects and schizotypal individuals will therefore have an advantage on the task and therefore show *less* negative priming.

The negative priming methodology has a special significance because it is one of a very small band of experimental procedures which are able to predict *better* performance than control subjects in schizophrenic and related groups. This feature enables the experimenter to circumvent the worry with most cognitive tasks used in this field: that the performance difference observed (expected to show up as deficits) might be due to non-specific factors that have nothing to with schizophrenia itself.

The possibility of predicting behavioural *superiority* in what is mostly regarded as a defect state has important implications for how we construe schizophrenia as illness, and what view we take of its dimensionality. Here, a rough-and-ready formulation that has guided some thinking about this is the notion – drawn from cognitive psychology – that there are individual differences in the threshold at which information becomes accessible to, or allowed into, consciousness. In schizophrenia this has been interpreted as having potentially detrimental effects: schizophrenic subjects actually have difficulty in what Frith (1979) once described as 'limiting the contents of consciousness'. This would then be seen to account for the mental 'flooding' often reported by schizophrenic subjects – the inability to constrain associations and the overinclusive thinking that is ultimately responsible for their delusional ideas. But the weakness of cognitive inhibition that allegedly underlies this may be detrimental only in the real-life situation. Away from that, in the limited environment of the experimental laboratory, it could be beneficial, even in the clinically schizophrenic state; hence, the better than normal performance on tasks such as negative priming. As a corollary to that,

in moderate degree, as a trait characteristic of schizotypy, weaker than average cognitive inhibition might be perfectly healthy, contributing – so the argument goes – to processes such as creativity, through its involvement in divergent thinking. Here we have a good example of the inverted-U effect, whereby a functional property of the organism can have both advantageous and harmful consequences.

## BRAIN SYSTEMS IN SCHIZOPHRENIA

**The back–front, top–down axes** Attempts to identify brain areas or functional brain circuits that might be implicated in schizophrenia have proceeded along several lines. Some work has been an immediate, quite narrowly focused, extension of the kind of research referred to in the previous section, investigating possible neurobiological correlates of the psychology and psychophysiology seen to be disturbed in schizophrenia. Sensory gating provides a good example of this. Even when originally investigating the phenomenon under his label of 'input dysfunction', Venables proposed that the hippocampus was a critical brain structure. Recent research on an animal model of gating in the rat has confirmed that this is likely to be the case (Bickford-Wimer et al., 1990). By use of the same EEG P50 measure of gating as that employed in humans, it was found that certain neurons in the hippocampus were mainly responsible for the decrement in response to repeated stimuli. Among the neurotransmitters implicated in this effect, the inhibitory chemical, GABA, is known to play an important role.

Other brain research has proceeded along more traditional lines. This has sometimes taken the form of a simple medical search for the cause of disease; for example, through postmortem studies and, more recently, structural and functional brain imaging. Sometimes it has been more theoretically based, using imaging to look for correlates of the neuropsychological deficits reported in schizophrenia. Such deficits range across many cognitive skills, including attention, executive function, spatial ability, motor speed, sequencing, auditory processing, and most aspects of memory (Gur & Gur, 1995).

It is probably fair to say that nothing consistent about the brain in schizophrenia has emerged from what is an enormous – and, it has been said, 'indigestible' – mass of data. Consistent, that is, in the sense that, although individual studies have regularly shown differences between schizophrenic and control samples, replicable effects *across* investigations have remained elusive. So much so that one recent review of the literature concluded that there was no reliable evidence for a gross structural or functional cerebral abnormality that could be said to characterize schizophrenia as a diagnostic category (Chua & McKenna, 1995). The only exception was lateral ventricular enlargement. But that was relatively minor and judged, if it had significance, to be more of a vulnerability factor than an immediate cause of disease. Nevertheless, the

201

finding for ventricular enlargement is worth bearing in mind because it has frequently been quoted in the schizophrenia literature as a sign of risk for the disorder (Cannon & Marco, 1994).

The pessimistic conclusion reached in the review cited above is not quite as bad as it sounds because it fails to take account of the heterogeneity of schizophrenia and the fact that trying to find a single, common abnormality is almost certainly misplaced anyway. Is it not more likely that different neural circuitry underlies different symptom clusters? There is some support for the idea, two brain areas having been of particular interest in that regard. One is the *temporolimbic system* which for a long time has been thought relevant because of clinical observations that individuals with known temporal lobe pathology often shown schizophrenic-like symptoms. Neuroimaging evidence from schizophrenic subjects themselves support the connection and go even further in suggesting that it is specifically the *positive* symptoms that are associated with temporolimbic dysfunction (Bogerts, 1997).

Possible explanation of *negative* symptoms has been proposed via other neural circuitry, implicating the frontal lobes. Results here have typically led to the conclusion that schizophrenic subjects show 'hypofrontality', seen either as reduced activity relative to other brain regions, or as a failure of the prefrontal cortex and associated structures to be appropriately activated by cognitive tasks (Velakoulis & Pantelis, 1996). These observations from brain imaging parallel the poor performance of schizophrenic subjects when examined with conventional neuropsychological tests of frontal lobe function. Significantly, the performance deficits found on such tasks are much more marked in those schizophrenic subjects rated high in negative symptomatology (Mattson *et al.*, 1997). One suggestion, therefore, is that the cognitive failure observed in these individuals is an indirect one, due to *motivational* effects, mediated through the frontolimbic circuitry involved in drive and emotion – in this case at the low end, associated with anhedonia and negative symptomatology. There is an interesting connection here to findings discussed in Chapter 5 with respect to melancholic depression.

202

There has been some extension of the above research into investigations along the schizophrenia spectrum, including schizotypy. One of the most intriguing studies is a recent one by Buchsbaum and colleagues. Focusing on prefrontal and temporal structure and function, these authors used magnetic image resonance (MRI) and positron emission tomography (PET) scans in a comparison of schizophrenic subjects, healthy control subjects, and individuals with the diagnosis of Schizotypal Personality Disorder (SPD). There were two findings of interest. First, the pattern of effects observed in the fully schizophrenic subjects was roughly similar to that reviewed above; no generalized difference in all cases for all of the brain sites monitored, but definite evidence of deficiency in frontal and temporal areas. Second, SPD subjects showed a 'compromise' profile, which was a mixture of that for schizophrenic subjects and that for healthy control subjects: midway between schizophrenic subjects and normal individuals for temporal function, but with little deficit in prefrontal areas. The authors concluded that there was evidence that schizophrenia and SPD do indeed lie on a continuum, and further speculated that those individuals in the personality disorder part of the spectrum have some protective factor – identified in this case as effective prefrontal functioning – which guards them against full psychotic breakdown (Buchsbaum *et al.*, 2002).

**The horizontal axis** A different neurobiological perspective (literally) on schizophrenia/schizotypy is that the clue to it all lies in some feature of the lateralization of the brain (*Schizophrenia Bulletin*, 1999). The idea is an old one, originating in early nineteenth-century writings about mental illness as a 'warring' between the two halves of the brain. The proposal was given some scientific credibility by the subsequent discovery that the cerebral hemispheres are indeed specialized for different psychological functions: first that the left hemisphere is dominant for speech and language and later that the 'silent' right hemisphere has a special involvement in, among other things, emotion. Subsequent, sometimes fanciful, simplifying of these left–right differences – for example, the contrasting of rational, linear and irrational, intuitive modes of cognitive processing – were easy meat for theories seeking to explain the chaotic, yet sometimes creative, psychology of madness. More sober scientific studies did not confirm this neat, romantic picture But nor did they entirely undermine it and over the years laterality explanations of psychosis have proliferated, coming into and going out of fashion more often than any other theory.

As with research on the other brain axes, left–right differences have been investigated from many points of view, with the same, or equivalent, methodologies. Needless to say, an equally dyspeptic mass of data has accumulated and similar differences of opinion on interpretation offered. As theories of schizophrenia, these have traditionally divided into three types. One – that the disorder is primarily a *left* brain dysfunction – is based on the well-documented evidence that schizophrenic subjects perform poorly on verbal tasks, coupled to claims from neuroimaging studies that they show abnormal left hemisphere activity (Gur & Chin, 1999). A second hypothesis is that schizophrenia is actually a *right* hemisphere disorder (Cutting, 1990). This, it is argued, is consistent with the perceptual and attentional symptoms of schizophrenia and with certain aspects of language disturbance, for example metaphor and humour, that are mediated by the right hemisphere. In this case, some of the impaired performance seen on left hemisphere tasks would be explained as due to interference from emotional arousal 'spilling over' from the right side of the brain. The third class of theory is that schizophrenia is associated with some kind of disturbed interaction between the two hemispheres.

203

Of the three possibilities, the last, although the most open-ended and most difficult to disprove, is the one that has received most attention in recent years. The general proposition is that schizophrenia is associated with incomplete lateralization of the brain – in practical terms, reduced left hemisphere dominance for language There are several sources of evidence for this theory (Sommer *et al.*, 2001). Two types of data are illustrative.

The first concerns the anatomy of the *planum temporale*, a small structure in the temporal lobe encompassing Wernicke's language area. In the majority of people the *planum temporale* is larger on the left than on the right side of the brain. However, it has been reported that in schizophrenic subjects this asymmetry is less; the structure is more often of similar size in both temporal lobes (Petty *et al.*, 1995).

A second source of evidence for reduced laterality in schizophrenia comes from studies of hand preference. Although a crude index of laterality, handedness is relatively easily measured and has therefore given rise to many studies. The results appear, on the face of it, rather variable; but recent reappraisal of the findings suggests that there is a general theme: a tendency for schizophrenic subjects to show more *mixed* (though, interestingly, not more left) handedness (Satz & Green, 1999). Similar findings have been reported in several studies of healthy schizotypes selected by questionnaire (Shaw *et al.*, 2001).

As with other perspectives on the brain in schizophrenia, there is the usual problem of heterogeneity and the fact that not all cases will conform to the generalizations made on the basis of average effects. Few writers in laterality research have addressed this question. An exception is Gruzelier (2002), who has made a special point of studying and speculating about it in both schizophrenia and schizotypy. His conclusion is that schizophrenics (and schizotypes) show a disproportionate tendency to shift, due to labile arousal, towards either left or right extremes of cerebral dominance. According to him, these correspond to two syndromes (or, in normal schizotypy, behavioural profiles): 'active' (left dominant over right) with largely positive symptoms and 'withdrawn' (right dominant over left), with largely negative symptoms.

Lastly, an imaginative interpretation of laterality theory that deserves mention is Crow's recent evolutionary model of schizophrenia (Crow, 1997). He argues simply that the genetic basis for schizophrenia is the same as the genetic basis of language. Language, he says, emerged as a single speciation event in evolution with the lateralization of the brain. Since, according to him, schizophrenia is first and foremost a language-related dysfunction the disorder then began to occur as a result of incomplete lateralization – or what he refers to as 'hemispheric indecision' – in the neurodevelopment of some feature of language. The theory therefore represents a new twist on a now well-rehearsed idea that schizophrenia is the price that *Homo sapiens* pays for the evolution of some otherwise adaptive qualities, in this case language capacity (see also Nettle, 2001).

## MANIC DEPRESSION

## THE UNITARY PSYCHOSIS ISSUE

Earlier we introduced the notion of unitary psychosis, the idea that schizophrenia and manic depression (or bipolar affective disorder) might simply form two broad varieties of madness. Several types of evidence have been put forward in favour of the theory (Taylor, 1992). These include the following:

- Genetic considerations, currently seen as one of the strong points of research on psychosis, do not particularly support a distinction being made between bipolar and schizophrenic psychosis. For instance, there appears to be no clear tendency for each to 'breed true' in families.

- At the level of symptoms there is considerable overlap between the two forms of psychosis, with what has been called no 'point of rarity' between them; that is to say, no evidence of a bimodal distribution when the symptoms of both manic depression and schizophrenia are plotted together (Kendell & Brockington, 1980).

- Many treatments (for example, drugs) are equally useable in schizophrenia and manic depression.

- Monitoring the clinical status of individual psychotic patients over time reveals that some may shift back and forth across the two diagnoses, or show mixtures of the symptoms of each. The last point is recognized in the psychiatric glossaries, in the existence of *schizoaffective psychosis*, a hybrid of schizophrenic and manic depressive features.

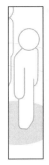

But what about other, more objective, evidence, for the unitary view, such as laboratory-based measures that might tap some common underlying process? Here, as well, overlap between the two conditions has been observed. Indeed, one expert commentator – whose general remarks on schizophrenia are also illuminating – was quite firmly of this opinion:

205

> Time after time research workers have compared groups of schizophrenics and normal controls and found some difference between the two which they assumed to be a clue to the aetiology of schizophrenia, only for someone else, years later, to find the same abnormality in patients with affective disorders. Of all the dozens of biological abnormalities reported in schizophrenia in the last 50 years, none has yet proved specific to that syndrome. (Kendell, 1991)

Several quite different examples – their discovery spanning some three decades – illustrate Kendell's point:

- Overinclusiveness – the loose associative thinking classically ascribed to schizophrenia – also occurs, probably to a greater degree, in mania (Andreasen & Powers, 1974)

- Enlarged brain ventricles – which, according to the review we quoted earlier, are the only distinguishing neuropathological feature common to schizophrenia – have also been reported in affective disorder (Pearlson *et al.*, 1984).

- Follow-up of individuals scoring highly on the positive features of schizotypy are very likely, if they develop psychotic experiences, to show mood disorder (Chapman *et al.*, 1994).

- Aberrations in sensory gating found in schizophrenia have also been observed in bipolar patients. This has been demonstrated by use of two measures of gating: eye tracking and pre-pulse inhibition of the startle response (Tien *et al.*, 1996; Perry *et al.*, 2001).

None of the above proves the unitary theory, of course, and we must not lose sight of the fact that the overall clinical manifestation of manic depression is different from that of schizophrenia. But – and this is the point – it differs no more than the range of symptoms to be found in what we should remind ourselves are properly called 'the schizophrenias'. So that might be a reason to accept the unitary theory as the default position about the psychoses, given the absence of any good evidence to the contrary. On the other hand, expanding the boundaries of one unknown to encompass another unknown could be counterproductive. For the moment therefore the choice remains one of clinical practicality, research aim, and preferred theoretical stance.

## DIMENSIONALITY OF MANIC DEPRESSION

Irrespective of whether or not manic depression is a subvariety of a single psychosis, the same questions can be raised about its dimensionality, as with schizophrenia. Compared with the latter, however, much less work has been carried out. This is not to say that the topic has no history. Indeed, manic depression was explicitly referred to in what was one of the first attempts to link personality to psychotic disorder: that by Kretschmer (1925), who in the early part of the last century proposed a single continuum running from schizophrenia to manic depression, with normal variants of each lying in between. On the manic depression side he used the terms 'cycloid' and 'cyclothymic' to describe the subclinical and personality equivalents. It was this theory that Eysenck revamped in order to arrive at his own dimension of psychoticism, taking in both schizophrenia and manic depression.

On the psychiatric side, some of Kretschmer's terminology has survived in the diagnostic glossaries; to be found, for example, in the DSM as *cyclothymic disorder*, defined by mood swings similar to, but of a lesser degree, than those found in full bipolar affective illness. This is mostly all that the DSM has to say about dimensionality in bipolar disorder. In that regard, there is an interesting contrast with schizophrenia, with its well-recognized connections to the personality disorders. The only acknowledgement of this for manic depression in the DSM is a brief reference to Borderline Personality Disorder, a point we shall return to shortly.

Outside the official psychiatric glossaries, there have been a number of attempts to arrive at classifications that take into account associations between temperament and bipolar disorder, and hence partly address the question of one being a disposition to the other. These systems have often built upon historical typologies and terminology, making use of descriptors such as cyclothymia. Or, more recently, they have involved applying the newer temperament constructs of writers such as Cloninger, whose work we came across in chapters 3 and 4.

Studies administering the Cloninger scales to patients with affective disorder have produced rather complicated findings (see Barrantes *et al.*, 2001). This is partly due to variations in the clinical diagnosis of samples tested – whether patients were in mania, depression, or a mixed state. But some differences in pre-morbid temperament have been found, along the lines one might expect; for example greater novelty seeking in bipolar subjects. One particular study is of interest because the authors gave the Cloninger scales to both bipolar patients and patients diagnosed as Borderline Personality Disorder (Atre-Vaidya & Hussain, 1999). Their aim was to discover whether the two types of disorder are distinct or whether they lie on a continuum. These authors concluded that the former was the case, bipolar subjects differing from borderline subjects in several ways that could not be explained as one being more severe than the other.

Despite these authors' negative findings, the theory that BPD and manic depression *are* related is currently a strong idea in psychiatry. At least one eminent authority on the affective disorders has come down in its favour, proposing a 'bipolar spectrum' that can encompass borderline personality (Akiskal, 1996). Others, reporting on clinical evidence, have confirmed the model (Deltito *et al.*, 2001). Further investigation is needed, conducted in the style of that currently adopted in schizotypy research, to decide whether the bipolar spectrum is an affective disorder equivalent of the schizophrenia spectrum.

## CONCLUSIONS

Even from our brief coverage in this chapter, it is clear that the bulk of the research on psychosis has concentrated on its schizophrenic form and any

207

conclusions reached here will mostly apply to that. What, in fact, can we conclude? There is certainly continuing disagreement on many issues, the consensus still being on some rather general points. No one would dispute the heterogeneity of schizophrenia and few would now wish to propose that there is one factor that can account for all of its manifestations. An accepted scenario is that the condition represents a final common path for a range of psychobiological influences that produce effects which we choose to bundle together under the single heading of 'schizophrenia' (meaning 'the schizophrenias'). Otherwise, much of the origin of schizophrenia remains unexplained.

An aspect that is increasingly being emphasized is the developmental trajectory of the illness (Walker & Bollini, 2002). Schizophrenia is notable in (mostly) appearing as a disorder in adolescence or early adulthood. One argument, therefore, is that some predisposing trait or set of traits (schizotypy) lies dormant until triggered into action by hormonal and other changes occurring in adolescence. The focus of these models is very much on the neurobiology and genetics of schizophrenia and schizotypy, aspects that we, too, have stressed in this chapter. However, it would be misleading to regard constructs such as schizotypy as fixedly genetic, or of interest only in a narrow biological context. It is known, for example, that even mild early trauma can increase the tendency in adulthood to superstitious belief and magical ideation – two of the hallmarks of schizotypal thinking (Lawrence *et al.*, 1995). This might be particularly significant in the light of evidence for a history of child abuse in many schizophrenic subjects (Greenfield *et al.*, 1994). It is probable that future research on schizotypy will need to look more closely at how the traits associated with it emerge during development; as has been done with other dimensions of personality and temperament.

No theory can satisfactorily account for the variability found across the schizophrenia spectrum; the fact that some highly schizotypal individuals show one schizophrenic profile and others a different one. Or – and this is especially intriguing – the observation that yet others (in fact, most of those evidently at high risk) do not become clinically psychotic at all. When trying to explain these variations it is usual to fall back on generalities about the influence of modifiers, such as intelligence, gender, independently mediated personality traits, age, and environmental influences, ranging from family rearing to peri-natal brain damage. It is safe to conclude that one or more of these variables will help to shape the form of the illness, or its failure to appear.

Whichever aetiological model applies, a common problem remains for the definition of schizophrenia as a disorder. Many people who never succumb to illness nevertheless experience its positive 'symptoms', such as hallucinations or weird beliefs. How we interpret this apparently healthy aspect of schizophrenia defines a boundary of opinion about the interpretation of its dimensionality. Is 'schizotypy' a varying defect state, sometimes sufficiently

208

compensated for so that the individual for all intents and purposes passes for normal? Or is it a genuinely adaptive trait, with several possible outcomes, one of which is schizophrenic illness? And, if we do accept the idea of a healthy form, at what point, in what circumstances, or with what combination of moderating variables do we label the state 'illness'? Since it would appear that cognitive changes of a schizophrenic kind are not in themselves sufficient to 'cause' schizophrenia, it may be – as the evidence begins to suggest – that there also needs to be some drastic *affective* change that shapes and directs the cognitions into behaviours and experiences that are sick and maladaptive. It is perhaps no coincidence that it was the 'splitting' of thought and emotion that was being referred to by Bleuler when labelling these unusual disorders of mental life, 'schizophrenia'.

It might seem an act of madness in itself for some writers to attempt to extend the mix of uncertain fact and tentative theory that still surrounds schizophrenia, to include manic depression. The dilemma is that the evidence in favour of a unitary psychosis is not insubstantial; this is true both for the clinical syndromes and at the personality level. It could therefore seem quite arbitrary – and an historical accident – that the demands for a neat classification of mental illness should have dictated the separation of two apparently overlapping expressions of insanity Yet, in the absence of a clear picture of what constitutes 'schizophrenia/schizotypy', is it helpful to broaden the remit even further to the larger construct, 'psychosis/psychoticism'? Some very disparate opinions about what is actually meant by 'psychoticism' certainly give one pause for thought, as the following illustrates.

Crow (1986) and Eysenck (1992) are two authors who, embracing the unitary psychosis theory, have both proposed a way in which schizophrenia and bipolar affective disorder may be subsumed under one heading. Both have visualized a continuum of psychosis running from the normal, through manic depression, to schizophrenia, the latter being regarded as the more severe abnormality. Crow's interpretation is in line with his evolutionary theory of brain lateralization and language specialization: the partial or complete failure of this process results, he would argue, in a spectrum of cognitive aberration that is responsible for a range of psychotic disorders, of which the most serious is schizophrenia. Eysenck's interpretation of the same normal–clinical continuum was totally different. He argued that the underlying trait is affective and interpersonal and has to do with empathic feelings, or lack of them, towards others. According to him the psychosis continuum starts with empathy (at the healthy end), which diminishes as one goes through criminality, affective disorder, then schizoaffective disorder, to unsocialized hostility at the schizophrenic extreme.

The contrast between the Crow and Eysenck theories could not be greater, articulating the very varied ways in which different observers have tried to grasp at the essence of some very puzzling disorders. Crow and Eysenck cannot both be right if, as seems to be the case, each is wishing to argue that his account *exclusively* explains psychosis. Yet, between them perhaps they too have stumbled unwittingly on the two facets of psychobiology – cognition and affect – which we need to consider if we are to advance our understanding of psychosis.

# CHAPTER 10
## FINAL REMARKS

This book has tried to bring together two topics that, intuitively, seem very close but which, in practice, often remain apart – most of all, surprisingly, in clinical psychology. It is generally in personality psychology, academic abnormal psychology, and occasionally in psychiatry that the ideas we have discussed here now surface – but even then only occasionally and in fragmented form. In Chapter 1 we outlined the historical reasons for this, when explaining some past realignments of clinical psychology, abnormal psychology, and psychiatry in relation to one another. Considerations of professional rôle, and the 'cognitive revolution', caused clinical psychology to retreat from concern with issues about personality differences, especially where these invoke biology. This, we believe, has sometimes left clinical psychologists marooned without a convincing explanation, if and when they try to give a full account of why the patients they treat have come to be as they are. A good example is one we quoted in Chapter 4 when discussing Beck's account of personality-disordered individuals. Beck's characterizations of the various mental sets of such people are invaluable in defining targets for cognitive therapy. But is it not important to have as rounded an explanation as possible of the origins of the cognitions and behaviours being treated? In that respect Beck's formulation is lacking.

Personality theory of the kind we have mostly drawn upon here is, if anything, now nearer to biological psychiatry. This is ironic, given its past history in the Eysenckian school's vigorous challenge to doctors over the medical model and the disease approach to psychological disorders. What has brought the two disciplines closer together of late is a common interest in the biology of abnormal functioning, and the realization that there is, or should be, no contest between psychology and psychiatry when trying to establish a science of psychological disorders. Of course, the respective contributions of psychology and psychiatry are still different – radically so in the account of some disorders, especially psychotic illness. But even there we can discern some convergence of viewpoint with, say, the idea of dimensionality creeping into medical explanations of serious disorders, such as schizophrenia.

The *rapprochement* between psychology and psychiatry we refer to has partly been made possible by occasionally redefining 'personality' more narrowly, as 'temperament'. The latter's biological connotation clearly sits well with an increasingly biological psychiatry; once it is realized that a temperament theory of disposition to psychological disorder is not, as we saw in Chapter 2, a million miles away from models of susceptibility to physical diseases of a systemic type. It would be very limiting, nevertheless, if that were all there was in the title of this book. Although many of the theories we have quoted here might make it seem like that, Cloninger, in particular, is quick to remind us otherwise; temperament is but one part of personality. We have tried throughout to pass that message on to the reader, by insisting that all of the disorders we have dealt with – as well as the dispositions to them – have to be regarded as *psychobiological*. They involve neurophysiologically based mechanisms, some genetics, a large degree of life experience (some of it random) and immediate life events; all of these can conspire, in the unlucky, to bring about the deviations in cognitive, behavioural, and biological function that we label psychological disorders. Joining the various parts together into an integrated explanation of personality and disorder is not, of course, easy. But at least we hope we have done more than just pay lip service to the principle, by regularly reminding the reader of alternative ways of approaching the topics we have discussed, and the need always to keep an open view of them.

We trust that we have done the same in dealing with another common criticism of biological explanations of behaviour: that they are unacceptably reductionist. We have tried to indicate that early temperament is really only the starting point for change and that, even where there are strong genetic propensities, these do not establish a fixed trajectory for personality; they merely set a trend. It is true that, once the individual reaches adulthood, a pattern of behaviour is in place; and if he or she happens to lie on the outskirts of some tendency to disorder then that behaviour pattern might (but actually need not) be abnormal. Whether we even judge it abnormal is not merely dictated by the biology; it rests on several other criteria as well, of both a personal and a socio-cultural kind. Reference to the individual's biology is not therefore reductionist; it merely recognizes one of many influences that can shape the human personality and points to one of several ways in which we can, and need to, examine it.

It would be satisfying to think that all possible facets of explanation have been equally represented here. That is not true and we make no apology for it.

A book like this has to have a central theme and for ours we chose a certain kind of theory of individual differences: one that concentrates on the biology of personality the extremes of which make a natural connection to disordered behaviour. We have concentrated on that approach because we believe – and we hope we have shown – that there is a coherent story to be told that helps our understanding of both the normal and the abnormal in personality. What, then, have we learned?

One of the most important discoveries, perhaps, is how remarkably few brain circuits are needed to account for a wide range of personality differences and psychological disorders. At least that is true at the level of motivational systems that steer behaviour and underpin the major variations in temperament. Our favourite example here is sensitivity to reward This appears to lie at the emotional core of many clinical conditions: as heightened sensitivity in several Cluster B personality disorders, in some addictive behaviours, in eating disorders, and probably in mania; and as anhedonia in risk for other addictive behaviours, certain forms of psychotic-like depression, and some parts of the schizophrenia syndrome. The place of reward sensitivity in these conditions varies. In psychosis it defines avolitional mood states that have detrimental effects on intellectual functioning. In the personality disorders it constitutes an habitual way of responding to the world. In those who abuse substances, whether food or drugs, it promotes behaviours meant to stabilize the irregularities of mood which abnormal degrees of unsatisfied hedonic need can bring about.

Of course, there is much more to these disorders than a commonality in motivational style. Each of them has its own particular aetiology: the negative symptom schizophrenic is not merely depressed and the borderline patient who abuses drugs has a different history from one who is eating-disordered or another who self-mutilates. But it is a beginning and could provide a focus for research on common mechanisms that cut across the conventional psychiatric categories. For the latter sometimes get in the way of attempts to find causes of disorder – a legacy of old-fashioned medical models that are predicated on the idea of circumscribed diseases having well-defined and mutually exclusive aetiologies.

213

There is a broader implication here for psychiatric nosology and the way disorders are classified in glossaries like the DSM. In previous chapters we have frequently commented on two weaknesses in these guidebooks. One is the sometimes considerable heterogeneity that can be observed among conditions listed under the same heading; which is true, for example, of all of the disorders discussed in this book. The other flaw is the comorbidity often found between different conditions. Comorbidity is a particular problem in Axis II of the DSM. Several of the personality disorders overlap so much that giving them different labels seems pointless. Far better to find a way of organizing personality deviations around some feature or features, such as shared temperamental – and hence motivational – dimensions which they have in common. This would clearly not exhaust the variety of ways in which personalities can be disordered, but it would provide a starting point from which to proceed to a more rationally based classification.

It is sometimes the *lack* of comorbidity that is worrying. Notable – and rather surprising – is the tendency for Obsessive–Compulsive Disorder not to overlap as much as one would expect with Obsessive–Compulsive Personality Disorder. This is certainly counterintuitive and seems to stem from the heterogeneity of OCD and the fact that under that label we are probably dealing with more than one disorder. Some forms seem to belong more in the schizophrenia spectrum and others among the anxiety disorders, with which OCD has traditionally been grouped. Again, it would be an advantage to have a classification based more on knowledge of underlying mechanisms, where necessary cutting across existing clinical categories.

The above suggestions do not demand abandoning traditional ways of classifying psychological disorders. To do so would be counterproductive. After all, both the DSM and the ICD are built upon a long history of accumulated clinical observation and, like the classic theory of temperaments, can scarcely be entirely wrong. Our point has more to do with the evolution of such systems in the light of new knowledge. The constructors of the DSM are relatively conservative, as we noted earlier in this book when commenting on their reluctance to adopt a dimensional view of the personality disorders – to an outsider a startlingly obvious way of construing them. It is the slow uptake of relevant knowledge – some of it from outside psychiatry – that perhaps could be remedied.

We have said little or nothing about treatment in this book. This is because our intention, on the abnormal side, has been to concentrate on the *origins* of psychological disorders. However, what we have presented does have implications for treatment and we will conclude by briefly considering that topic.

On the face it, the consequences for treatment of what we have written might seem to be mainly pharmacological, emphasizing the use of drugs to modify behaviour. But that is not true – certainly not exclusively so – and even where pharmacology might seem relevant, this is not the case in any straightforward sense. The clue here lies, not in the biological aspects of the theories we discussed, but in the continuity of normal with abnormal. Once a model is accepted in which healthy personality shades into illness, even with perceptible jumps, it becomes difficult to accept the simple medical formulation that still prevails in psychiatry, of merely matching drug to disorder. On the drug issue, therefore, there are several ways in which the dimensional approach could be seen to depart from the conventional medical treatment strategy.

First of all, it would follow that drugs, if they are used, would need to be carefully titrated to the biological status of the individual. We already know

from work mentioned early in the book that individuals differ enormously in their tolerance of and susceptibility to psychotropic drugs. This is rarely taken into account, in any systematic way, in medical practice.

Second, the psychobiological view of disorder that has been promoted here would expect that cognitive behavioural and pharmacological procedures would combine to produce optimum treatment strategies. This already happens, for example in the use of tranquillizers to make certain kinds of desensitization procedure possible in highly anxious patients, or in the use of neuroleptic agents to ensure that psychotic subjects are sufficiently accessible for cognitive manipulations of their delusional beliefs. But the separation of the cognitive from the biological is still greater than it should be.

Third, the dimensional perspective raises some special issues about the psychotic disorders in particular. Dimensionality does, if anything and in several ways, work rather against a pharmacological approach to treatment. Consider a broad interpretation of the schizophrenia spectrum, supported by the existence of techniques that purport to identify individuals at risk before they break down. A logical consequence of this, already in practice, is early detection, coupled to treatment interventions that may involve drugs. The ethics and the efficacy of this preventative approach are still under review. The conclusions may not be as straightforward as they seem, given the several possible outcomes – healthy and unhealthy – of schizotypal risk.

Lastly, and away from the drug scene, there is one further treatment implication of what we have discussed here; for some therapists it will almost certainly be controversial. We refer to the fact that, by the time adulthood is reached, temperament and the personality traits that have developed on top of that will have placed a limit on the capacity of the individual to alter his or her behaviour. Response to treatment – whether psychological or, through the placebo effect, pharmacological – is very influenced by the individual's desire to improve. People who are anxious or whose lives are disrupted by disabling symptoms, are highly motivated to get better and the treatment works in that direction. But in other conditions this is often not the case. The most dramatic example would be Antisocial Personality Disorder; but the list could be expanded to include aberrant behaviours that come for treatment – for example, gambling – that are also driven by impulsiveness, sensation seeking, or the need for pleasure. The motives of such people are understandable but sometimes even the person regrets the way these are expressed. Is it feasible or even possible to change the habit patterns of such individuals? Another approach to their 'treatment' might be to encourage them into more personally and socially acceptable ways of channelling their temperamental energies: persuade the gambler, for example, to risk his or her money on the stock market, rather than throw it away on fruit machines.

When we think about it, if left to their own devices that is how individuals actually conduct themselves and how society helps shape their rôles in life.

Those of psychopathic temperament are attracted to risky pursuits or manipulative endeavours that are perfectly within the law; schizoids become librarians; the anxious and obsessive turn their perfectionism into products of excellence. Even the potentially psychotic, if they have talent and are protected from the worst in life, can survive their tendency to disorder, and consequently flourish. Perhaps in some cases the aim of prevention and treatment should be to give these natural individual differences a gentle hand, rather than try to shift people towards an impossible norm of behaviour that their temperaments do not allow.

# References

Aharon, I., Etcoff, N., Ariely, D., Chabris, C. F., O'Connor, E. & Breiter, H. C. (2001) Beautiful faces have variable reward value: fMRI and behavioral evidence. *Neuron* 32: 537–551.

Akiskal, H. S. (1996) The prevalent clinical spectrum of bipolar disorders beyond DSM-III. *Journal of Clinical Psychopharmacology* 16 (Suppl. 1), 4–14.

Allen, T. J., Moeller, G., Rhoades, H. M. & Cherek, D. R. (1998) Impulsivity and history of drug dependence. *Drug and Alcohol Dependence* 50: 137–145.

Amaral, D. G. (2002) The primate amygdala and the neurobiology of social behavior: Implications for understanding social anxiety. *Biological Psychiatry* 51: 11–17.

American Psychiatric Association (1994) *Diagnostic and Statistical Manual of Mental Disorders* (fourth edition). Washington, DC: American Pyschiatric Association.

American Psychiatric Association (2000) *Diagnostic and Statistical Manual of Mental Disorders* (fourth edition – text revision). Washington DC: American Psychiatric Association.

Andersen, A. E. (1990) *Males with Eating Disorders*. New York: Brunner/Mazel.

Andersen, A. E., Cohn, L., and Holbrook, T. (2000) Making Weight: Men's Conflicts with Food, Weight, Shape and Appearance. Calrlsbad, CA: Gurze Books

Andreasen, N. C. & Olsen, S. (1982) Negative versus positive schizophrenia. Definition and validation. *Archives of General Psychiatry* 39: 789–794.

Andreasen, N. J. C. & Powers, P. S. (1974) Overinclusive thinking in mania and schizophrenia. *British Journal of Psychiatry* 125: 452–456.

Arndt, S., Alliger, R. J. & Andreasen, N. C. (1991) The distribution of positive and negative symptoms: the failure of a two-dimensional model. *British Journal of Psychiatry* 158: 317–322.

Atre-Vaidya, N. & Hussain, S. M. (1999) Borderline personality disorder and bipolar mood disorder: two distinct disorders or a continuum? *Journal of Nervous and Mental Disease* 187: 313–315.

Badiani, A., Oates, M. M., Day, H. E. W., Watson, S. J., Akil, H. & Robinson, T. E. (1998) Amphetamine-induced behavior, dopamine release, and c-fos mRNA expression: modulation by environmental novelty. *Journal of Neuroscience* 18: 10,579–10,593.

Bannister, D. & Fransella, F. (1971) *Inquiring Man: The Theory of Personal Constructs*. London: Croom Helm.

Barlow, D. H. & Campbell, L. A. (2000) Mixed anxiety-depression and its implications for models of mood and anxiety disorders. *Comprehensive Psychiatry* 41: 55–60.

Barrantes, N., Colom, F. & Claridge, G. (2001) Temperament and personality in bipolar affective disorders. In: E. Vieta (Ed.). *Bipolar Disorders: Clinical and Therapeutic Progress*. Madrid: Editorial Médica Panamericana; 217–242.

Bastiani, A. M., Rao, R., Weltzin, T. & Kaye, W. H. (1995) Perfectionism in anorexia nervosa. *International Journal of Eating Disorders* 17: 147–152.

Baumgarten, H. G. & Grozdanovic, Z. (1998) Role of serotonin in obsessive–compulsive disorder. *British Journal of Psychiatry* 173 (Suppl. 35): 13–20.

Bayer, T. A., Falkai, P. & Maier, W. (1999) Genetic and non-genetic vulnerability factors in schizophrenia: the basis of the 'two-hit hypothesis'. *Journal of Psychiatric Research* 33: 543–548.

Bebbington, P. E. (1998) Epidemiology of obsessive–compulsive disorder. *British Journal of Psychiatry* 173 (Suppl. 35): 2–6.

Bechara, A., Dolan, S., Denburg, N., Hindes, A., Anderson, S. W. & Nathan, P. E. (2001) Decision-making deficits, linked to a dysfunction ventromedial prefrontal cortex, revealed in alcohol and stimulant abusers. *Neuropsychologia* 39: 376–389.

Beck, A. T. (1986) Cognitive therapy: a sign of retrogression or progress. *Behavior Therapist* 9: 2–3.

Beck, A. T., Freeman, A. & associates (1990) *Cognitive Therapy of Personality Disorders*. New York, NY: The Guilford Press.

Beck, R. & Perkins, T. S. (2001) Cognitive content-specificity for anxiety and depression: A meta-analysis. *Cognitive Therapy and Research* 25: 651–663.

Becker, D. (1997) *Through the Looking Glass. Women and Borderline Personality Disorder*. Oxford: Westview Press.

Bejerot, S. & Humble, M. (1999) Low prevalence of smoking among patients with obsessive–compulsive disorder. *Comprehensive Psychiatry* 40: 268–272.

Bejerot, S., Ekselius, L. & von Knorring, L. (1998a) Comorbidity between obsessive–compulsive disorder (OCD) and personality disorders. *Acta Psychiatrica Scandinavica* 97: 398–402.

Bejerot, S., Schlette, P., Ekselius, L., Adolfsson, R. & von Knorring, L. (1998b)

Personality disorders and relationship to personality dimensions measured by the Temperament and Character Inventory in patients with obsessive–compulsive disorder. *Acta Psychiatrica Scandinavica* 98: 243–249.

Belke, T. W. (1996) Investigating the reinforcing properties of running: Or running is its own reward. In: W. F. Epling & W. D. Pierce (eds.) *Activity Anorexia: Theory, Research, and Treatment.* Mahwah, NJ: Lawrence Erlbaum Publishers; 45-55.

Berman, S., Ozkaragoz, T., Young, R.M., and Noble, E.P. (2002). $D_2$ dopamine receptor gene polymorphism discriminates two kinds of novelty seeking. *Personality and Individual Differences* 33: 867-882.

Bergh, C. & Sodersten, P. (1996) Anorexia nervosa, self-starvation and the reward of stress. *Nature Medicine* 2: 21–22.

Berridge, V. (1997) Two tales of addiction: opium and nicotine. *Human Psychopharmacology – Clinical and Experimental* 12: S45–S52.

Berridge, K. C. & Robinson, T. E. (1995) The mind of an addicted brain: neural sensitization of wanting versus liking. *Current Directions in Psychological Science* 4: 71–76.

Berrios, G. E. (1995) Conceptual problems in diagnosing schizophrenic disorders. In: J. A. Den Boer, H. G. M. Westenberg & H. M. van Praag (eds). *Advances in the Neurobiology of Schizophrenia.* Chichester: John Wiley; 7–25.

Bevins, R. A., Besheer, J., Palmatier, M. I., Jensen, H. C., Pickett, K. S. & Eurek, S. (2002) Novel-object place conditioning: behavioural and dopaminergic processes in expression of novelty reward. *Behavioural and Brain Research* 129: 41–50.

Bickford-Wimer, P. C., Nagamoto, H., Johnson, R., Adler, L. E., Egan, M., Rose, G. M. & Freedman, R. (1990) Auditory sensory gating in hippocampal neurons: a model system in the rat. *Biological Psychiatry* 27: 183–192.

Black, D. W. & Noyes, R. (1997) Obsessive–compulsive disorder and Axis II. *International Review of Psychiatry* 9: 111–118.

Blair, C. (2002) Integrating cognition and emotion in a neurobiological conceptualization of children's functioning at school entry. *American Psychologist* 57: 111–127.

Blair, R. J. R. (1995) A cognitive developmental approach to morality: investigating the psychopath. *Cognition* 57: 1–29.

Blair, R. J. R. (1999) Responsivness to distress cues in the child with psychopathic tendencies. *Personality and Individual Differences* 27: 135–145.

Blair, R. J. R., Sellars, C., Strickland, I., Clark, F., Williams, A. O., Smith, M. & Jones, L. (1995) Emoton attributions in the psychopath. *Personality and Individual Differences* 19: 431–437.

Blair, R. J. R., Jones, L., Clark, F & Smith, M. (1997) The psychopathic individual: a lack of responsiveness to distress cues? *Psychophysiology* 34: 192–198.

Blatt (1995). The destructiveness of perfectionism. *American Psychologist* 50: 1003-1020.

Bleuler, E. (1911) *Dementia Praecox or the Group of Schizophrenias* (trans. J. Zinkin, 1950). New York, NY: International Universities Press.

Bogerts, B. (1997) The temporolimbic system theory of positive schizophrenic symptoms. *Schizophrenia Bulletin* 23: 423–435.

Bogetto, F., Venturello, S., Albert, U., Maina, G. & Ravizza, L. (1999) Gender-related clinical differences in obsessive–compulsive disorder. *European Psychiatry* 14: 1–8.

Bouricius, J. K. (1989) Negative symptoms and emotions in schizophrenia. *Schizophrenia Bulletin* 15: 201–208.

Brady, K. T., Myrick, I. I. & McElroy, S. (1998) The relationship between substance abuse disorders, impulse control disorders, and pathological aggression. *American Journal of Addiction*s 7: 221–230.

Breier, A., Kestler, L., Adler, C., Elman, I., Wiesenfel, N., Malhotra, A. & Pickar, D. (1998) Dopamine $D_2$ receptor density and personal detachment in healthy subjects. *American Journal of Psychiatry* 155: 1440–1442.

Broadhurst, P. L. (1975) The Maudsley reactive and non-reactive strains of rats: a survey. *Behavior Genetics* 5: 299–319.

Broocks, A., Liu, J. & Pirke, K. M. (1990) Semistarvation-induced hyperactivity compensates for decreased norepinephrine and dopamine turnover in the mediobasal hypothalamus of the rat. *Journal of Neural Transmission* 79: 113–124.

Brown, T. A., Chorpin, B. P. & Barlow, D. H. (1998) Structural relationships among dimensions of the DSM-IV anxiety and mood disorders and dimensions of negative affect, positive affect, and autonomic arousal. *Journal of Abnormal Psychology* 107: 179–192.

Brunello, N., den Boer, J. A., Judd, L. L., Kasper, S., Kelsey, J. E., Lader, M., Lecrubier, Y., Lepine, J. P., Lydiard, R. B., Mendlewicz, J., Montgomery, S. A., Racagni, G., Stein, M. B. & Wittchen, H-U. (2000) Social phobia: Diagnosis and epidemiology, neurobiology and pharmacology, comorbidity and treatment. *Journal of Affective Disorders* 60: 61–74.

Buchsbaum, M. S., Nenadic, I., Hazlett, E. A., Spiegel-Cohen, J., Fleischman, M. B., Akhavan, A., Silverman, J. M. & Siever, L. J. (2002) Differential metabolic rates in prefrontal and temporal Brodmann areas in schizophrenia and schizotypal personality disorder. *Schizophrenia Research* 54: 141–150.

Burke, R. J. (2000) Workaholism in organizations: the role of personal beliefs and fears. *Anxiety, Stress and Coping* 13: 53–64.

Burt, S. A., McGue, M., Iacano, W., Cornings, D. and MacMurray, J. (2002). An examination of the association between D2D4 and D2D2 polymorphisms and personality traits. *Personality and Individual Differences*. 33: 849-859

Buss, A. H. & Plomin, R. (1984) *Temperament: Early Developing Personality Traits.* Hillsdale, NJ: Erlbaum.

220

Cadenhead, K. S. & Braff, D. L. (2002) Endophenotyping schizotypy: a prelude to genetic studies within the schizophrenia spectrum. *Schizophrenia Research* 54: 47–57.

Caldji, C., Tannenbaum, B., Sharma, S., Francis, D., Plotsky, P. M. & Meaney, M. J. (1998) Maternal care during infancy regulates the development of neural systems mediating the expression of fearfulness in the rat. *Proceedings of the National Academy of Sciences* 95: 5335–5340.

Cannon, T. D. & Marco, E. (1994) Structural brain abnormalities as indicators of vulnerability to schizophrenia. *Schizophrenia Bulletin* 20: 89–102.

Cannon, W. B. (1953) *Bodily Changes, in Pain, Hunger, Fear and Rage.* Boston, MA: Charles T. Branford.

Cardinal, R. N., Pennicott, D. R., Sugathapala, C. L., Robbins, T. W. & Everitt, B. J. (2001) Impulsive choice induced in rats by lesions of the nucleus accumbens core. *Science*: 292: 2499–2501.

Carver, C. S. & White, T. L. (1994) Behavioural inhibition, behavioural activation, and affective responses to impending reward and punishments: the BIS/BAS scales. *Journal of Personality and Social Psychology* 67: 319–333.

Casper, R. C., Hedeker, D. & McClough, J. F. (1992) Personality dimensions in eating disorders and their relevance for subtyping. *Journal of the American Academy of Child and Adolescent Psychiatry* 31: 830–840.

Cattell, R. B. (1965) *The Scientific Analysis of Personality.* Harmondsworth: Penguin.

Chamove, A. S., Eysenck, H. J. & Harlow, H. F. (1972) Personality in monkeys: factor analysis of rhesus social behaviour. *Quarterly Journal of Experimental Psychology* 24: 496–504.

Chapman, L. J., Chapman, J. P., Kwapil, T. R., Eckblad, M. & Zinsere, M. C. (1994) Putatively psychosis-prone subjects 10 years later. *Journal of Abnormal Psychology* 103: 171–183.

Childress, A. C., Brewerton, T. D., Hodges, E. L. & Jarrell, M. P. (1993) The Kid's Eating Disorder Survey (KEDS): a study of middle school students. *Journal of the American Academy of Child and Adolescent Psychiatry* 32: 843–850.

Childress, A. R., Mozley, P. D., McElgin, W., Fitzgerald, J., Reivich, M. & O'Brien, C. P. (1999) Limbic activation during cue-induced cocaine craving. *American Journal of Psychiatry* 156: 11–18.

Chua, S. E. & McKenna, P. J. (1995) Schizophrenia – a brain disease? A critical review of structural and functional cerebral abnormality in the disorder. *British Journal of Psychiatry* 166: 563–582.

Chutuape, M. A. D. & Dewit, H. (1995) Preferences for ethanol and diazepam in anxious individuals – an evaluation of the self-medication hypothesis. *Psychopharmacology* 121: 91–103.

Claridge, G. (1967) *Personality and Arousal.* Oxford: Pergamon.

Claridge, G. (1995) *Origins of Mental Illness.* Cambridge, MA: Malor Books.

Claridge. G. (Ed.) (1997) *Schizotypy: Implications for Illness and Health*. Oxford: Oxford University Press.

Claridge, G. & Clark, K. (1982) Covariation between two-flash threshold and skin conductance level in first-breakdown schizophrenics: relationships in drug-free patients and effects of treatment. *Psychiatry Research* 6: 371–380.

Claridge, G. & Davis, C. (2001) What's the use of neuroticism? *Personality and Individual Differences* 31: 383–400.

Claridge, G. & Herrington, R. N. (1960) Sedation threshold, personality, and the theory of neurosis. *Journal of Mental Science* 106: 1568–1583.

Claridge, G. & Mangan, G. (1983) Genetics of human nervous system functioning. In: J. L. Fuller & Simmel, E. C. (eds). *Behavior Genetics*. Hillsdale, NJ: Erlbaum.

Claridge, G., McCreery, C., Mason, O., Bentall, R., Boyle, G., Slade, P. & Popplewell, D. (1996) The factor structure of 'schizotypal' traits: a large replication study. *British Journal of Clinical Psychology* 35: 103–115.

Clark, D. B., Pollock, N., Bukstein, O. G., Mezzih, A. C., Bromberger, J. T. & Donovan, J. E. (1997) Gender and comorbid psychopathology in adolescents with alcohol dependence. *Journal of the American Academy of Child and Adolescent Psychiatry* 36: 1195–1203.

Clark, D. M. (1986) A cognitive approach to panic. *Behaviour Research and Therapy* 24: 461–470.

Clark, L. A., Watson, D. & Mineka, S. (1994) Temperament, personality, and the mood and anxiety disorders. *Journal of Abnormal Psychology* 103: 103–116.

Cleckley, H. (1976) *The Mask of Sanity* (fifth edition). St Louis, MI: Mosby.

Cloninger, C. R. (1987) A systematic method for clinical description and classification of personality variants. *Archives of General Psychiatry* 44: 573–588.

Cloninger, C. R. (1998) The genetics and psychobiology of the seven-factor model of Personality. In: K. R. Silk (Ed.). *Biology of Personality Disorders*. Washington, DC: American Psychiatric Press.

Cloninger, C. R. (2000) Biology of personality dimensions. *Current Opinions in Psychiatry* 13: 611–616.

Cloninger, C. R., Przybeck, T. R., Svrakic, D. M. & Wetzel, R. D. (1994) *The Temperament and Character Inventory (TCI): A Guide to its Development and Use*. Washington, DC: Washington University, Center for Psychobiology of Personality.

Cloninger, C. R., Svrakic, D. M. & Przybeck, T. R. (1993) A psychobiological model of temperament and character. *Archives of General Psychiatry* 50: 975–990.

Connor, K. M. & Davidson, J. R. T. (1998) Generalized anxiety disorder: neurobiological and pharmacotherapeutic perspectives. *Biological Psychiatry* 44: 1286–1294.

Cooke, D. J., Forth, A. E. & Hare, R. D. (1998) *Psychopathy: Theory, Research, and Implications for Society*. Dordrecht, The Netherlands: Kluver.

Cooper, C. (1998) *Individual Differences*. London: Arnold.

Costa, P. T. Jr. & McCrae, R. R. (1992*) Revised NEO Personality Inventory (NEO-PI-R)*. Odessa, FL: Psychological Assessment Resources.

Coupland, N. J. (2001) Social phobia, etiology, neurobiology, and treatment. *Journal of Clinical Psychiatry* 62: 25–35.

Crabbe, J. C. (2002) Genetic contributions to addiction. *Annual Review of Psychology* 53: 435–462.

Crino, R. C. (1999) Obsessive–compulsive spectrum disorders. *Current Opinion in Psychiatry* 12: 151–155.

Crow, T. J. (1985) The two-syndrome concept – origins and current status. *Schizophrenia Bulletin* 11: 471–486.

Crow, T. J. (1986) The continuum of psychosis and its implication for the structure of the gene. *British Journal of Psychiatry* 149: 419–429.

Crow, T. J. (1997) Is schizophrenia the price that *Homo sapiens* pays for language? *Schizophrenia Research* 28: 127–141.

Cutting, J. (1990) *The Right Cerebral Hemisphere and Psychiatric Disorders*. Oxford: Oxford University Press.

Dackis, C. A. & Gold, M. S. (1985) New concepts in cocaine addiction: the dopamine depletion hypothesis. *Neuroscience and Biobehavioral Reviews* 9: 469–477.

Davidson, R. J., Pizzagalli, D., Nitschke, J. B. & Putnam, K. (2002) Depression: perspectives from affective neuroscience. *Annual Review of Psychology* 53: 545–574.

Davis, C. (1997a) Eating disorders and hyperactivity: a psychobiological perspective. *Canadian Journal of Psychiatry* 42: 168–175.

Davis, C. (1997b) Normal and neurotic perfectionism in eating disorders: an interactive model. *International Journal of Eating Disorders* 22: 421–426.

Davis, C., Blackmore, E. & Fox, J. (2001) 'Looking Good' – Family Focus on Attractiveness and the Risk for Eating Disorders. Presentation at the annual meeting of the Eating Disorder Research Society, New Mexico, November.

Davis, C. & Claridge, G. (1998) The eating disorders as addiction: a psychobiological perspective. *Addictive Behaviors* 23: 463–475.

Davis, C., Claridge, G. & Brewer, H. (1996) The two faces of narcissism: personality dynamics of body esteem. *Journal of Social & Clinical Psychology* 15: 153–166.

Davis, C., Claridge, G. & Cerullo, D. (1997) Personality factors and weight preoccupation: a continuum approach to the association between eating disorders and personality disorders. *Journal of Psychiatric Research* 31: 467–480.

Davis, C., Kennedy, S. H., Ralevski, E. & Dionne, M. (1994) The role of physical activity in the development and maintenance of eating disorders.

223

*Psychological Medicine* 24: 957–967.

Davis, C., Strachan, S. & Berkson, M. (2002) Sensitivity to Reward and Emotional Eating: Implications for Overweight and Obesity. Presentation made at the annual conference of the Eating Disorder Research Society, Charleston, SC, November.

Davis, C. & Woodside, D. B. (2002) Sensitivity to rewarding effects of food and exercise in the eating disorders. *Comprehensive Psychiatry* 43: 189–194.

Davis, C., Woodside, D. B. & Olmsted, M. P. (1999) Psychopathology in the eating disorders: the influence of physical activity. *Journal of Applied Biobehavioral Research* 4: 139–156.

Davis, M. (1997) Neurobiology of fear responses: the role of the amygdala. *Journal of Neuropsychiatry and Clinical Neurosciences* 9: 382–402.

Davis, M. (1998) Are different parts of the extended amygdala involved in fear versus anxiety? *Biological Psychiatry* 44: 1239–1247.

Dawes, M. A., Tarter, R. E. & Kirisci, L. (1997) Behavioral self-regulation: correlates and 2 year follow-ups for boys at risk for substance abuse. *Drug and Alcohol Dependence* 45: 165–176.

Deep, A. L., Nagy, L. M., Weltzin, T. E., Rao, R. & Kaye, W. H. (1995) Premorbid onset of psychopathology in long-term recovered anorexia nervosa. *International Journal of Eating Disorders* 17: 291–297.

DeHaas, R. A., Calamari, J. E., Bair, J. P. & Martin, E. D. (2001) Anxiety sensitivity and drug or alcohol use in individuals with anxiety and substance use disorders. *Addictive Behaviors* 26: 787–801.

Delgado, P. L. (2000) Depression: a case for a monoamine deficiency. *Journal of Clinical Psychiatry* 61 (Suppl. 6): 7–11.

Delgado, P. L. & Moreno, F. A. (1998) Different roles for serotonin in anti-obsessional drug action and the pathophysiology of obsessive–compulsive disorder. *British Journal of Psychiatry* 173 (Suppl. 35): 21–25.

Deltito, J., Martin, L., Riefkohl, J., Austria, B., Kissilenko, A., Corless, C. & Morse, P. (2001) Do patients with borderline personality disorder belong to the bipolar spectrum? *Journal of Affective Disorders* 67: 221–228.

Depue, R. A. & Collins, P. F. (1999) Neurobiology of the structure of personality: dopamine, facilitation of incentive motivation, and extraversion. *Behavioral and Brain Science* 22: 491–569.

Dess, N. K. (1997) Ingestion after stress: evidence for a regulatory shift in food-rewarded operant performance. *Learning and Motivation* 28: 342–356.

Diaferia, G., Bianchi, I., Bianchi, M. L., Cavedini, P., Erzegovesi, S. & Bellodi, L. (1997) Relationship between obsessive–compulsive personality disorder and obsessive–compulsive disorder. *Comprehensive Psychiatry* 38: 38–42.

Di Chiara, G. (1999) Drug addiction as dopamine-dependent associative learning disorder. *European Journal of Pharmacology* 375: 13–30.

Drevets, W. C. (1998) Functional neuroimaging studies of depression: the anatomy of melancholia. *Annual Review of Medicine* 49: 341–361.

Drewnowski, A., Hopkins, S. A. & Kessler, R. L. (1988) The prevalence of bulimia nervosa in the US college student population. *American Journal of Public Health* 78: 1322–1325.

Edell, W. S. (1995) The psychometric measurement of schizotypy using the Wisconsin scales of psychosis-proneness. In: G. A. Miller (Ed.). *The Behavioural High-risk Paradigm in Psychopathology*. New York, NY: Springer.

Eisen, J. L., Phillips, K. A. & Rasmussen, S. A. (1999) Obsessions and delusions: the relationship between obsessive–compulsive disorder and the psychotic disorders. *Psychiatric Annals* 29: 515–522.

Eley, T. C. & Gregory, A. M. (in press) The genetics of anxiety in children. In: T. Morris & J. March (eds). *Anxiety Disorders in Children and Adolescents*. New York, NY: The Guilford Press.

el-Guebaly, N. & Hodgins, D. (1998) Substance-related cravings and relapses: clinical implications. *Canadian Journal of Psychiatry* 43: 29–36.

Epling, W. F. & Pierce, W. D. (1996) *Activity Anorexia: Theory, Research, and Treatment*. Hillsdale, NJ: Erlbaum.

Eysenck, H. J. (1952) *The Scientific Study of Personality*. London: Routledge & Kegan Paul.

Eysenck, H. J. (1957) *Dynamics of Anxiety and Hysteria*. London: Routledge & Kegan Paul.

Eysenck, H. J. (1960) Classification and the problem of diagnosis. In: H. J. Eysenck (Ed.). *Handbook of Abnormal Psychology* (First edition). London: Pitman.

Eysenck, H. J. (Ed.). (1963) *Experiments with Drugs*. Oxford: Pergamon.

Eysenck, H. J. (1967) *The Biological Basis of Personality*. Springfield, ILL: Charles C. Thomas.

Eysenck, H. J. (Ed.). (1973) *Handbook of Abnormal Psychology* (Second edition). London: Pitman.

Eysenck, H. J. (1992) The definition and measurement of psychoticism. *Personality and Individual Differences* 13: 757–785.

Eysenck, H. J. & Eysenck, M. W. (1985) *Personality and Individual Differences*. New York: Plenum Press.

Eysenck, H. J. & Eysenck, S. B. G. (1976a) *Manual of the Eysenck Personality Questionnaire*. London: Hodder & Stoughton.

Eysenck, H. J. & Eysenck, S. B. G. (1976b) *Psychoticism as a Dimension of Personality*. London: Hodder & Stoughton.

Eysenck, H. J. & Eysenck, S. B. G. (1991) *Manual of the Eysenck Personality Scales*. London: Hodder & Stoughton.

Fairburn, C. G. & Beglin, S. J. (1990) Studies of epidemiology of bulimia nervosa. *American Journal of Psychiatry* 147: 401–408.

Fairburn, C. G., Shafran, R. & Cooper, Z. (1999) A cognitive behavioural theory of anorexia nervosa. *Behaviour Research and Therapy* 37: 1–13.

Farmer, A. E., McGuffin, P. & Gottesman, I. I. (1987) Twin concordance for

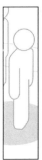

DSM-III schizophrenia: scrutinizing the validity of the definition. *Archives of General Psychiatry* 44: 634–641.

Favaro, A. & Santonastaso, P. (1998). Impulsive and compulsive self-injurious behavior in bulimia nervosa: prevalence and psychological correlates. *Journal of Nervous and Mental Disease* 186: 157–165.

Figueroa, E. & Silk, K. R. (1997) Biological implications of childhood sexual abuse in borderline personality disorder. *Journal of Personality Disorders* 11: 71–92.

Foulds, G. A. (1965) *Personality and Personal Illness*. London: Tavistock.

Foulds, G. A. (1971) Personality deviance and personal symptomatology. *Psychological Medicine* 1: 222–233.

Fowles, D. C. (1987) Application of a behavioural theory of motivation to the concepts of anxiety and impulsivity. *Journal of Research in Personality* 21: 417–435.

Freud, S. (1940) *An Outline of Psychoanalysis*. Harmondsworth: Penguin.

Frith, C. D. (1979) Consciousness, information processing and schizophrenia. *British Journal of Psychiatry* 134: 225–235.

Funtowicz, M. N. & Widiger, T. A. (1995) Sex bias in the diagnosis of personality disorders: a different approach. *Journal of Psychopathology and Behavioral Assessment* 17: 145–165.

Gainetdinov, R. R., Jones, S. R. & Caron, M. G. (1999) Functional hyperdopaminergia in dopamine transporter knock-out mice. *Biological Psychiatry* 46: 303–311.

Gamberino, W. C. & Gold, M. S. (1999) Neurobiology of tobacco smoking and other addictive disorders. *Addictive Disorders* 22: 301–312.

Gantt, W. H., Pickenhain, L. & Zwingmann, Ch. (eds) (1970) *Pavlovian Approach to Psychopathology*. Oxford: Pergamon.

Germans, M. K. & Kring, A. M. (2000) Hedonic deficit in anhedonia: support for the role of approach motivation. *Personality and Individual Differences* 28: 659–672.

Gianoulakis, C. (1998) Alcohol-seeking behavior. *Alcohol Health & Research World* 22: 202–210.

Ginovart, N., Farde, L., Halldin, C. & Swahn, C. G. (1999) Changes in striatal D2 receptor density following chronic treatment with amphetamine as assessed with PET in nonhuman primates. *Synapse* 31: 154–162.

Glass, M. J., Billington, C. J. & Levine, A. S. (1999) Opioids and food intake: distributed functional neural pathways? *Neuropeptides* 33: 360–368.

Goldman, D. (1996) High anxiety. *Science* 274: 1483.

Goldner, E. M., Cockell, S. J. & Srikameswaran, S. (2002) Perfectionism and eating disorders. In G. L. Flett & P. L. Hewitt (eds). *Perfectionism: Theory, Research, and Treatment*. Washington, DC: American Psychological Association; 319–340.

Gordon, H. W. (2002) Early environmental stress and biological vulnerability

to drug abuse. *Psychoneuroendocrinology* 27: 115–126.

Gorman, J. M., Kent, J. M., Sullivan, G. M. & Coplan, J. D. (2000) Neuroanatomical hypothesis of panic disorder, revisited. *American Journal of Psychiatry* 157: 493–505.

Gosling, S.D. (2001) From mice to men: what can we learn about personality from animal research? *Psychological Bulletin* 127: 45–86.

Gottesman, I. I. (1991) *Schizophrenia Genesis: the Origins of Madness*, New York, NY: W. H. Freeman.

Gottesman, I. I. & Shields, J. (1982) *Schizophrenia: The Epigenetic Puzzle.* Cambridge: Cambridge University Press.

Graeff, F. G. (2002) On serotonin and experimental anxiety. *Psychopharmacology* 163: 467–476.

Grant, S., Contoreggi, C. & London, E. D. (2000) Drug abusers show impaired performance in a laboratory test of decision making. *Neuropsychologia* 38: 333–342.

Grant, B. F., Harford, T. C. (1995) Comorbidity between DSM-IV alcohol-use disorders and major depression – results of a national survey. Drug Alcohol Depen 39 (3): 197–206.

Gray, J. A. (1981) A critique of Eysenck's theory of personality. In: H. J. Eysenck (Ed.). *A Model for Personality.* Berlin: Springer-Verlag.

Gray, J. A. (1982) *The Neuropsychology of Anxiety.* Oxford: Clarendon Press.

Greenfield, S. F., Strakowski, S. M., Tohen, M., Batson, S. C. & Kolbrener, M. L. (1994) Childhood abuse in first-episode psychosis. *British Journal of Psychiatry* 164: 831–834.

Griffiths, M. (2001) Sex on the internet: observations and implications for Internet sex addiction. *Journal of Sex Research* 38: 333–342.

Grilo, C. M., Walker, M. L., Becker, D. F., Edell, W. S. & McGlashan, T. H. (1997) Personality disorders in adolescents with major depression, substance use disorders, and coexisting major depression and substance abuse disorders. *Journal of Consulting and Clinical Psychology* 65: 328–332.

Gross, C., Zhuang, X., Stark, K., Ramboz, S., Oosting, R., Kirby, L., Santarelli, L., Beck, S. & Hen, R. (2002) Serotonin$_{1A}$ receptor acts during development to establish normal anxiety-like behaviour in the adult. *Nature* 416: 396–400.

Gruzelier, J. (2002) A Janusian perspective on the nature, development and structure of schizophrenia and schizotypy. *Schizophrenia Research* 54: 95–103.

Gur, R. E. & Chin, S. (1999) Laterality in functional brain imaging studies of schizophrenia. *Schizophrenia Bulletin* 25: 141–156.

Gur, R. C. & Gur, R. E. (1995) The potential of physiological neuroimaging for the study of schizotypy: experiences from applications to schizophrenia. In: A. Raine, T. Lencz & S. A. Mednick (eds). *Schizotypal Personality.* Cambridge: Cambridge University Press; 406–425.

227

Halmi, K. A., Eckert, E., Marchi, P., Sampugnaro, V., Apple, R. & Cohen, J. (1991) Comorbidity of psychiatric diagnoses in anorexia nervosa. *Archives of General Psychiatry*, 48; 712–718.

Hare, R. D. (1986) Twenty years of experience with the Cleckley psychopath. In: W. H. Reid, D. Dorr, J. I. Walker & J. W. Bonner III (eds). *Unmasking the Psychopath*. New York, NY: WW Norton.

Hare, R. D. (1993) *Without Conscience*. New York, NY: The Guilford Press.

Hare, R. D., Harpur, T. J., Hakstian, A. R., Forth, A. E., Hart, S. D. & Newman, J. P. (1990) The revised Psychopathy Checklist: reliability and factor structure. *Psychological Assessment* 2: 338–341.

Hebb, D. O. (1955) Drives and the CNS (conceptual nervous system). *Psychological Review* 62: 243–254.

Heinz, A. (1999) Anhedonia – a general nosology correlation of a dysfunction of the dopaminergic reward system? *Nervenarzt* 70: 391–398.

Henderson, N. J. & Huon, G. F. (2002) Negative affect and binge eating in overweight woman. *British Journal of Health Psychology* 7: 77–87.

Henriques, J. B. & Davidson, R. J. (2000) Decreased responsiveness to reward in depression. *Cognition and Emotion* 14: 711–724.

Herpertz, S. C., Kunert, H. J., Schwenger, U. B. & Sass, H. (1999) Affective responsiveness in borderline personality disorder: a psychophysiological approach. *American Journal of Psychiatry* 156: 1550–1556.

Hertel, P. T. (2002) Cognitive biases in anxiety and depression: introduction to the Special Issue. *Cognition and Emotion*, 16: 321–330.

Herzog, D. B., Dorer, D. J., Keel, P. K., Selwyn, S. E, Ekblad, E. R., Flores, A. T., Greenwood, D. N., Brwell, R. A. & Keller, M. B. (1999) Recovery and relapse in anorexia and bulimia nervosa: a 7.5 year follow-up study. *Journal of the American Academy of Child and Adolescent Psychiatry* 38: 829–837.

Heubner, H. F. (1993) *Endorphins, Eating Disorders and Other Addictive Behaviors*. New York, NY: WW Norton.

Hewitt, P. L., Flett, G. L. & Ediger, E. (1995) Perfectionism traits and perfectionistic self-presentation in eating disorder attitudes, characteristics, and symptoms. *International Journal of Eating Disorders* 18: 317–326.

Heyman, G. M. (1996) Resolving the contradictions of addiction. *Behavioral and Brain Sciences* 19: 561–610.

Hirschfeld, R. M. A. (2000) History and evolution of the monoamine hypothesis of depression. *Journal of Clinical Psychiatry* 61 (Suppl. 6): 4–6.

Hoehn-Saric, R. & Greenberg, B. D. (1997) Psychobiology of obsessive–compulsive disorder: anatomical and physiological considerations. *International Review of Psychiatry* 9: 15–29.

Holden, C. (2001) 'Behavioral' addictions: do they exist? *Science* 294: 980–982.

Holden, N. L. (1990) Is anorexia nervosa an obsessive–compulsive disorder? *British Journal of Psychiatry* 157: 1–5.

228

Holderness, C. C., Brooks-Gunn, J. & Warren, M. P. (1994) Co-morbidiity of eating disorders and substance abuse: review of the literature. *International Journal of Eating Disorders* 16: 1–34.

Holeva, V. & Tarrier, N. (2001) Personality and peritraumatic dissociation in the prediction of PTSD in victims of road traffic accidents. *Journal of Psychosomatic Research* 51: 687–692.

Hollander, E. (1996) Obsessive–compulsive disorder-related disorders: the role of selective serotonergic reuptake inhibitors. *International Clinical Psychopharmacology* 11 (Suppl. 5): 75–87.

Hollander, E. & Wong, C. M. (1995) Obsessive–compulsive spectrum disorders. *Journal of Clinical Psychiatry* 56 (Suppl. 4): 3–6.

Hollander, E. & Evers, M. (2001). New developments in impulsivity. *Lancet* 358: 949–950.

Holsboer, F. (2000) The corticosteroid receptor hypothesis of depression. *Neuropsychopharmacology* 23: 477–501.

Hudziak, J. J., Boffeli, T. J., Kriesman, J. J., Battaglia, M. M., Stanger, C. & Guze, S. B. (1996) Clinical study of the relation of borderline personality disorder to Briquet's syndrome (hysteria), somatization disorder, antisocial personality disorder and substance abuse disorders. *American Journal of Psychiatry* 153: 1598–1606.

Hughes, J. R., Hatsukami, D. K., Mitchell, J. E. & Dahlgren, L. A. (1986) Prevalence of smoking among psychiatric outpatients. *American Journal of Psychiatry* 143: 993–997.

Insel, T. R. (2002) Social Anxiety: from laboratory studies to clinical practice. *Biological Psychiatry* 51: 1–3.

Jackson, M. (1997) Benign schizotypy? The case of spiritual experience. In: G. Claridge (Ed.). *Schizotypy: Implications for Illness and Health*. Oxford: Oxford University Press; 227–250.

Jentsch, J. D. & Taylor, J. R. (1999) Impulsivity resulting from frontostriatal dysfunction in drug abuse: implications for the control of behavior by reward-related stimuli. *Psychopharmacology* 146: 373–390.

Jentsch, J. D., Roth, R. H. & Taylor, J. R. (2000) Object retrieval/detour deficits in monkeys produced by prior subchronic phencyclidine administration: evidence for cognitive impulsivity. *Biological Psychiatry* 48: 415–424.

John, O. P. (1990) The 'Big Five' factor taxonomy: dimensions of personality in the natural languages and in questonnaires. In: L. A. Pervin (Ed.). *Handbook of Personality: Theory and Research*. New York, NY: The Guilford Press; 66–100.

Johns, J. H. & Quay, H. C. (1962) The effect of social reward on verbal conditioning in psychopathic and neurotic military offenders. *Journal of Consulting and Clinical Psychology* 26: 217–220.

Johns. L. C. & van Os, J. (2001) The continuity of psychotic experiences in the general population. *Clinical Psychology Review* 21: 1125–1141.

229

Johnson, R. D. (1995) Opioid involvement in feeding-behavior and the pathogenesis of certain eating disorders. *Medical Hypotheses* 45: 491–497.

Jorm, A. F., Christensen, H., Henderson, A. S., Jacomb, P. A., Korten, A. E. & Rodgers, B. (2000) Predicting anxiety and depression from personality: is there a synergistic effect of neuroticism and extraversion? *Journal of Abnormal Psychology* 109: 145–149.

Just, N., Abramson, L. Y. & Alloy, L. B. (2001) Remitted depression studies as tests of the cognitive vulnerability hypotheses of depression onset: a critique and conceptual analysis. *Clinical Psychology Review* 21: 63–83.

Kagan, J. (1989) The concept of behavioral inhibition to the unfamiliar. In: J. S. Reznick (Ed.). *Perspectives on Behavioral Inhibition.* Cambridge, MA: The John D. and Catherine T. MacArthur Foundation Series on Mental Health and Development; 1–23.

Kashdan, T. B. & Herbert, J. D. (2001) Social anxiety disorder in childhood and adolescence: current status and future directions. *Clinical Child and Family Psychology* 4: 37–62.

Katzmarzyk, P. T. & Davis, C. (2001) Thinness and body shape of *Playboy* centerfolds from 1978 to 1998. *International Journal of Obesity* 25: 590–592.

Kaye, W. H. (1997) Anorexia nervosa, obsessional behavior, and serotonin. *Psychopharmacology Bulletin* 33: 335–344.

Kaye, W. H. (1999) The new biology of anorexia and bulimia nervosa: implications for advances in treatment. *European Eating Disorder Review* 7: 157–161.

Kaye, W. H., Weltzin, T. E. & Hsu, L. G. (1993) Relationship between anorexia nervosa and obsessive and compulsive behaviors. *Psychiatric Annals* 23: 365–373.

Kaye, W. H., Frank, G. K., Meltzer, C. C., Price, J. C., McConaha, C. W., Crossan, P. J., Klump, K. L. & Rodes, L. (2001) Altered serotonin$_{2A}$ receptor activity in women who have recovered from bulimia nervosa. *American Journal of Psychiatry* 158: 1152–1155.

Kaye, W. H., Strober, M. & Rhodes, L. (2002) Body image disturbance and other core symptoms in anorexia and bulimia nervosa. In: D. J. Castle & K. A. Phillips (eds). *Disorders of Body Image.* Petersfield, UK: Wrightson Biomedical Publishing; 67–82.

Kendell, R. E. (1991) The major functional psychoses: are they independent entities or part of a continuum? Philosophical and conceptual issues underlying the debate. In: A. Kerr & H. McClelland (eds). *Concepts of Mental Disorder. A Continuing Debate.* London: Gaskell; 1–16.

Kendell, R. E. & Brockington, J. F. (1980) The identification of disease entities and the relationship between schizophrenia and affective psychosis. *British Journal of Psychiatry* 137: 324–331.

Kendler, K. S., MacLean, C., Neale, M., Kessler, R., Health, A. & Eaves, L.

(1991) The genetic epidemiology of bulimia nervosa. *American Journal of Psychiatry* 148: 1627–1637.

Kendler, K. S., Neale, M. C., Kessler, R. C., Heath, A. C. & Eaves, L. J. (1992) Major depression and generalized anxiety disorder. *Archives of General Psychiatry* 49: 716–722.

Kendler, K. S., Myers, J. M. & Prescott, C. A. (2002) The etiology of phobias. An evaluation of the stress-diathesis model. *Archives of General Psychiatry* 59: 242–248.

Kessler, R. C., Crum, R. M., Warner, L. A., Nelson, C. B., Schulenberg, J. & Anthony, J. C. (1997) Lifetime co-occurrence of DSM-III-R alcohol abuse and dependence with other psychiatric disorders in the national comorbidity survey. *Archives of General Psychiatry* 54: 313–321.

Keys, A. (1950). *The Biology of Human Starvation*. Minneapolis, MN: University of Minnesota Press.

Khantzian, E. J. (1997) The self-medication hypothesis of substance use disorders: a reconsideration and recent applications. *Harvard Review of Psychiatry* 4: 231–244.

Kiehl, K. A., Smith, A. M., Hare, R. D., Mendrek, A., Forster, B. B., Brink, J. & Liddle, P. F. (2001) Limbic abnormalities in affective processing by criminal psychopaths as revealed by functional magnetic resonance imaging. *Biological Psychiatry* 50: 677–684.

King, J. A., Abend, S. & Edwards, E. (2001) Genetic predisposition and the development of post-traumatic stress disorder in an animal model. *Biological Psychiatry* 50: 231–237.

King, J. E. & Figueredo, A. J. (1997) The five-factor model plus dominance in chimpanzee personality. *Journal of Research in Personality* 31: 257–271.

Kline, P. (1972) *Fact and Fantasy in Freudian Theory*. London: Metheun.

Klump, K. L., Bulik, C. M., Pollics, C., Halmi, K. A. Fichter, M. M., Berrettini, W. H., Devlin, B., Strober, M., Kaplan, A., Woodside, D. B., Treasure, J., Shabbout, M., Lilenfeld, L. R. R., Plotnicov, K. H. & Kaye, W. H. (2000) Temperament and character in women with anorexia nervosa. *Journal of Nervous and Mental Disease*, 188, 559–567.

Koff, E. & Sangani, P. (1997) Effect of coping style and negative body image on eating disturbance. *International Journal of Eating Disorders* 22: 51–56.

Koob, G. F. & Le Moal, M. (1997).

Kosten, T. A. & Ambrosio, E. (2002) HPA axis function and drug addictive behaviors: insights from studies with Lewis and Fischer 344 inbred rats. *Psychoneuroendocrinology* 27: 35–69.

Kosten, T. A., Miserendino, M. J. D. & Kehoe, P. (2000) Enhanced acquisition of cocaine self-administration in adult rats with neonatal isolation stress experience. *Brain Research* 875: 44–50.

Kraepelin, E. (1919) *Dementia Praecox and Paraphrenia* (trans. R. M. Barclay). Edinburgh: Churchill Livingstone.

Kretschmer, E. (1925) *Physique and Character* (trans. W. J. H. Sprott). London: Kegan, Trench & Trubner.

Kroeze, S. & van den Hout, M. A. (2000) Selective attention for hyperventilatory sensations in panic disorder. *Journal of Anxiety Disorders* 14: 563–581.

Kwapil, T. R. (1998) Social anhedonia as a predictor of the development of schizophrenia-spectrum disorders. *Journal of Abnormal Psychology* 107: 558–565.

Kwapil, T. R., Miller, M. B., Zinser, M. C., Chapman, J. & Chapman, L. (1997) Magical ideation and social anhedonia as predictors of psychosis proneness: a partial replication. *Journal of Abnormal Psychology* 106: 491–495.

Laing, R. D. (1960) *The Divided Self.* London: Tavistock.

Lawrence, T., Edwards, C., Barraclough, N., Church, S. & Hetherington, F. (1995) Modelling childhood causes of paranormal belief and experience: childhood trauma and childhood fantasy. *Personality and Individual Differences* 19: 209–215.

LeDoux, J. (1998) Fear and the brain: where have we been, and where are we going? *Biological Psychiatry* 44: 1229–1238.

Lenzenweger, M. F. (1993) Explorations in schizotypy and the psychometric high-risk paradigm. In L. J. Chapman, J. P. Chapman & D. C. Fowles (eds). *Progress in Experimental Personality and Psychopathology Research Vol 2.* New York, NY: Springer; 66–116.

Leonard, B. E. (2000) Evidence for a biochemical lesion in depression. *Journal of Clinical Psychiatry* 2000 (Suppl. 6): 12–17.

Lerman, C., Caporaso, N. E., Audrain, J., Main, D., Bowman, E. D., Lockshin, B., Boyd, N. R. & Shields, P. G. (1999) Evidence suggesting the role of specific genetic factors in cigarette smoking. *Health Psychology* 18: 14–20.

Leshner, A. I. (1997) Addiction is a brain disease, and it matters. *Science* 278: 45–47.

Leshner, A. I. (1999) Science is revolutionizing our view of addiction – and what to do about it. *American Journal of Psychiatry* 156: 1–3.

Leshner, A. I. & Koob, G. F. (1999) Drugs of abuse and the brain. *Proceedings of the Association of American Physicians* 111: 99–108.

Lester, D. & Kaplan, S. (1994) The Depression–Happiness scale: happiness is not hypomania. *Psychological Reports* 74: 858.

Lett, B. T. & Grant, V. L. (1996) Wheel running induces conditioned taste aversion in rats trained while hungry and thirsty. *Physiology & Behavior* 59: 699–702.

Levine, D., Marziali, E. & Hood, J. (1997) Emotion processing in borderline personality disorders. *Journal of Nervous and Mental Disease* 185: 240–246.

Levy, D. L., Holman, P. S., Matthysse, S. & Mendell, N. R. (1993) Eye tracking dysfunction and schizophrenia: a critical perspective. *Schizophrenia Bulletin* 19: 461–506.

232

Lewis, G. & Appleby, L. (1988) Personality disorder: the patients psychiatrists dislike. *British Journal of Psychiatry* 153: 44–49.

Li, D., Chokka, P. & Tibbo, P. (2001) Toward an integrative understanding of social phobia. *Journal of Psychiatry & Neuroscience* 26: 190–202.

Lindenmayer, J-P., Bernstein-Hyman, R. & Grochowski, S. (1994) A new five factor model of schizophrenia. *Psychiatric Quarterly* 65: 299–322.

Loehlin, J.C. (1992) *Genes and Environment in Personality Development*. London: Sage.

Maier, W., Falkai, P. & Wagner, M. (1999) Schizophrenia-spectrum disorders. In: M. Maj (Ed.). *WPA Series in Evidence Based Psychiatry. Vol 2. Schizophrenia*. Chichester: John Wiley; 312–371.

Majewska, M. D. (2002) HPA axis and stimulant dependence: an enigmatic relationship. *Psychoneuroendocrinology* 27: 5–12.

Mangan, G. (1982) *The Biology of Human Conduct*. Oxford: Pergamon.

Marazziti, D. (2001) What came first: dimensions or categories? *British Journal of Psychiatry* 178: 478–479.

Marrazzi, M. A. & Luby, E. D. (1986) An auto-addiction opioid model of chronic anorexia nervosa. *International Journal of Eating Disorders* 5: 191–208.

Marazziti, D., Akiskal, H. S., Rossi, A. & Cassano, G. B. (1999) Alteration of the platelet serotonin transporter in romantic love. *Psychological Medicine* 29: 741–745.

Marcus, D. & Weiner, M. (1989) Anorexia nervosa reconceeptualized from a psychosocial transactional perspective. *American Journal of Orthopsychiatry*, 59, 346-354.

Maren, S. (2001) Neurobiology of Pavlovian fear conditioning. *Annual Review of Neuroscience* 24: 897–931.

Markou, A., Kosten, T. R. & Koob, G. F. (1998) Neurobiological similarities in depression and drug dependence: a self-medication hypothesis. *Neuropsychopharmacology* 18: 135–174.

Martin-Bivens, C. L. & Olster, D. H. (1999) Opioid receptor blockade promotes weight loss and improves the display of sexual behaviors in obese Zucker female rats. *Pharmacology Biochemistry and Behavior* 63: 515–520.

Mason, O., Claridge, G. & Jackson, M. (1995) New scales for the assessment of schizotypy. *Personality and Individual Differences* 18: 7–13.

Mason, O., Claridge, G. & Williams, L. (1997) Questionnaire measurement. In: G. Claridge (Ed.). *Schizotypy: Implications for Illness and Health*. Oxford: Oxford University Press; 19–37.

Masten, A. S. (1994) Resilience in individual development: successful adaptation despite risk and adversity. In: M. Wang & E. Gordon (eds). *Risk and Resilience in Inner City America*. Hillsdale, NJ: Erlbaum; 3–25.

Mataix-Cols, D., Rauch, S. L., Manzo, P. A., Jenike, M. A. & Baer, L. (1999) Use of factor-analyzed symptom dimensions to predict outcome with serotonin reuptake inhibitors and placebo in the treatment of obsessive–compulsive disorder. *American Journal of Psychiatry* 156: 1409–1416.

Matthews, G. & Deary, I. J. (1998) *Personality Traits.* Cambridge: Cambridge University Press.

Mattson, D. T., Berk, M. & Lucas. M. D. (1997) A neuropsychological study of prefrontal lobe function in the positive and negative subtypes of schizophrenia. *Journal of Genetic Psychology* 158: 487–494.

Maynard, T. M., Sikich, L., Lieberman, J. A. & LaMantia, A-S. (2001) Neural development, cell-cell, signaling, and the 'two-hit' hypothesis of schizophrenia. *Schizophrenia Bulletin* 27: 457–476.

McCreery, C. & Claridge, G. (2002) Healthy schizotypy: the case of out-of-the-body experiences. *Personality and Individual Differences* 32: 141–154.

McGuffin, P., Farmer, A. E. & Gottesman, I.I. (1987) Is there really a split in schizophrenia? The genetic evidence. *British Journal of Psychiatry* 150: 581–592.

McIlwraith, R. D. (1998) 'I'm addicted to television': the personality, imagination, and TV watching patterns of self-identified TV addicts. *Journal of Broadcasting & Electronic Media* 42: 371–386.

McNally, R. J. (2000) Information-processing abnormalities in obsessive–compulsive disorder. In: W. K. Goodman, M. V. Rudorfer & J. D. Maser (eds). *Obsessive Compulsive Disorder. Contemporary Issues in Treatment.* Hillsdale, NJ: Lawrence Erlbaum Associates.

Meehl, P. E (1962) Schizotaxia, schizotypy, schizophrenia. *American Psychologist* 17: 827–838.

Meehl, P. E. (1975) Hedonic capacity: some conjectures. *Bulletin of the Menninger Clinic* 39: 295–307.

Meehl, P. E. (1990) Toward and integrated theory of schizotaxia, schizotypy, and schizophrenia. *Journal of Personality Disorders* 4: 1–99.

Merikangas, K. R., Mehta, R. L., Molnar, B. E., Walter, E. E., Swendsen, J. D., Aguilar-Gaziola, S., Bijl, R., Borges, G., Caraveo-Anduaga, J. J., Dewit, D. J., Kolody, B., Vega, W. A., Wittchen, H-U. & Kessler, R. C. (1998) Comorbidity of substance use disorders with mood and anxiety disorders: results of the international consortium in psychiatry epidemiology. *Addictive Behaviors* 23: 893–907.

Millon, T. & Davis, R. (2000) *Personality Disorders in Modern Life.* New York, NY: John Wiley.

Millon, T., Davis, R. D. & Millon, C. (1996) *The Millon Clinical Multiaxial Instrument – III Manual.* Minnetonka, MN: National Computer System.

Mitzman, S. F., Slade, P. & Dewey, M. E. (1994) Preliminary development of a questionnaire designed to measure neurotic perfectionism in the eating disorders. *Journal of Clinical Psychology* 50: 516–522.

Moeller, F. G., Dougherty, D. M., Barratt, E. S., Schmitz, J. M., Swann, A. C.

234

& Grabowski, J. (2001) The impact of impulsivity on cocaine use and retention in treatment. *Journal of Substance Abuse Treatment* 21: 193–198.

Moore, M. C. & Zebb, B. J. (1999) The catastrophic misinterpretation of physiological distress. *Behaviour Research and Therapy* 37: 1105–1118.

Moritz, S. & Mass, R. (1997) Reduced cognitive inhibition in schizotypy. *British Journal of Clinical Psychology* 36: 365–376.

Morris, P. H., Gale, A. & Duffy, K. (2002) Can judges agree on the personality of horses. *Personality and Individual Differences* 33: 67–81.

Muller, M. B. & Keck, M. E. (2002) Genetically engineered mice for studies of stress-related clinical conditions. *Journal of Psychiatric Research* 36: 53–76.

Nebylitsyn, V. D. & Gray, J. A. (eds). (1972) *Biological Bases of Individual Behaviour*. New York, NY: Academic Press.

Nettle, D. (2001) *Strong Imagination: Madness, Creativity and Human nature*. Oxford: Oxford University Press.

Nigg, J. T. & Goldsmith, H. H. (1994) Genetics of personality disorders: perspectives from personality and psychopathology research. *Psychological Review* 115: 346–380.

Noble, E. P., Blum, K., Ritchie, T., Montgomery, A. & Sheridan, P. J. (1991) Allelic association of the $D_2$ dopamine receptor gene with receptor-binding characteristics in alcoholism. *Archives of General Psychiatry* 48: 648–654.

Norton, G. R. (2001) Substance use/abuse and anxiety sensitivity. What are the relationships? *Addictive Behaviors* 26: 935–946.

Norton, G. R., Rockman, G. E., Ediger, J., Pepe, C., Goldberg, S., Cox, J. & Asmundson, G. J. G. (1997) Anxiety sensitivity and drug choice in individuals seeking treatment for substance abuse. *Behaviour Research and Therapy* 35: 859–862.

Nyborg, H. (Ed.) (1997) *The Scientific Study of Human Nature, Tribute to Hans J Eysenck at Eighty*. Oxford: Elsevier.

O'Dwyer, A-M. & Marks, I. (2000) Obsessive–compulsive disorder and delusions revisited. *British Journal of Psychiatry* 176: 281–284.

Oldham, J. M., Skodol, A. E., Kellman, H. D., Hyler, S. E., Doidge, N., Rosnick, L. & Gallaher, P. E. (1995) Comobidity of Axis I and Axis II disorders. *American Journal of Psychiatry* 152: 571–578.

Ollendick, T. H. & Hirshfeld-Becker, D. R. (2002) The developmental psychopathology of social axiety. *Biological Psychiatry*, 51, 44–58.

Oquendo, M. A. & Mann, J. J. (2000) The biology of impulsivity and suicidality. *Psychiatric Clinics of North America* 23: 11–25.

Orford, J. (2001) *Excessive Appetites*. Chichester: John Wiley & Sons.

Palanza, P. (2001) Animal models of anxiety and depression: how are females different? *Neuroscience and Biobehavioral Reviews* 25: 219–233.

Paris, J. (1994) *Borderline Personality Disorder. A Multidimensional Approach*. Washington, DC: American Psychiatric Press.

Parkinson, J. A., Crofts, H. S., McGuigan, M., Tomic, D. L., Everitt, B. J. &

235

Roberts, A. C. (2001) The role of the primate amygdala in conditioned reinforcement. *Journal of Neuroscience* 21: 7770–7780.

Pavlov, I. P. (1928) *Lectures on Conditioned Reflexes*. (trans. W. H. Gantt). New York: Liveright Publishing Corporation.

Pavlov, I. P. (1955) *Selected Works*. (trans. S. Belsky). Moscow: Foreign Languages Publishing House.

Pearlson, G. D., Garbacz, D. J., Tompkins, R. H., Ahn, H. S., Gutterman, D. F., Veroff, A. E. & DePaulo, J. R. (1984) Clinical correlaters of lateral ventricular enlargement in bipolar affective disorder. *American Journal of Psychiatry* 141: 253–256.

Penas-Lledo, E., Vaz, F. J., Ramos, M. I. & Waller, G. (2002) Impulsive behaviors in bulimic patients: relation to general psychopathology. *International Journal of Eating Disorders* 32: 98–102.

Perry, W., Minassian, A., Feifel, D. & Braff, D. L. (2001) Sensorimotor gating deficits in bipolar disorder patients with acute psychotic mania. *Biological Psychiatry* 50: 418–424.

Peters, E. (2001) Are delusions on a continuum? The case of religious and delusional beliefs. In: I. Clarke (Ed.). *Psychosis and Spirituality: Exploring the New Frontier*. London: Whurr Publishers.

Petty, R. G., Barta, P. E., Pearlson, G. D., McGilchrist, I. K., Lewis, R. W., Tien, A. Y., Pulver, A., Vaughn, D. D., Casanova, M. F. & Powers, R. E. (1995) Reversal of asymmetry of the planum temporale in schizophrenia. *American Journal of Psychiatry* 152: 715–721.

Phillips, E.D. (1987) *Aspects of Greek Medicine*. London: Croom Helm.

Piazza, P. V., Deminiere, J. M., Le Moal, M. & Simon, H. (1989) Factors that predict individual vulnerability to amphetamine self-administration. *Science* 24: 1511–1513.

Pickering, A. D. & Gray, J. A. (1999) The neuroscience of personality. In: L. A. Pervin & O. P. John (eds). *Handbook of Personality: Theory and Research* (Second edition). New York, NY: The Guilford Press.

Pierson, A., le Houezec, J., Fossaert, A., Dubal, S. & Jouvent, R. (1999) Frontal reactivity and sensation seeking: an ERP study in skydivers. *Progress in Neuropsychopharmacology and Biological Psychiatry* 23: 447–463.

Pigott, T. A. (1998) Obsessive–compulsive disorder: symptom overview and epidemiology. *Bulletin of the Menninger Clinic* 62 (Suppl. A): A4–A32.

Pine, D. S. & Cohen, J. A. (2002) Trauma in children and adolescents: risk and treatment of psychiatric sequelae. *Biological Psychiatry* 51: 519–531.

Pinel, J. P., Assanand, S. & Lehman, D. R. (2000) Hunger, eating, and ill health. *American Psychologist* 55: 1105–1116.

Plomin, R. (1986) *Development, Genetics, and Psychology*. Hillsdale, NJ: Erlbaum.

Plomin, R. & Dunn, J. (1986) *The Study of Temperament: Changes, Continuities and Challenges*. Hillsdale, NJ: Erlbaum.

Plomin, R., Owen, M. J. & McGuffin, P. (1994) The genetic basis of complex human behaviours. *Science* 264: 1733–1739.

Polivy, J. & Herman, P. C. (2002) Causes of eating disorders. *Annual Review of Psychology* 53: 187–213.

Post, R. M. & Ballenger, J. C. (1981) Kindling models for the progressive development of psychopathology: sensitization to electrical, pharmacological and psychological stimuli. In: H. W. Van Praag, M. H. Lader, O. J. Rafaelson & E. J. Sachar (eds). *Handbook of Biological Psychiatry*. Vol IV. New York, NY: Marcel Dekker; 609–651.

Poulton, R., Thomson, W. M., Davies, S., Kruger, E., Brown, R. H. & Silva, P. A. (1997) Good teeth, bad teeth and fear of the dentist. *Behaviour Research and Therapy* 35: 327–334.

Poulton, R., Davies, S., Menzies, R. G., Langley, J. D. & Silva, P. A. (1998) Evidence for a non-associative model of the acquisition of a fear of heights. *Behaviour Research and Therapy* 36: 537–544.

Poulton, R., Waldie, K. E., Menzies, R. G., Craske, M. G. & Silva, P. A. (2001) Failure to overcome 'innate' fear: a developmental test of the non-associative model of fear acquisition. *Behaviour Research and Therapy* 39: 29–43.

Purdon, C. (1999) Thought suppression and psychopathology. *Behaviour Research and Therapy* 37: 1029–1054.

Rachman, S. (1978) *Fear and Courage*. San Francisco, CA: W. H. Freeman & Co.

Rado, S. (1953) Dynamics and classification of disordered behavior. *American Journal of Psychiatry* 110: 406–416.

Raine, A., Lencz, T. & Mednick, S. A. (eds) (1995) *Schizotypal Personality*. Cambridge: Cambridge University Press.

Ramboz, S., Oosting, R., Amara, D. A., Kung, H. F. & Blier, P. (1998) Serotonin receptor 1A knockout: an animal model of anxiety-related disorder. *Proceedings of the National Academy of Sciences USA* 95: 4472–4481.

Rasmussen, S. A. (1994) Obsessive compulsive spectrum disorders. *Psychiatry* 55: 89–91.

Robinet, P. M., Rowlett, J. K. & Bardo, M. T. (1998) Individual differences in novelty-induced activity and the rewarding effects of novelty and amphetamine in rats. *Behavioural Processes* 44: 1–9.

Robinson, R. (1998) Obsessive–compulsive disorders in children and adolescents. *Bulletin of the Menninger Clinic* 62 (Suppl. A): A49–A64.

Robinson, T. E. & Berridge, K. C. (1993) The neural basis of drug craving: an incentive-sensitization theory of addiction. *Brain Research Reviews* 18: 247–291.

Rosenberg, R. (1989) Kindling and panic disorder. In: T. G. Bolwig & M. R. Trimble (eds). *The Clinical Relevance of Kindling*. Chichester: John Wiley.

Rothenberg, A. (1986) Eating disorder as a modern obsessive–compulsive syndrome. *Psychiatry* 49: 45–53.

Rothman, R. B., Partilla, J. S., Dersch, C. M., Carroll, F. I., Rice, K. C. & Baumann, M. H. (2000) Methamphetamine dependence: medication development efforts based on the dual deficit model of stimulant addiction. In: *Neurobiological Mechanisms of Drugs of Abuse: Cocaine, Ibogaine, and Substituted Amphetamines.* New York, NY: New York Academy of Sciences; 71–81.

Rowe, D. C., Stever, C., Gard, J. M. C., Cleveland, H. H., Sanders, M. L., Abramowitz, A., Kozol, S. T., Mohr, J. H., Sherman, S. L. & Waldman, I. D. (1998) The relation of the dopamine transporter gene (DAT1) to symptoms of internalizing disorders in children. *Behavior Genetics* 28: 215–225.

Roy, A. (Ed.) (1982) *Hysteria.* Chichester: John Wiley.

Rubenstein, C. S., Pigott, T. A., L'Heureux, F., Hill, J. L. & Murphy, D. L. (1992) A preliminary investigation of the lifetime prevalence of anorexia and bulimia nervosa in patients with obsessive compulsive disorder. *Journal of Clinical Psychiatry* 53: 309–314.

Rutledge, T. & Linden, W. (1998) To eat or not to eat: affective and physiological mechanisms in the stress–eating relationship. *Journal of Behavioral Medicine* 21: 221–240.

Salkovskis, P. M. (1985) Obsessive–compulsive problems: a cognitive–behavioural analysis. *Behaviour Research and Therapy* 25: 571–583.

Saxena, S., Brody, A. L., Schwartz, J. M. & Baxter, L. R. (1998) Neuroimaging and frontal–subcortical circuitry in obsessive–compulsive disorder. *British Journal of Psychiatry* 173 (Suppl. 35): 26–37.

Satz, P. & Green, M. F. (1999) Atypical handedness in schizophrenia. *Schizophrenia Bulletin* 25: 63–78.

*Schizophrenia Bulletin* (1999) Vol 25, No 1. Issue theme: Is schizophrenia a lateralised brain disorder?

*Schizophrenia Bulletin* (2000) Vol 26, No 3. Part issue theme on schizotypy.

Schmitz, S., Sandino, K. J., Plomin., R., Fulker, D. W. & DeFries, J. C. (1996) Genetic and environmental influences on temperament in middle childhood: analyses of teacher and tester ratings. *Child Development* 67: 409–422.

Schneider, K. (1959) *Clinical Psychopathology.* New York, NY: Grune & Stratton.

Schneier, F. R., Liebowitz, M. R., Abi-Dargham, A., Zea-Ponce, Y., Lin, S-H. & Laruelle, M. (2000) Low dopamine $D_2$ receptor binding potential in social phobia. *American Journal of Psychiatry* 157: 457–459.

Schork, E. J., Eckert, E. D. & Halmi, K. A. (1994) The relationship between psychopathology, eating disorder diagnosis, and clinical outcome at 10-year follow-up in anorexia nervosa. *Comprehensive Psychiatry* 35: 113–123.

Schroeder, M. L., Wormsworth, J. A. & Livesley, W. J. (1992) Dimensions of personality disorder and their relationships to the big five dimensions of personality. *Psychological Assessment* 4: 47–53.

238

Schroeter, K., Dahme, B. & Nutzinger, D-O. (2002) Self-injurious behavior in women with eating disorders. *American Journal of Psychiatry* 159: 408–411.

Seligman, M. E. P. (1971) Phobias and preparedness. *Behaviour Therapy* 2: 307–320.

Shachnow, J., Clarkin, J., DiPalma, C. S., Thurston, F., Hull, J. & Shearin, E. (1997) Biparental psychopathology and borderline personality disorder. *Psychiatry* 60: 171–181.

Shafer, A. B. (2001) Relation of the Big Five to the EASI scales and the Thurstone Temperament Schedule. *Personality and Individual Differences* 31: 193–204.

Shagass, C. & Jones, A. L. (1958) A neurophysiological test for psychiatric diagnosis: results in 750 patients. *American Journal of Psychiatry* 114: 1002–1009.

Shaw, J., Claridge, G. & Clark, K. (2001) Schizotypy and the shift from dextrality: a study of handedness in a large non-clinical sample. *Schizophrenia Research* 50: 181–189.

Showalter, E. (1987) *The Female Malady*. London: Virago.

Skoog, G. & Skoog, I. (1999) A 40-year follow-up of patients with obsessive–compulsive disorder. *Archives of General Psychiatry* 56: 121–127.

Slaughter, J. R., Slaughter, K. A., Nichols, D., Holmes, S. E. & Martens, R. P. (2001) Prevalence, clinical manifestations, etiology, and treating depression in Parkinson's disease. *Journal of Neuropsychiatry and Clinical Neurosciences* 13: 187–196.

Small, D. M., Zatore, R. J., Dagher, A., Evans, A. C. & Jones-Gotman, M. (2001) Changes in brain activity related to eating chocolate. *Brain* 124: 1720–1733.

Snyder, S. (2002) Serotonin sustains serenity. *Nature* 416: 377–380.

Sommer, I., Aleman, A., Ramsey, N., Bouma, A. & Kahn, R. (2001) Handedness, language lateralisation and anatomical asymmetry in schizophrenia. Meta-analysis. *British Journal of Psychiatry* 178: 344–351.

Steiger, H., Gauvin, L., Israel, M., Koerner, N., Ng-Ying-Kin, N. M. K., Paris, J. & Young, S. N. (2001c) Association of serotonin and cortisol indices with childhood abuse in bulimia nervosa. *Archives of General Psychiatry* 58: 837–843.

Steiger, H., Jabalpurwala, S. & Champagne, J. (1996) Axis II comorbidity and developmental adversity in bulimia nervosa. *Journal of Nervous and Mental Disease* 184: 555–560.

Steiger, H., Koerner, N., Engelberg, M. J., Israel, M., Kin, N, M. & Young, S. N. (2001a) Self-destructiveness and serotonin function in bulimia nervosa. *Psychiatry Research* 103: 15–26.

Steiger, H., Young, S. N., Ng, Y. K., Koerner, N. M. K., Israel, M., Lageix, P. & Paris, J. (2001b) Implications of impulsive and affective symptoms for serotonin function in bulimia nervosa. *Psychological Medicine* 31: 85–95.

239

Stein, M. B. (1998) Neurobiological perspectives on social phobia: from affiliation to zoology. *Biological Psychiatry* 44: 1277–1285.

Stein, D. J., Westenberg, H. G. M. & Liebowitz, M. R. (2002) Social anxiety disorder and generalized anxiety disorder: serotonergic and dopaminergic neurocircuitry. *Journal of Clinical Psychiatry* 63 (Suppl. 6): 12–19.

Steptoe, A., Lipsey, Z. & Wardle, J. (1998) Stress, hassles and variations in alcohol consumption, food choice and physical exercise. A diary study. *British Journal of Health Psychology* 3: 51–63.

Stewart, S. H. & Kushner, M. G. (2001) Introduction to the special issue on 'anxiety sensitivity and addictive behaviors'. *Addictive Behaviors* 26: 775–785.

Street, H., Sheeran, P. & Orbell, S. (1999) Conceptualizing depression: an integration of 27 theories. *Clinical Psychology and Psychotherapy* 6: 175–193.

Strober, M., Freeman, R. & Morrell, W. (1999) Atypical anorexia nervosa: separation from typical cases in course and outcome in a long-term prospective study. *International Journal of Eating Disorders* 25: 135–142.

Summerfeldt, L. J., Huta, V. & Swinson, R. P. (1998) Personality and obsessive–compulsive disorder. In: R. P. Swinson, A. S. Rachman & M. A. Richter (eds). *Obsessive–Compulsive Disorder: Theory, Research, and Treatment.* New York, NY: Guilford.

Summerfeldt, L. J., Richter, M. A., Antony, M. M. & Swinson, R. P. (1999) Symptom structure in obsessive–compulsive disorder: a confirmatory factor-analytic study. *Behaviour Research and Therapy* 37: 297–311.

Svrakic, D. M., Whitehead, C., Przybeck, T. R. & Cloninger, R. (1993) Differential diagnosis of personality disorders by the seven-factor model of temperament and character. *Archives of General Psychiatry* 50: 991–999.

Szabo, C. P. (1996) *Playboy* centrefolds and eating disorders – from male pleasure to female pathology. *South African Medical Journal* 86: 838–839.

Szasz, T.S. (1974) *The Myth of Mental Illness.* Oxford: Oxford University Press.

Szechtman, H., Sulis, W. & Eilam, D. (1998) Quinpirole induces compulsive checking behavior in rats: a potential animal model of obsessive–compulsive disorder (OCD). *Behavioral Neuroscience* 6: 1475–1485.

Talbot, M. (2000) The shyness syndrome. *The New York Times Magazine*, June 24, 11–12.

Taylor, J. R. & Jentsch, D. (2001) Repeated intermittent administration of psychomotor stimulant drugs alters the acquisition of Pavlovian approach behavior in rats: differential effects of cocaine, *d*-amphetamine and 3,4-methylenedioxymethampetamine ('Ecstasy'). *Biological Psychiatry* 50: 137–143.

Taylor, M. A. (1992) Are schizophrenia and affective disorder related? A selective literature review. *American Journal of Psychiatry* 149: 22–32.

Terry-Short, L. A., Owens, R. G., Slade, P. D. & Dewey, M. E. (1995) Positive and negative perfectionism. *Personality and Individual Differences* 18: 663–668.

Thiel, A., Broocks, A., Ohlmeier, M., Jacoby, G. E. & Schussler, G. (1995) Obsessive–compulsive disorder among patients with anorexia nervosa and bulimia nervosa. *American Journal of Psychiatry* 152: 72–75.

Thom, R. (1975) *Structual Stability and Morphogenesis*. Reading, MA: WA Benjamin, Inc.

Tien, A.Y., Ross, D. E., Pearlson, G. & Strauss, M. E. (1996) Eye movements and psychopathology in schizophrenia and bipolar disorder. *Journal of Nervous and Mental Disease* 184: 331–338.

Tienari, P. (1991) Gene–environment interaction in adoptive families. In: H. Häfner & W. F. Gattaz (eds). *Search for the Causes of Schizophrenia* (Vol II). Berlin: Springer-Verlag; 126–143.

Tiller, J., Schmidt, U., Ali, S., *et al.* (1995) Patterns of punitiveness in women with eating disorders. *Int J Eat Disorder* 17 (4): 365-371

Tomarken, A. J. & Keener, A. D. (1998) Frontal brain asymmetry and depression: a self-regulatory perspective. *Cognition and Emotion* 12: 387–420.

Torrubia, R., Ávila, C., Molton, J. & Caseras, X. (2001) The Sensitivity to Punishment and Sensitivity to Reward Questionnaire (SPSRQ) as a measure of Gray's anxiety and impulsivity dimensions. *Personality and Individual Differences* 31: 837–862.

Treasure, J. L. & Owen, J. B. (1997) Intriguing links between animal behavior and anorexia nervosa. *International Journal of Eating Disorders* 21: 307–311.

Tremblay, L. K., Naranjo, C. A., Cardenas, L., Herrmann, N. & Busto, U. E. (2002) Probing brain reward system function in major depressive disorder. *Archives of General Psychiatry* 59: 409–415.

Tsuang, M. T., Stone, W. S., Tarbox, S. I. & Faraone, S. V. (2002) An integration of schizophrenia with schizotypy: identification of schizotaxia and implications for research on treatment and prevention. *Schizophrenia Research* 54: 169–175.

Van't Hof, S. & Nicolson, M. (1996) The rise and fall of a fact: the increase in anorexia nervosa. *Sociology of Health and Illness* 18: 581–608.

Velakoulis, D. & Pantelis, C. (1996) What have we learned from functional imaging studies in schizophrenia? The role of frontal, striatal and temporal areas. *Australian and New Zealand Journal of Psychiatry* 30: 195, 209.

Venables, P. H. (1964) Input dysfunction in schizophrenia. In: B. A. Maher (Ed.). *Progress in Experimental Personality Research*. New York, NY: Academic Press; 1–41.

Verdoux, H., Geddes, J. R., Takei, N., Lawrie, S. M., Bovet, P., Eagles, J. M., Heun, R., McCreadie, R. G., McNeil, T. F., O'Callaghan, E., Stöber, G., Willinger, U., Wright, P. & Murray, R. M. (1997) Obstetric complications and age at onset in schizophrenia: an international collaborative meta-analysis of individual patient data. *American Journal of Psychiatry* 154: 1220–1227.

241

Verheul, R. & van den Brink, W. (2000) The role of personality pathology in the aetiology and treatment of substance use disorders. *Current Opinion in Psychiatry* 13: 163–169.

Vitousek, K. & Manke, F. (1994) Personality variables and disorders in anorexia nervosa and bulimia nervosa. *Journal of Abnormal Psychology* 103: 137–147.

Volkow, N. D., Ding, Y-S., Fowler, J. S. & Wang, G-J. (1996a) Cocaine addiction: hypothesis derived from imaging studies with PET. *Journal of Addictive Disorders* 15: 55–71.

Volkow, N. D., Fowler, J. S., Hitzemann, R. & Wang, G-J. (1996b) Neurochemical mechanisms underlying responses to psychostimulants. *National Institute on Drug Abuse Research Monograph* 159: 322–348.

Volkow, N. D., Wang, G-J., Fowler, J. S., Logan, J., Gatley, S. J., Gifford, A., Hitzemann, R., Ding, Y-S. & Pappas, N. (1999) Prediction of reinforcing responses to psychostimulants in humans by brain dopamine D2 receptor levels. *American Journal of Psychiatry* 156: 1440–1443.

Wade, D., Kyrios, M. & Jackson, H. (1998) A model of obsessive–compulsive phenomena in a nonclinical sample. *Australian Journal of Psychology* 50: 11–17.

Wagner, A. W. & Linehan, M. M. (1999) Facial expression recognition ability among women with borderline personality disorder: implications for emotion regulation? *Journal of Personality Disorders* 13: 329–344.

Waldman, I. D., Rowe, D. C., Abramowitz, A., Kozel, S. T., Mohr, J. H., Sherman, S. L., Cleveland, H. H., Sanders, M. L., Gard, J. M. C. & Stever, C. (1998) Association and linkage of the dopamine transporter gene and attention-deficit hyperactivity disorder in children: heterogeneity owing to diagnositc subtype and severity. *American Journal of Human Genetics* 63: 1767–1776.

Walker, E. & Bollini, A. M. (2002) Pubertal neurodevelopment and the emergence of psychotic symptoms. *Schizophrenia Research* 54: 17–23.

Walsh, A. E. S., Oldman, A. D., Franklin, M., Fairburn, C. G. & Cowen, P. J. (1995) Dieting decreases plasma trytophan and increases prolactin response to *d*-fenfluramine in women but not men. *Journal of Affective Disorders* 33: 89–97.

Wang, G-J., Volkow, N. D., Logan, J., Pappas, N. R., Wong, C. T., Zhu, W., Netusil, N. & Fowler, J. S. (2001) Brain dopamine and obesity. *Lancet* 357: 354–357.

Watkins, P. C. (2002) Implicit memory bias in depression. *Cognition and Emotion* 16: 381–402.

Watson, D., Wiese, D., Vaidya, J. & Tellegen, A. (1999) The two general activation systems of affect: structural findings, evolutionary considerations, and psychobiological evidence. *Journal of Personality and Social Psychology* 76: 820–838.

Wegner, D. M., Schneider, D. J., Carter, S. R. & White, T. (1987) Paradoxical effects of thought suppression. *Journal of Personality and Social Psychology* 53: 5–13.

Weinberger, D. R. (2002) Biological phenotypes and genetic research on schizophrenia. *World Psychiatry* 1: 2–6.

Wexler, B. E., Lyons, L., Lyons, H. & Mazure, C. M. (1997) Physical and sexual abuse during childhood and development of psychiatric illnesses during adulthood. *Journal of Nervous and Mental Disease* 185: 522–524.

White, T. L. & Depue, R. A. (1999) Differential association of traits of fear and anxiety with norepinephrine- and dark-induced pupil reactivity. *Journal of Personality and Social Psychology* 77: 863–877.

Widiger, T. A. & Costa, P. T. Jr (1994) Personality and personality disorders. *Journal of Abnormal Psychology* 103: 78–91.

Wiederman, M. W. & Pryor, T. (1996) Substance use and impulsive behaviors among adolescents with eating disorders. *Addictive Behaviors* 21: 269–272.

Wilhelm, S., McNally, R. J., Baer, L. & Florin, I. (1996) Directed forgetting in obsessive-compulsive disorder. *Behaviour Research and Therapy* 34: 633–641.

Williams, L. & Beech, A. (1997) Investigations of cognitive inhibitory processes in schizophrenia and schizotypy. In: G. Claridge (Ed.). *Schizotypy: Implications for Illness and Health*. Oxford: Oxford University Press; 63–79.

Williams, J. M. G., Watts, F. N., MacLeod, C. & Mathews, A. (1997) *Cognitive Psychology and Emotional Disorders*. (Second edition). Chichester: John Wiley.

Williamson, S. E., Harpur, T. J. & Hare, R. D. (1991) Abnormal processing of affective words by psychopaths. *Psychophysiology* 28: 260–273.

Willner, P. (1997) Validity, reliability and utility of the chronic mild stress model of depression: a 10-year review and evaluation. *Psychopharmacology* 134: 319–329.

Willner, P., Benton, D., Brown, E., Cheeta, S., Davies, G., Morgan, J. & Morgan, M. (1998) 'Depression' increases 'craving' for sweet rewards in animal and human models of depression and craving. *Psychopharmacology* 136: 272–283.

Wills, T. A., Windle, M. & Cleary, S. D. (1998) Temperament and novelty seeking in adolescent substance use: convergence of dimensions of temperament with constructs from Cloninger's theory. *Journal of Personality and Social Psychology* 74: 387–406.

Wise, R. A. (1982) Neuroleptics and operant behaviour: the anhedonia hypothesis. *Behavioral and Brain Sciences* 5: 39–87.

Wise, R. A. & Bozarth, M. A. (1987) A psychomotor stimulant theory of addiction. *Psychological Review* 94: 469–492.

Wiseman, C. V., Gray, J. J., Mosimann, J. E. & Ahrens, A. H. (1992) Cultural expectations of thinness in women: an update. *International Journal of Eating Disorders* 11: 85–89.

Withers, N. W., Pulvirenti, L., Koob, G. F. & Gillin, J. C. (1995) Cocaine abuse and dependence. *Journal of Clinical Psychopharmacology* 15: 63–78.

Woodcock, A. & Davis, M. (1978) *Catastrophe Theory*. New York, NY: Dutton.

World Health Organization (1992) *ICD: The ICD-10 Classification of Mental and Behavioural Disorders–Clinical Descriptions and Diagnostic Guidelines.* Geneva: World Health Organization.

Yehuda, R., McFarlane, A. C. & Shaleve, A. Y. (1998) Predicting the development of post-traumatic stress disorder from the acute response to a traumatic event. *Biological Psychiatry* 44: 1305–1313.

Young, L. J. (2002) The neurobiology of social recognition, approach, and avoidance. *Biological Psychiatry* 51: 18–26.

Zacharko, R. M. (1994) Stressors, the mesolimbic system, and anhedonia: implications for PTSD. In: M. M. Murburg (Ed.). *Catecholamine Function in Posttraumatic Stress Disorder: Emerging Concepts*. Progress in Psychiatry, No. 42. Washington, DC: American Psychiatric Press; 99–130.

Zanarini, M. C., Williams, A. A., Lewis, R. E., Reich, R. B., Vera, S. C., Marino, M. F., Levin, A., Young, L. & Frankenburg, F. R. (1997) Reported pathological childhood experiences associated with the development of borderline personality disorder. *American Journal of Psychiatry* 154: 1101–1106.

Zeeman, E. C. (1976) Catastrophe theory. *Scientific American* 24: 65–83.

Zelenski, J. M. & Larsen, R. J. (1999) Susceptibility to affect: a comparison of three personality taxonomies. *Journal of Personality* 67: 761–791.

Zuckerman, M. (1994) *Behavioural Expressions and Biosocial Bases of Sensation Seeking*. New York, NY: Cambridge University Press.

Zuckerman, M. (1996) The psychobiological model for impulsive unsocialized sensation seeking: a comparative approach. *Neuropsychobiology* 34: 125–129.

# Index

## AUTHOR INDEX

Aharon, I. 137
Aitre-Vaidya, N. 207
Akiskal, H.S. 207
Allen, T.J. 149
Amaral, D.G. 97
Ambrioso, E. 152
Andersen, A.E. 156
Andreasen, N.C. 186, 200
Appleby, L. 61
Arndt, S. 187

Badiani, A. 144
Ballenger, J.C. 25
Bannister, D. 8
Barlow, D.H. 89
Bastiani, A.M. 167
Baumgarten, H.G. 119
Bayer, T.A. 195
Bebbington, P.E. 116
Bechara, A. 140
Beck, A.T. 72-3, 102, 110, 211
Beck, R. 89
Becker, D. 64
Beech, T. 200
Bejerot, S. 113, 125
Belke, T.W. 179
Bergh, C. 176
Berman, S. 57
Berridge, K.C. 133, 175
Berridge, V. 132
Berrios, G.E. 185
Bevins, R.A. 144
Bickford-Wimer, P.C. 201
Black, D.W. 125
Blair, C. 148
Blair, R.J.R. 79-80

Blatt, S.J. 127
Bleuler, E. 184-5, 187, 209
Bogerts, B. 202
Bogetto, F. 116
Bollini, A.M. 208
Bouricius, J.K. 187
Bozarth, M.A. 175
Brady, K.T. 149
Braff, D.L. 199
Broadhurst, P.L. 40
Brockington, J.F. 205
Broocks, A. 179
Brown, T.A. 102
Brunelllo, N. 104, 170
Buchsbaum, M.S. 203
Burke, R.J. 133
Burt, S.A. 56
Buss, A.H. 57

Cadenhead, K.S. 199
Caldji, C. 98
Campbell, L.A. 89
Cannon, T.D. 202
Cannon, W.B. 29-30
Cardinal, R.N. 129
Carver, C.S. 44
Casper, R.C. 170
Cattell, R.B. 16, 49
Chamove, A.S. 39
Chapman, L.J. 206
Chappa, H. 24
Childress, A.R. 135, 159
Chin, S. 203
Chua, S.E. 201
Chutuape, M.A.D. 177
Claridge, C. 5, 36, 51, 55, 65, 81, 170, 175, 178, 190, 191, 192
Clark, D.B. 149

Clark, D.M. **99, 102, 121**
Clark, K. **192**
Clark, L.A. **88**
Cleckley, H. **75-8**
Cloninger, C.R. **44-6, 48, 49, 51, 52, 55,**
 **56, 59, 70-1, 143, 145, 148, 207, 212**
Cohen, J.A. **106**
Collins, P.F. **44, 109**
Connor, K.M. **103**
Cooke, D.J. **77**
Cooper, C. **17**
Costa, P.T. **48-9, 68**
Coupland, N.J. **105**
Crabbe, J.C. **142**
Crino, R.C. **129**
Crow, T.J. **187, 204, 209**
Cutting, J. **203**

Dackis, C.A. **131, 134, 139**
Davidson, J.R.T. **103**
Davidson, R.J. **89, 109, 110**
Davis, C. **51, 156, 158, 164, 168, 170, 171,**
 **172, 173, 175, 176, 177, 178, 179**
Davis, M. **28**
Davis, M. **97, 105**
Davis, R. **71**
Dawes, M.A. **150**
Deary, I.J. **54**
Deep, A.L. **168**
DeHaas, R.A. **150**
Delgado, P.L. **108, 119, 120**
Depue, R.A. **95, 96, 109**
Dess, N.K. **173**
Dewit, H. **177**
Diaferia, G. **126**
Di Chiara, G. **134**
Drevetts, W.C. **89**
Drewnowski, A. **159**
Dunn, J. **58**

Edell, W.S. **191**
Eisen, J.L. **115**
Eley, T.C. **58**
el-Guebaly, N. **135**
Epling, W.F. **163, 178**
Evers, M. **129**
Eysenck, H.J. **7, 8, 16-20, 29, 31, 33-8,**
 **40, 47, 51, 52, 62, 143, 150, 206,**
 **209, 211**

Eysenck, M.W. **16**
Eysenck, S.B.G. **17, 37**

Fairburn, C.G. **155, 166**
Farmer, A.E. **194**
Favaro, A. **169**
Foulds, G.A. **19-20, 66**
Fowles, D.C. **44**
Fransella, F. **8**
Freud, S. **2-3**
Figueredo, A.J. **49**
Figueroa, E. **85**
Frith, C.D. **200**
Funtowicz, M.N. **64**

Gainerdinov, R.R. **138**
Gamberino, W.C. **138, 144**
Gantt, W.H. **35**
Germans, M.K. **143**
Ginovart, N. **141**
Glass, M.J. **173**
Gold, M. **131, 135, 138, 139, 144**
Goldman, D. **56**
Goldner, E.M. **168**
Goldsmith, H.H. **14, 69, 84**
Gordon, H.W. **153**
Gosling, S.D. **39**
Gottesman, I.I. **193, 194**
Grant, B.F. **175**
Grant, S. **140**
Grant, V.L. **179**
Gray, J.A. **35, 40-4, 46, 47, 51, 52, 143,**
 **148**
Green, M.F. **204**
Greenberg, B.D. **127**
Greenfield, S.F. **208**
Gregory, A.M. **58**
Griffiths, M. **132**
Grilo, C.M. **149**
Gross, C. **92, 103**
Grozdanovic, Z. **119**
Gruzelier, J. **204**
Gur, R.C. **201**
Gur, R.E. **201, 203**

Halmi, K.A. **165**
Hare, R.D. **77-9**
Harford, T.C. **175**
Hebb, D.O. **5**

246

Heinz, A. **144**
Henderson, N.J. **173**
Henriques, J.B. **109, 110**
Herbert, J.D. **104**
Herman, P.C. **168, 169**
Herpertz, S.C. **85**
Herrington, R.N. **37**
Hertel, P.T. **89**
Herzog, D.B. **162, 176**
Heubner, H.F. **176**
Hewitt, P.L. **168**
Heyman, G.M. **175**
Hirshfield, R.M.A. **107**
Hodgins, D. **135**
Hoean-Sarie, R. **127**
Holden, C. **133, 147**
Holden, N.L. **164**
Holderness, C.C. **175**
Holeva, V. **106**
Hollander, E. **128, 129, 169**
Holsboer, F. **92**
Hudziak, J.J. **82**
Hughes, J.R. **196**
Humble, M. **113**
Huon, G.F. **173**
Husain, S.M. **207**

Jentsch, J.D. **139, 149**
John, O.P. **48**
Johns, J.H. **77**
Johnson, R.D. **173**
Jones, A.L. **37**
Jorm, A.F. **102**
Just, N. **89, 110**

Kagan, J. **104**
Kaplan, S. **183**
Kashdan, T.B. **104**
Katzmarzyk, P.T. **158**
Kaye, W.H. **160, 164, 174**
Keck, M.E. **92**
Keener, A.D. **109**
Kendell, R.E. **205, 206**
Kendler, K.S. **88, 100, 101, 155**
Kessler, R.C. **175**
Keys, A. **160-1**
Khantzian, E.J. **142, 150, 177**
Kiehl, K.A. **79**
King, J.A. **106**

King, J.E. **49**
Klump, K.L. **164**
Koff, E. **173**
Koob, G.F. **136, 138, 142, 175**
Kline, P. **3**
Kosten, T.A. **152, 153**
Kraepelin, E. **185**
Kretschmer, E. **206, 207**
Kring, A.M. **143**
Kroeze, S. **99**
Kushner, M.G. **103, 151**
Kwapil, T.R. **197**

Laing, R.D. **6-7, 8**
Larsen, R.J. **143**
Lawrence, T. **208**
LeDoux, J. **97, 99**
Le Moal, M. **175**
Lenzenweger, M.F. **190**
Leonard, B.E. **108**
Lerman, C. **145**
Leshner, A.I. **135, 136, 138, 142, 175**
Lester, D. **183**
Lett, B.T. **179**
Levine, D. **86**
Lewis, G. **61**
Li, D. **105**
Linden, W. **173**
Linehan, M.M. **85**
Loehlin, J.C. **49, 54**
Luby, E.D. **176**

Maier, W. **188**
Majewska, M.D. **152**
Mangan, G. **35, 55**
Manke, F. **169, 175**
Mann, J.J. **148**
Marazziti, D. **115, 120**
Marco, E. **202**
Marcus, D. **171**
Maren, S. **97**
Markou, A. **110, 177**
Marks, I. **115**
Marrazzi, M.A. **176**
Marrin-Bevins, C.L. **173**
Mason, O. **191**
Mass, R. **200**
Masten, A.S. **2**
Mataix-Cols, D. **114**

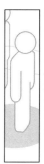

Matthews, G. 54
Mattson, D.T. 202
Maynard, T.M. 27
McCrae, R.R. 48-9
McCreery, C. 190
McGuffin, P. 194
McIlwraith, R.D. 133
McKenna, P.J. 201
McNally, R.J. 123
Meehl, P.E. 143, 190
Merikangas, K.R. 150
Millon, T. 71-2
Mitzman, S.F. 173
Moeller, F.G. 149
Moore, M.C. 99
Moreno, F.A. 119, 120
Morris, P.H. 49
Moritz, S. 200
Muller, M.B. 92

Nebylitsyn, V.D. 35
Nettle, D. 204
Nicolson, M. 159
Nigg, J.T. 14, 69, 84
Noble, E.P. 145
Norton, G.R. 151
Noyes, R. 125
Nyborg, H. 16

O'Dwyer, A-M 115
Oldham, J.M. 82
Olsen, S. 186
Olster, D.H. 173
Oquendo, M.A. 148
Orford, J. 132, 133
Owen, J.B. 163

Palanza, P. 91, 93
Pantelis, C. 202
Paris, J. 26, 82-4, 86
Parkinson, J.A. 139
Pavlov, I.P. 34-5, 39, 135
Pearlson, G.D. 206
Penas-Lledo, E. 169
Perkins, T.S. 89
Perry, W. 206
Petty, R.G. 204
Phillips, E.D. 32
Piazza, P.V. 152

Pickering, A.D. 42
Pierce, W.D. 163, 178
Pierson, A. 146
Pigott, T.A. 116
Pine, D.S. 106
Pinel, J.P. 177
Plomin, R. 55, 57, 58
Polivy, J. 168, 169
Post, R.M. 25
Poulton, R. 100, 101
Powers, P.S. 206
Pryor, T. 175
Purdon, C. 111

Quay, H.C. 77

Rachman, S. 100
Rado, S. 190
Raine, A. 190
Ramboz, S. 103
Rasmussen, S.A. 129
Robinet, P.M. 152
Robinson, R. 117
Robinson, T.E. 133, 175
Rosenberg, R. 25
Rothenberg, A. 165
Rothman, R.B. 145
Rowe, D.C. 145
Roy, A. 64
Rubenstein, C.S. 165
Rutledge, T. 173

Salkovskis, P. 121
Sangani, P. 173
Santonastaso, P. 169
Satz, P. 204
Saxena, S. 108
Schmitz, J.M. 58
Schnieder, K. 184-5
Schneier, F.R. 105
Schroeter, K. 169
Schork, E.J. 162
Seligman, M.E.P. 42, 92-3
Shachnow, J. 84
Shafer, A.B. 58
Shagass, C. 37
Shaw, J. 204
Shields, J. 194
Showalter, E. 64

Silk, K.R. **85**
Slaughter, J.R. **144**
Small, D.M. **137**
Snyder, S. **103**
Sommer, I. **204**
Sondersten, P. **176**
Steiger, H. **169, 174**
Stein, M.B. **104, 105**
Steptoe, A. **173**
Stewart, S.H. **103, 151**
Street, H. **111**
Strober, M. **176**
Summerfeldt, L. **114, 124**
Svrakic, D.M. **70**
Szasz, T. **6, 7, 8**
Szechtman, H. **120**

Tarrier, N. **106**
Taylor, J.R. **139, 149**
Taylor, M.A. **204**
Terry-Short, L.A. **167**
Tiller, J. **169**
Thiel, A. **165**
Thom, R. **27**
Tien, A.Y. **206**
Tiffany, S.T. **175**
Tomarken, A.J. **109**
Torrubia, R. **44**
Treasure, J.L. **163**
Tremblay, L.K. **110**
Tsuamg, M.T. **197**

van den Brink, W. **142**
van den Hout, M.A. **99**
Van't Hof, S. **159**
Velakoulis, D. **202**
Venables, P.H. **198-9, 201**
Verdoux, H. **195**
Verheul, R. **142**
Vitousek, K. **169, 175**

Volkow, N.D. **145-6, 152**

Wade, D. **127**
Wagner, A.W. **85**
Waldman, I.D. **145**
Walker, E. **208**
Wang, G-J. **177**
Watkins, P.C. **111**
Watson, D. **44, 109**
Wegner, D.M. **111**
Weinberger, D.R. **195-6**
Weiner, M. **171**
Wernicke, C. **204**
Wexler, B.E. **82**
White, T.L. **44, 95, 96**
Widiger, T.A. **64, 68**
Wiederman, M.W. **175**
Wilhelm, S. **123**
Williams, J.M.G. **85**
Williams, L. **200**
Williamson, S.E. **79**
Willner, P. **91, 94, 110**
Wills, T.A. **146, 150**
Wise, R.A. **144, 175**
Wiseman, C.V. **158**
Withers, N.W. **137**
Wong, C.M. **128, 169**
Woodcock, A. **28**
Woodside, D.B. **164, 176**

Yehuda, R. **106**
Young, L.J. **104**

Zacharko, R.M. **144**
Zanarini, M.C. **82**
Zebb, B.J. **99**
Zeeman, E.C. **28**
Zelenski, J.M. **143**
Zuckerman, M. **46-8, 49, 51, 52, 62, 143**

# SUBJECT INDEX

ACTH 151
activity 58
activity anorexia 163
addiction
  chronicity of 140-1
  clinical features of 133-5
  cognitive theory of 151
  conditioning in 135
  eating disorders and 175-6
  impulsivity and 147-50
addictive personality 150, 175
aggression 48, 51, 52, 148, 149
agoraphobia see phobias
agreeableness 49, 68
alcohol 131, 170
Alzheimer's disease 14
amphetamine 132
amplification theory 26, 82-4
amygdala 79, 80, 97ff, 139, 148
anhedonia (see also sensitivity to reward)
  94, 107, 134, 143-4, 146, 191, 197,
  202
animal research
  addiction 134, 137-8, 144, 152, 153
  anxiety 91-2
  depression 92-5
  eating disorders 163, 179
  five-factor theory 49-50
  temperament
anorexia nervosa (see also eating disorders)
  128, 156
anti-psychiatry 6-7
antisocial personality disorder (see also
  psychopathy) 64, 70, 74ff, 128, 215
anxiety (see also anxiousness and
  fearfulness) 4, 40ff, 150-2
anxiety disorders 15, 18, 36-7, 88-90,
  101, 102
anxiety sensitivity 102-3, 151
anxiousness 103, 105, 170ff
ARAS 36, 37
arousal 36, 43, 78
ascending reticular activating system see
  ARAS
assortative mating 54
auto-addiction opioid theory 176
avoidant personality disorder 69, 70

Axis I disorders 13
Axis II disorders (see also personality
  disorders) 12-14

barbiturates 37
basal ganglia 117-18
behavioural activation system (BAS) 42-4,
  107
behavioural inhibition system (BIS) 41-4,
  104-5, 107, 149
behaviour genetics see genetics
benzodiazepine 98
'big five' theory see five-factor theory
binge eating disorder (see also eating
  disorders) 157
bipolar disorder 15, 18, 183, 186, 205ff
bipolar spectrum 207
body dysmorphic disorder 128
body image 171-2
borderline personality disorder 63, 68, 70,
  74, 80-6, 128, 182, 207
brain imaging see neuroimaging
bulimia nervosa (see also eating disorders)
  157

caffeine 132
catastrophe theory 27-8
catatonia 186
character 44ff
chocolate 137
chronic mild stress model 92, 94-5
cingulate gyrus 79
clinical psychology 7-8, 211
cocaine 131, 135-6, 137, 151
cognitive behaviour therapy 8, 72, 211
cognitive disorganisation scale (O-LIFE) 191
cognitive inhibition 200-1
comorbidity 13-14, 65, 74, 82, 125,
  213-14
compulsivity 128, 133
conceptual nervous system 5, 35
conditioning 45, 93, 98ff, 135, 139,
  148-149
conscientiousness 49
conversion hysteria 64-5
co-operativeness 45, 70, 71
corticotrophin-releasing hormone (or factor)
  98
cortisol 153

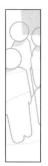

creativity **189, 203**
cyclothymia **206**

delusional disorder **186**
delusions **197**
dementia praecox **185**
depression (*see also* melancholy) **15, 88-9**
  animal models of **92-5**
  cognitive model of **110-12**
  monoamine hypothesis of **107-110**
desensitisation **140**
deviant traits **66**
Diagnostic and Statistical Manual *see* DSM
dichotomous thinking **160**
dissociative disorders **15, 64-5**
dopamine **42, 46, 48, 56, 109-10, 121,**
    **137-8, 144-6, 177**
drug abuse *see* substance abuse
DSM **12ff, 28, 213-214**

EAS(I) dimensions **58**
eating disorders
  cultural influences on **159**
  exercise and **176ff**
  media influences on **158ff**
  in men **156**
  personality in **164ff**
  personality disorders and **82, 165-6**
  sensitivity to reward theory of **175ff**
Ecstasy **147**
EEG **36, 46, 199, 201**
Einheitpsychose theory *see* unitary psychosis
electroencephalogram *see* EEG
emotionality **58**
emotional reactivity **40**
emotional Stroop *see* Stroop test
emotional processing **85-6**
empathy **79**
endophenotype **196-7, 199**
environment
  gene-environment interaction **54**
  shared v unshared **53-4, 55**
epistasis **54, 56**
evoked potential **199, 201**
executive function **139, 201**
exercising **178**
experimental psychopathology **197ff**
extraversion *see* introversion-extraversion
eye movement *see* SPEM

factor analysis **17**
fear conditioning **98ff**
fearfulness **96ff**
first rank symptoms **184, 194**
five-factor theory **49ff, 68-70**
flight of ideas **183**
fMRI *see* neuroimaging
Freudian theory **2-3**
frontal lobes **67**
functional magnetic resonance imaging *see*
    neuroimaging

GABA **46, 48, 201**
galvanic skin response *see* skin conductance
gambling **129, 133**
gender **62, 64, 116, 161**
gene-environment interaction **54**
generalized anxiety disorder **88-90, 101-2**
genetics **5-6**
  behaviour genetics **53-55**
  of dopamine system **57, 145**
  QTL genetics **57**
  of schizophrenia **193ff, 205**
  of serotonin **56, 92**
glutamate **46, 138**

hallucinations **183, 184, 197, 208**
haloperidol **121**
harm avoidance **45-6, 51, 52, 56, 70, 71, 85**
healthy schizotypy **190, 208-9**
hebephrenia **186**
hemisphere asymmetry
  in melancholy **108-9**
  in psychopathy **78**
  in schizophrenia **203ff, 209**
hemisphere indecision **204**
heritability **53**
heroin **137**
hippocampus **79, 88-9, 201**
histrionic personality disorder **64, 70, 74**
HPA axis **92, 106, 176**
Huntington's chorea **14, 119**
hyperactivity **156**
hyperfrontality **128**
hypertension **22-3**
hypofrontality **128, 202**
hypothalamic-pituitary-adrenal axis *see* HPA
    axis
hypothalamus **151**

251

hysteria **15, 37, 64-5**

ICD (*see also* psychiatric classification) **12, 17-19, 28, 49, 65, 214**
impulse disorders **17-18, 128**
impulsive nonconformity scale (O-LIFE) **191**
impulsivity **38, 40ff, 51, 52, 58, 82-3, 85, 128, 143, 147-50, 168ff**
inhibition **35, 199-200**
International Classification of Mental and Behavioural Disorders *see* ICD
introversion-extraversion **3, 17, 33ff, 36, 49**
introvertive anhedonia scale (O-LIFE) **191**
inverted-U function *see* U-shaped function

kindling **25-6**
'knock-out' mouse *see* transgenic mice

latent inhibition **100**
latent schizophrenia **80**
laterality *see* hemisphere asymmetry
learned helplessness **92-4**
LHPA axis **151ff**
limbic system (*see also* mesolimbic system) **36, 37, 42, 80, 117-18**
locus cereleus **98**

magical ideation **197, 208**
magnetic resonance imaging *see* neuroimaging
manic-depression *see* bipolar disorder
marijuana **131, 132**
medical model **20ff**
melancholy **95**
 anhedonia and **107**
 biology of **107-10**
 cognitive models of **110-12**
mesolimbic dopamine pathway **109-10, 137**
mesolimbic system (*see also* limbic system) **42, 137**
methylphenidate (Ritalin) **152**
molecular genetics *see* genetics
monoamine hypothesis **107-10**
MRI *see* neuroimaging

narcissism (*see also* narcissistic personality disorder) **3**
narcissistic personality disorder **63, 67, 74**
negative symptoms **187, 197, 202, 204**

nervous type theory **35, 189**
neuroimaging
 functional magnetic resonance imaging (fMRI) **79, 202**
 positron emission tomography (PET) **46, 135, 152, 177, 202**
neurological disease **14-15**
neurotic disorders
 and psychotic disorders compared **15-16**
neuroticism **17-19, 33, 49, 51, 56, 68-9, 71**
neuroticism-anxiety **47-8, 51**
nicotine (*see also* smoking)
noradrenaline **46, 48, 179**
norepinephrine *see* noradrenaline
nosology (*see also* psychiatric classification) **11**
novelty seeking **45-6, 51, 52, 70, 85, 144**
 genetics of **56**
 bipolar disorder and **207**
nucleus accumbens **110, 129, 138-9, 148**

obsessionality **3, 165ff**
obsessive compulsive disorder **14, 15, 63, 65, 74, 214**
 anxiety disorder and **113ff**
 biological model of **117ff**
 cognitive model of **121-4**
 eating disorders and **165ff**
 personality factors in **124-7**
 personality disorders comorbidity **125-6**
 spectrum **128-30**
obsessive-compulsive personality disorder **14, 63, 65, 69, 74, 125-6, 165-6, 214**
O-LIFE **191**
open field test **40, 91, 152**
openness to experience **49, 50**
opiates (*see also* heroin) **131**
overinclusiveness **206**
Oxford Liverpool Inventory of Experience and Feelings *see* O-LIFE

panic disorder **24-5, 90, 96, 99, 150**
paraldehyde **197**
paranoia **186**
paranoid personality disorder **188**
Parkinson's disease **105**
perceptual aberration **197**
perfectionism **127, 167-8, 172-3**

persistence **45-6, 70**
personality
  Eysenck's theory of **16-20, 34-37**
  genetics of **53ff**
  as predisposition to illness **20-3**
  traits defined **19-20**
personality disorders (*see also* individual
    disorders) **13-14**
  cognitive approach to **72-3**
  dimensionality of **66-7**
  gender and **62, 64**
  genetics of **69**
  psychotic disorder and **62**
  reinforcement theory of **71-2**
  types in DSM **62ff**
PET *see* neuroimaging
phobias
  agoraphobia **4, 90**
  social phobia **90, 103-5, 170**
  specific phobia **90, 100-1**
pituitary gland **151**
planum temporale **204**
positive feedback **23-5**
positive symptoms **187, 197, 202, 204,
    208**
positron emission tomography *see*
    neuroimaging
post traumatic stress disorder **85, 90,
    105-6**
prefrontal cortex **117-18, 139-40, 202**
pre-pulse inhibition **199, 206**
pseudoneurotic schizophrenia **80**
psychiatric classification (*see also* DSM *and*
    ICD) **11-16, 212**
psychopathy (*see also* antisocial personality
    disorder) **75-80**
  animal research in **79**
  EEG in **79**
  Hare checklist **77-8**
psychosexual stages **2-3**
psychosis (*see also* schizophrenia *and* bipolar
    disorder)
  defined **15-16**
  and psychoticism **37, 182**
psychoticism **17-18, 37-8, 182, 186, 207,
    209**
psychotropic drugs **36-7**

quantitative trait loci genetics (QTL) **57**

quasi-dimensional model **188ff**
quinpirole preparation **120**

radical psychiatry **6-7**
reinforcement sensitivity theory **41ff**
Revised Psychopathy Checklist (PCL-R) **78**
reward dependence **45-6, 51, 52, 70, 71**
reward sensitivity *see* sensitivity to reward
Ritalin **152**

scar hypothesis **124**
schizoaffective psychosis **205, 209**
schizoid personality disorder **63, 68, 69,
    70, 71, 188**
schizophrenia (*see also* psychosis) **15, 18**
  bipolar disorder and **205ff**
  brain systems in **201ff**
  dimensionality of **187ff**
  experimental psychopathology of **197ff**
  first rank symptoms in **184**
  negative v positive symptoms in **187**
schizophrenia spectrum **189, 208**
schizotypal personality disorder (*see also*
    schizotypy) **63, 67, 74, 188, 189,
    193, 202**
schizotypy **188ff, 204, 208**
sedation threshold **36-7, 55**
self-directedness **45, 70, 71**
self-esteem **163**
self-medication **150ff**
self-transcendence **45, 70**
sensation seeking **46-8, 52**
sensitivity to punishment **41, 51**
sensitivity to reward **41, 51, 143-7, 152,
    175ff**
sensitization **140, 141**
sensory gating
  in psychopathy **78-9**
  in bipolar disorder **206**
  in schizophrenia **199, 201**
serotonin (5-HT) **46, 48, 56, 85, 92, 103,
    105, 107-8,119-20, 128, 148, 153,
    169, 174**
serotonin reuptake inhibitor drugs (SRIs)
    **107-8, 119-21**
sexual abuse **82**
shared environment **53ff**
skin conductance **80, 192**
skinlessness **198**

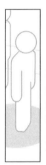

253

sleep threshold *see* sedation threshold
smoking (*see also* nicotine) **196**
smooth pursuit eye movement *see* SPEM
sociability **38, 51, 52, 58**
social anxiety disorder *see* social phobia
social phobia *see* phobias
somatoform disorders **15, 64-5**
spatial ability **201**
SPEM **196, 199, 206**
startle response **199, 206**
starvation
  semi-starvation study (Keys) **160-1**
  spontaneous **163**
stress-diathesis model **101**
Stroop test **123**
substance abuse (*see also* individual
    drugs *and* addiction) **84, 109-110,
    170**
symptoms, defined **20**
synaesthesia **198**

temperament
  animal equivalents of **39-40**
  and character compared **44-5**
  classic theory of **31-33**
  developmental aspects of **57-8**
  dimensions of **44-46**
  genetics of **53ff**

measurement of **44, 58**
and personality compared **38-40, 50-51,
    212**
Temperament and Character Inventory
    (Cloninger) **44**
temporal lobe epilepsy **67, 202**
temporal lobes **202-3**
temporolimbic system (*see also* limbic
    system) **202**
thought-action fusion **122**
thought suppression **111, 123**
toughening up **2**
traits, defined **19-20**
transgenic mice **91-2, 137-8**
twins **53, 194**
two-hit hypothesis **27**
Type I schizophrenia *see* positive symptoms
Type II schizophrenia *see* negative symptoms

unitary psychosis **185-6, 205ff**
universal addiction site **138-9**
unshared environment **53ff. 59, 84**
U-shaped function **23-4, 146, 201**
unusual experiences scale (O-LIFE) **191**

ventral tegmentum **138**
ventricular enlargement **202, 206**
violence inhibition mechanism **79-80**

254

**DATE DUE**

| JAN 0 3 2010 | | |
|---|---|---|
| | | |
| | | |
| | | |
| | | |
| | | |
| | | |
| | | |
| | | |
| | | |